Right Turn

RIGHT TURN

The Decline of the Democrats and the Future of American Politics

Thomas Ferguson and Joel Rogers

iw Hill and Wang / New York

A division of Farrar, Straus and Giroux

Library of Congress Cataloging-in-Publication Data
Ferguson, Thomas
Right turn.
Includes bibliographical references and index.
1. United States—Politics and government—
1945–   . 2. Democratic Party (U.S.)—History—
20th century. I. Rogers, Joel. II. Title.
E743.F39   1986   324.2736   86-12404

Acknowledgments

Many people helped us write this book.

For comments, criticisms, data, and other assistance, we are grateful to Robert Armstrong, Jack Beatty, Kai Bird, Robert Brenner, Stephen Bronner, Walter Dean Burnham, Daniel Cantor, Thomas Cavanaugh, Noam Chomsky, Richard Cloward, Charles Cnudde, Mary Anna Colwell, Bruce Cumings, Celia Eckhardt, John Evansohn, Rudy de la Garza, Joe Feagin, Richard Florida, Gary Freeman, James Galbraith, Benjamin Ginsberg, Thomas Graham, Richard Grossman, Max Holland, Cynthia Horan, J. Craig Jenkins, Stanley Kelley, John Kelly, James Kurth, Emily McKay, Colleen McMurray, Joseph Madison, Stephen Magee, Elliot Mandel, Ruth Milkman, Cheryl Morden, Victor Navasky, Alain Parguez, Sue Parilla, Frances Fox Piven, Marie Rickum, Robert Plotkin, Geoffrey Rips, Caleb Rossiter, Gail Russell, Sherle Schwenninger, Jeri Scofield, Martin Shefter, Rayman Solomon, Donald Torres, and Murray Waas.

The research on campaign contributions was partially supported by a grant from the Project for Investigative Reporting on Money and Politics. We are grateful to the Project and its director, James Boyd. At the Federal Election Commission, Michael Dickerson, Patricia Klein, and Lawrence Noble all helped enormously in fielding our many questions and requests. Gavan Duffy, Erik Devereux, and James Sidanius advised in the analysis of the data.

We were very fortunate in our publisher. Arthur Wang's enthusiasm launched us on this project, and his Olympian patience helped sustain us through it. Bill Newlin provided detailed editorial suggestions on more drafts of different parts of the book than he would care to remember, or than we would care to admit. It is much better for them.

We are particularly grateful to Joshua Cohen, Robert Johnson, and Benjamin Page for much advice and encouragement, and to Anne McCauley and Sarah Siskind for the most difficult task of all—putting up with the two of us during the writing of this book (and, we hope, beyond).

Like our other work together, what follows is fully a joint product. Once again, we have let the alphabet dictate the order of our names.

Thomas Ferguson
Joel Rogers

February 1986

Contents

Would it not be easier
. . . for the government
To dissolve the people
And elect another?

BERTOLT BRECHT
"The Solution"

Right Turn

Revisionist Democrats:

The Myth of the American

Public's Turn to the Right

On the morning of November 27, 1984, barely three weeks after Ronald Reagan's landslide reelection, twenty of the Democratic Party's leading fund-raisers held a private breakfast meeting in Washington, D.C. Over the past few years, this group had raised more money for their party's Presidential nominee than any other set of fund-raisers in Democratic history. As they gathered just a few blocks from the White House in a posh basement foyer of the Four Seasons Hotel, the nominee himself, Walter Mondale, came by to reminisce briefly about the campaign just past and thank them for their support.

But this was no political wake. The Democratic financiers had not come to Washington to recall their collective past, but to plan their collective future. As *The Washington Post* reported the next day, after hearing Mondale out, the group quickly settled down "to talk about 1988 and how they could have more policy influence in that campaign, how they might use their fund-raising skills to move the party toward their business oriented, centrist viewpoints."[1]

Exactly how the group intended to do this was not clear. One of the moneymen (there were no women), Daytona Beach real-estate developer E. William Crotty, had told a *Post* reporter before the meeting that he "wanted to talk about a plan whereby each member [of the group] would raise a quarter-million dollars over the next two years, then possibly direct the funds, totaling $6 to $10 million, toward a selected presidential candidate." After the meeting broke up, however, Crotty denied that specific dollar amounts had been discussed.

Another of those present, Bethesda developer Nathan Landow (who had personally raised more than $2 million for Mondale) insisted that it was still far too early to talk about specific candidates.[2]

Such particulars aside, the financiers emerged from the meeting with a distinct program—to move the party rightward—and a certain quiet confidence in their ability to implement it. As yet another developer, Chicago real-estate magnate Thomas Rosenberg, explained:

If you assume the people in the room are the major fund-raisers for the Democratic presidential race and that they have a desire to see a more moderate, centrist position by the candidates, we'll see what happens from there. . . . We are not trying to form our own special interest group to influence policies. . . . We don't have to do anything. We have a certain viewpoint that is, say, moderate or centrist. And we are major fund-raisers.[3]

Apart from the *Post*, the major media did not cover the financiers' meeting. Less than forty-eight hours later, however, an organization with close ties to key members of the Four Seasons group, the Coalition for a Democratic Majority, sponsored a forum on the 1984 elections and the future of the Democratic Party. Staged in a Senate hearing room, the proceedings were intended to make news, and they did.

Two speeches in particular by Democratic officeholders from the South and West—Arizona governor Bruce Babbitt and Virginia governor Charles Robb—dominated most press notices. Babbitt, a wealthy rancher and member of the Trilateral Commission, who is noted for his close ties to the elite "Phoenix 40" group of wealthy business figures in his home state, launched a sweeping attack on the New Deal principles that have guided the party for the last half century. "We must step away from the lazy orthodoxy that represents what we did 30 or 40 years ago," he told party members. "Your leaders are out of touch. Tell them to get outside of Washington and rediscover America."

Old Democratic convictions "that big business can only be checked by the countervailing power of big labor and big government," said Babbitt, were obsolete, and had already been rejected by the electorate. Strongly emphasizing the free play of what he claimed were "irresistible decentralizing forces in the American economy," Babbitt also denounced the party's recent stand in favor of a national industrial policy, and warned against offering "warmed-over versions" of New Deal initiatives to manage the economy. Instead, Babbitt suggested the Democratic Party of tomorrow should line up behind the new Reagan tax-reform proposal, which he described as preferable to alternatives offered by other Democrats, and "so good the Republicans won't have the courage to support it." That the Reagan tax plan, by eliminating the deduction for state and local income taxes, would desperately constrain many state social-welfare systems was no argument for the Democrats holding back. The principles behind the tax bill, Babbitt insisted, amounted to "classic federalism."

The comments of Virginia governor Charles Robb, whose own state party has been bitterly criticized by local labor leaders for its ties to coal operators and other business interests, also attracted considerable notice. "At the national level," Robb claimed, "we have become a party with too many messages. . . . We are the party of fairness. We are the party of the poor. We are the party of the worker, of the small farmer, of the urban dweller, of the renter. The list goes on and on." Robb was, however, prepared to consider a few more additions. The Democrats, he claimed, must "also be a party of business leaders, doctors, pharmacists, stockbrokers and other professionals." Demanding that the Democrats take a stronger stand in favor of more military spending, additional support for business, and further cuts in the domestic budget, Robb claimed that the crucial task facing the party was the recapture of the allegiance of conservative Southern whites. "Since Southerners still want to be Democrats," Robb asked rhetorically, "why not give them a chance?"[4]

Trumpeted widely in the press, Babbitt and Robb were soon echoed by other analysts in the business-sponsored think tanks and research institutes that dot downtown Washington. A few days after their speeches, for example, the affluent American Enterprise Institute (AEI) staged its own "Public Policy Week." Harvard professor Samuel P. Huntington, a vociferous advocate of the Vietnam War, a past member of the board of the Coalition for a Democratic Majority, and author of a controversial report to the Trilateral Commission that argued that American society suffered from an excess of democracy, presented his own analysis of Democratic troubles. Representative of what soon became a consensus view, it is worth quoting at length.[5]

While noting that "the identification of some groups with the contemporary Democratic Party goes back over a hundred years," Huntington took as his point of departure what he referred to as the "New Deal coalition of groups," whose

key components were southern whites, northern urban machines, a rapidly expanding labor movement, and the large numbers of recent immigrants and their children who became politically mobilized in the late 1920s and 1930s. This coalition was the heart of the Democratic Party from the early 1930s to the mid-1960s. Over time its elements began to defect and attenuate, but for 30 years it was the majority coalition in the country.[6]

In the 1960s, Huntington claimed, the slow disintegration of this Democratic coalition quickened.

First, the New Deal coalition lost its majority status in national elections. This was a result of many developments including the declining effectiveness and clout of the urban machines, the impact of upward mobility on the political allegiances of the children and grandchildren of immigrants, the leveling-off in numbers and decrease in political effectiveness of organized labor, and, most significantly, the declining support for Democratic presidential tickets among white southerners. Second, the control of the Democratic Party by the New Deal coalition was challenged by the rise of new groups that had become politically mobilized during the 1960s. . . . This New Politics stratum eventually included blacks, youth, women, liberal intellectuals, Hispanics, and others. . . . The defeat of Humphrey and the subsequent revision of the party gave these groups the opportunity to expand their influence within the party.[7]

Huntington argued that since the 1960s the "central political leadership of the Democratic Party" had decayed. Instead, narrowly focused interest groups had become increasingly prominent, and had successfully imposed on the party their commitment to "categorical representation,"

that is, the proposition that the interests of particular groups can be properly represented only by individuals who are themselves members of those groups, blacks by blacks, women by women, union members by union members. Since such people are unavoidably identified as the spokesmen for their groups, they are also virtually barred from understanding and representing the interests of other groups and from attempting to reconcile and integrate differing group interests into a broader perspective. . . . Carried to an extreme, categorical representation becomes, in a sense, anti-political since it denies the role of the political leader to extract, refine, and create the *res publica* that people have in common.[8]

In 1984, Huntington claimed, these "special interests" had led the party to disaster. By promoting a futile "downward reaching strategy" of attempting to increase voter participation by labor-union members, blacks, Hispanics, and the poor, they had wasted party resources while alienating more moderate voters, especially Southern whites:

The failure of the downward reaching strategy was most notable in the South. The Democrats had hoped that registration of new black voters would enable them to win back several southern states Reagan had carried by extraordinarily close margins in 1980. The Republicans, however, effectively countered the Democratic [registration] efforts. . . . The Democratic appeal to the blacks also sensitized whites to the Republican appeal and caused southern Democratic defection to a Republican presidential ticket to reach new heights. . . . As a result, Reagan carried every southern state by a margin of at least 15 percent, including those states which he had won by a whisker in 1980.[9]

Huntington urged the party to respond to the 1984 disaster by moving rightward. The special-interest groups that now dominate the party, he suggested, should be replaced by "a new trans-strata coalition of white southerners and moderate income workers from the New Deal stratum, the young professionals, independents and others in the emerging newly affluent stratum, and whatever elements can be recruited from the New Politics stratum." To consolidate this new coalition, he argued, the Democrats should be sure to put a Southerner or Westerner on the ticket in 1988. Most importantly, however, they should recognize the need to make "some adjustments in party positions on policy issues," including a revision of what he attacked as the party's excessively "liberal policy positions in foreign, economic, and social policy."[10]

Like the speeches of Robb and Babbitt, Huntington's AEI paper promptly found a larger audience. Written up the day after Christmas on the front page of *The Christian Science Monitor* as "news" under the headline "Democratic Party Analysts Take Measure of Special-Interest Group Splintering," his analysis soon appeared in *The Public Interest*, the famous neoconservative quarterly whose editorial board includes several members of the Coalition for a Democratic Majority, and which has in the past received large subsidies from a number of conservative foundations and personalities, including the archconservative Richard Scaife.[11]

By the time the paper appeared, however, its message was already on the verge of carrying the day. In its coverage of a late-January meeting in Washington to choose the new chair for the Democratic National Committee, *The New York Times* headlined: "Democrats Picking Leaders Are Pressed to Shift to the Right." Noting that "such historically liberal groups as the Americans for Democratic Action" were "noticeably absent from the policy debate," the *Times* reported that the

push for a more "moderate" image was being guided by the Coalition for a Democratic Majority and by a group of governors and state chairmen from the South and West, who say the party has become a captive of its Washington-based leadership and of its image as a party of factions more interested in Federal spending programs than broader national policy questions.[12]

By the spring of 1985, the forces of "moderation" were clearly visible. The new Democratic National Committee (DNC) chair, Paul Kirk, feuded openly with AFL–CIO president Lane Kirkland. Traditional Democratic liberals, including Senator Edward Kennedy, claimed to be "rethinking" their traditional commitments. A group of Southern and Western elected officials, prominently including Babbitt and Robb, Missouri representative Richard A. Gephardt, and Georgia senator Sam Nunn, defied Kirk's objections and formed an independent group, the Democratic Leadership Council, to promote more conservative candidates. "The moderate and conservative Democrats didn't make it past the first round in its primaries in 1984 and we want to change that," said Nunn, a major Democratic proponent of increased military spending who had backed John Glenn in the 1984 race. Alarmed, as a Kirk supporter put it, that "this group wants to take the cream of the party's leadership and leave Kirk with Jesse Jackson and the single-issue interest groups," the DNC chair countered with the formation of a Democratic Policy Commission with wider regional (and racial) representation. The Commission, said Kirk, was aimed at reclaiming "the mainstream values" preempted by the Republicans in 1984.[13]

Along with these maneuverings came a blizzard of post-election analyses, editorials, op-ed pieces, and the like, in which prominent journalists and academics joined elected officials in refining and then reiterating the new political consensus. American voters, it was said, had finally killed off the New Deal. To avoid becoming a permanent minority party at the national level, the Democrats had to stop resisting the drift of the majority of the electorate toward conservative, entrepreneurially oriented social and economic policies, increased military spending, and more actively anti-Communist, interventionist foreign policies. Simple electoral arithmetic required that the Democrats make more conservative appeals to those portions of their old (New Deal) mass base—particularly, Southern white males—who had defected to the Republicans..

To move in these new directions, of course, the party would have to break with the selfish policies promoted by its "special interests." Unfortunately, however, the "categorical representatives" of these groups had little interest in political compromise or a broader vision for the party, and would never recognize and make amends for the disaster they had wrought. As former DNC chair Robert Strauss summed up the consensus view of these "special interests" shortly after the election:

The defeat will mean nothing to them. The hunger of these groups will be even greater. Women, blacks, teachers, Hispanics. They have more power, more money than ever before. Do you think these groups are going to turn the party loose? Do you think labor is going to turn the party loose? Jesse Jackson? The others? Forget it.[14]

But as early as August 1985, despite the alleged power of these groups, DNC chair Kirk was able to report significant progress in loosening their grip on the Democratic Party. In what he suggestively described as a "stockholders report" to the Democratic Business Council—a group of prominent party backers to which many of the financiers at the Four Seasons meeting belong—Kirk hailed the Council as "the backbone of the Democratic Party's finances, and its intellectual resources," and reviewed the success of what *The Wall Street Journal* described as his "efforts to move the party toward the political center." Delaware senator Joseph Biden, a prominent "neoliberal," was also upbeat. As a result of Vietnam, the environmental movement, and the rise of special interests within the party, Biden said, the Democrats had gone through "a difficult phase," but after years of losing its way the party was coming to its senses. "The good times are coming," Biden promised the group, "and I mean that sincerely." Just how good those times might be became evident a few months later, when Biden, who had voted for the 1981 Reagan tax cuts, crossed the aisle once again to vote for a mandatory balanced budget by 1991. He was joined by twenty-six other Democratic senators, including such erstwhile liberals as Edward Kennedy.[15]

If the implications were less sweeping, one could simply accept revisionist prescriptions for Democratic "renewal" at face value. But the implications are great, and no such facile acceptance is possible. The proposals of the revisionist Democrats do not simply represent, as some commentators suggest, a long-overdue trimming of excesses that may have marked certain Great Society programs. Rather, as Babbitt and Robb openly proclaim, and many other revisionist Democrats imply more guardedly, they represent an abandonment of core political commitments that marked the New Deal itself—the belief that markets have limited competencies and, commonly, undesirable consequences; that the state can and should play an active role in regulating business and redressing income and welfare inequalities; that greater equality is not a bar to the economic growth; and that the rights of workers and their capacities for "self-help" should be protected. This rejection applies to more than abstract commitments. It extends as well to the chief institutional features of American politics that are most centrally identified with the New Deal—the progressive income tax, social-welfare programs, business regulation, and the protection of the only organized form of representation that most members of the lower and middle classes have ever had, namely unions.

Because so much is at stake, it is essential to make certain that the revisionists are reading the tea leaves correctly. We need to be sure that the contrast they draw between the old New Deal coalition and the less salubrious "New Politics" of the 1960s is not simply a projection of some millionaires' antipathy for social spending. We need to know whether powerful, benevolent, and visionary elected officials were really responsible for the policies of the New Deal, and whether the policy failures of the 1960s and 1970s truly reflected the dominance within the party of labor unions, black groups, women's rights organizations, Hispanic associations, and similar "special interests."

We need to find out if "downward-reaching" strategies calling for the mobilization of poor voters are really infeasible, and whether the last election demonstrated that fact; whether Walter Mondale's defeat really occurred because he was dominated by "special interests"; and whether it is really necessary to abandon civil rights and other commitments to black Americans in order to lure Southern whites back to the party. Before any of these questions can be sensibly addressed, however, we need to know if the revisionists' central claim—that a majority of the public shares a stable, well-informed consensus on the desirability of the right or center-right policies promoted by them—is really true.

We do not believe it is.

Policy Realignment without Electoral Realignment

At first glance, revisionist claims that voters have broken with the New Deal look quite compelling. In terms of recent legislation and executive action, it is hard to argue with the proposition that what might be called a "right turn" in American public policy has already taken place. Following some much less significant precedents established by both Democratic and Republican Administrations in the 1970s, the Reagan Administration has broken sharply with many of the major policies championed by New Deal-oriented Democratic (and even Republican) Presidents from the 1930s through the mid-1960s. It has passed massively regressive tax legislation. It has dramatically slashed social-welfare programs, and has made plain its desire for far deeper cuts. It has dismantled or gutted a host of regulatory programs, and abandoned the view that the federal government has a major positive role to play in guaranteeing the rights of minorities and the victims of discrimination. More than any other Administration since the 1930s, it has moved away from the New Deal tradition of multilateral internationalism and free trade. At a time when military outlays directly threaten the maintenance of social programs, it has sponsored the largest peacetime military buildup in U.S. history. And it has vastly increased the size of federal budget deficits, thus creating system-wide pressures for a reduction in the scope of federal activity.

Together, the policy initiatives of the Reagan Administration announce the end of the New Deal era in American politics. Since the Democratic Party originated that era, and set the agenda for national politics within it, these initiatives also announce the decline of the Democratic Party as the dominant force in American public life. What might be termed the "New Deal party system," within which the Democrats clearly held the upper hand, has finally collapsed. In policy terms, the American political system has "realigned." There has been a shift in the basic structure of American party politics.

But while there is overwhelming evidence of such a policy realignment, there is little direct evidence that mass public sentiment has turned against the domestic programs of the New Deal, or even the most important components of the Great Society, and little evidence either of a stable shift to the right in public attitudes on military and foreign policy. On the contrary, as poll after poll demonstrates, the basic structure of public opinion in the United States has remained relatively stable in recent years. To the extent that there have been changes in public opinion on particular issues, most have tended to run *against* the direction of public policy. Moreover, despite major Republican victories in 1980 and 1984, recent voting behavior and trends in partisan identification provide little evidence for an electoral realignment. We consider these points in turn.

Public Opinion

American public opinion has long been best described as both ideologically "conservative" *and* programmatically "liberal." That is, Americans are opposed to "big government" and respond favorably to the myths and symbols of competitive capitalism, in the abstract. When it comes to assessing specific government programs or the behavior of actual business enterprises, however, they support government spending in a variety of domestic areas and are profoundly suspicious of big business. Similarly, Americans are strongly anti-Communist and generally hostile to the Soviet Union, but they are wary of using force in the pursuit of U.S. foreign-policy objectives and anxious to live in peace with the U.S.S.R. This basic opinion structure may appear schizophrenic, but at least on domestic issues it probably reflects voter adaptation to a political system in which the government is interventionist but nonsocialist. In any case, it has been stable for at least a generation.[16]

Within this basic structure, moreover, the basic trend in public opinion over the past generation has been toward greater liberalism. During the 1970s, and particularly after 1973, the rate of *increase* in general support for liberalism slowed somewhat. In addition, as we will note below, there were some exceptions to the general liberal trend. But none of this amounts to a basic change in the basically liberal direction of public opinion. There has been no right turn in public opinion corresponding to the right turn in public policy.[17]

We begin with domestic issues. Revisionists commonly claim that voter support for traditional Democratic positions on typical "New Deal issues"—including government management of the economy; the protection of social security, the aged, and worker welfare; and, at least since the mid-1960s, medical care—has long been in decline and that the present weakness of the party at the national level is a belated consequence of that fact. Typically, it is argued that rising incomes in the post-New Deal era made voters more "middle class," both in the sense that the majority of Americans were living far better than their parents had (and therefore no longer supported social programs) and in the sense that they no longer responded positively to FDR-styled attacks on "economic royalists," made in the name of the "common man."[18]

The survey data, however, do not bear this argument out. A recent effort to map the "salience" (that is, the importance to voter choice of party or candidate) of such New Deal issues found remarkable stability in voter attitudes in Presidential elections between 1952 and 1976. In 1952, 85 percent of the voters found New Deal issues salient—that is, 85 percent of the electorate cited positions on such issues as something to like or dislike about the major parties and/or their candidates. This dropped to 76 percent of the electorate in 1956, but then varied only slightly over the next five elections at 74–77 percent of the electorate. Obviously, New Deal issues did not become less important to American voters. Moreover, among those who saw a position on New Deal issues as "biasing" their choice—that is, leading them to favor a particular party or candidate—the Democrats enjoyed the support of strong majorities in *every* election during the 1952–76 period. The average Democratic bias was just under 62 percent. Put otherwise, if all those elections had been decided solely on those issues, Democrats would have won them all by a landslide. Clearly, Democratic Party identification with "traditional" positions on New Deal issues was a major party strength, not weakness, during this period.[19]

The stability of such postwar attitudes aside, it is commonly argued

TABLE 1.1

Public Attitudes toward
Business and Government Regulation

ORC: *There is too much power concentrated in the hands of a few large companies for the good of the nation.*

AGREE

1969	1971	1973	1975	1977	1979
61%	66%	74%	78%	72%	79%

ORC: *Do you think business as a whole is making too much profit, a reasonable profit, or not enough profit?*

	1969	1971	1973	1975	1977	1979
Too much	38%	26%	35%	35%	50%	51%
Reasonable	47	54	50	39	37	38
Not enough	4	6	3	6	9	8
No opinion	11	12	12	10	4	3

ORC: *In all industries where there is competition, do you think companies should be allowed to make all the profit they can, or should the government put a limit on the profits companies can make?*

	1971	1973	1975	1976	1979
No limits	55%	48%	36%	39%	34%
Limit profits	33	40	55	55	60
No opinion	12	12	9	6	6

Source: *Opinion Research Corporation (ORC), as in note 20.*

that the public moved sharply to the right during the late 1970s on most domestic issues and that a ground swell of popular opposition to government regulation of business and domestic spending programs was an important cause of Reagan's election in 1980. In fact, no such ground swell occurred. As Table 1.1 indicates, public skepticism toward business, and support for government regulation of it, actually increased on several dimensions during the 1970s.[20]

Nor was there any evidence of an upsurge in support for domestic spending cuts. Averaging responses across different spending areas, in

1980 the National Opinion Research Center (NORC) found that only 21 percent of Americans thought that "too much" was being spent on environmental, health, education, welfare, and urban-aid programs—the same percentage that held that belief in 1976, 1977, and 1978. The percentage of Americans thinking "too little" was spent on those programs was also remarkably stable over the 1976–80 period, dropping only from 44 to 42 percent, while the combined percentage thinking the amount spent was "too little" or "about right" was never lower than 72 percent.[21]

As the rollback in regulation and cutbacks in domestic spending became evident during Reagan's first term, the public increased its support for regulatory and social programs. A *Los Angeles Times* poll in 1982, for example, asked respondents if they would favor "keeping" or "easing" regulations that President Reagan "says are holding back American free enterprise." Even with the question posed this way, the percentage favoring "keeping" outweighed that favoring "easing" regulations regarding the environment (49–28%), industrial safety (66–18%), the teenage minimum wage (58–29%), auto emission and safety standards (59–29%), federal lands (43–27%), and offshore oil drilling (46–29%). In 1983, the *Times* again asked about regulatory policy, finding that only 5 percent of Americans found regulations "too strict," while 42 percent thought they were "not strong enough." The CBS News/*New York Times* poll, meanwhile, found that support for the extreme proposition that "protecting the environment is so important that requirements and standards cannot be too high, and continuing environmental improvements must be made regardless of cost," increased from 45 to 58 percent between 1981 and 1983.

The movement in support of social spending programs was similar. An NBC News poll found that those agreeing with the statement that Reagan was "going too far in attempting to cut back or eliminate government social programs" rose from 37 to 52 percent over 1981–83. Comparing the results of a 1982 survey with one commissioned in 1978, the Chicago Council on Foreign Relations found a remarkable 26 percentage point jump in those wishing to "expand" rather than "cut back" welfare and relief programs, typically the easiest target of attack among social spending programs. Support for government action to assist the unemployed was particularly broad. By early 1983, a CBS News/*New York Times* poll found that 74 percent of the public supported a jobs program even if it meant increasing the size of the federal deficit.[22]

Nor were such sentiments swamped by the Reagan recovery or abandoned in the 1984 landslide for the incumbent President. Even on the eve of Reagan's second inauguration, with his approval rating at a record 68 percent and drums beating loudly about the huge federal deficit, a *Washington Post*/ABC News poll found that only 35 percent of Americans favored substantial cuts in social programs to reduce the deficit (although 65 percent believed such cuts were on the way). Representative was a CBS News/*New York Times* poll conducted shortly after the reelection, which compared responses then to its post-election survey in 1980:

There is no suggestion in this poll that the American public has grown more conservative during the four years of the Reagan administration. If anything, there is more willingness now to spend money on domestic programs and a better assessment of the social programs of the 1960's.[23]

The *Times* went back a year later, with similar results. Reporting on a January 1986 survey, again done jointly with CBS News, it found that voter attitudes showed "no consistent evidence of change, certainly not in a conservative direction," over the course of the Reagan Presidency:

Fewer people (40 percent versus 51 percent as Mr. Reagan was coming into office) think that welfare recipients could get along without welfare payments. Fewer people (51 percent versus 63) believe that government creates more problems than it solves. . . . Even more significantly, perhaps, fully 66 percent think the government should spend money now on efforts similar to those of the Great Society programs to help the poor people in the United States. That finding seems to run counter to many Democrats' view that there is no longer any political mileage in such Federal poverty programs.[24]

On "social issues'" as well, American attitudes betray no evidence of a right turn. In general, religion, feminism, civil liberties, abortion, and race relations are the policy areas in which the public has shown the sharpest increase in liberalism since World War II. The rate of increase slowed during the post-1973 period, but at no time did the public actually become more conservative on these issues. And on several of the key questions highlighted by the Reagan Administration, the public became more liberal over the course of Reagan's first term. Regarding abortion, for example, an NBC News exit poll in 1984 found that two-thirds of the electorate endorse the legalization of abortion, with the decision "left to the woman and her physician," while only a quarter do not. Just after the election, an ABC News poll found that the share of Americans supporting the relatively radical position that women should have a right to abortion on demand, "no matter what the reason," actually increased over Reagan's first term, rising from 40 to 52 percent between 1981 and 1985, while the percentage opposing abortion on demand declined from 59 to 46 percent. According to a *Los Angeles Times* poll, only 23 percent of the electorate supported a constitutional amendment prohibiting abortion, and only 32 percent of those who voted for Reagan endorsed his policy on abortion. On other social issues, Louis Harris reports that Americans oppose requiring school prayer by 51–43 percent, while supporting passage of the Equal Rights Amendment by 60–34 percent. Nor are most Americans enthusiasts of Jerry Falwell, the most prominent leader of the religious right. A 1984 *Los Angeles Times* exit poll found only 16 percent of the voters approving of the minister.[25]

Recent trends in public attitudes toward affirmative action bear special notice, if only because of the Reagan Administration's sustained attack on affirmative action and the revisionists' repeated insistence on public revulsion at such "special interests" as women and minorities. In 1978, Louis Harris reported, only 45 percent of the public agreed that "if there are no affirmative action programs helping women and minorities in employment and education, then these groups will continue to fail to get their share of jobs and higher education, thereby continuing past discrimination in the future"; 36 percent disagreed. By 1982, the split on this question showed 57–39 majority support; by September 1985, it showed 71–27 percent support. Those favoring a "federal law requiring affirmative action programs for women and minorities in employment and education, provided there are no rigid quotas," increased to 67–18 percent by 1984; by 1985, majority support had risen to 75–21 percent. Here, too, the movement of public opinion has been directly opposite the movement of public policy.[26]

Once again, in noting the generally liberal trend in American public opinion on domestic issues in recent years, we are not arguing that this trend was universal. American support for harsher sentencing of criminals has increased dramatically over the past two decades, and this may be taken as a trend toward greater conservatism. Resistance to tax hikes—although not demands for tax reduction—increased during the 1970s, and very likely worked to soften support for increased social spending, at least in some areas. Given all the countervailing trends, however, it would obviously be mistaken to generalize from these two exceptions, and considered on their own terms, neither serves to help the revisionist case.

Increased support for punishing criminals dates from the mid-1960s. It coincides with the real and dramatic increase in crime observable since that time, and not with the much later right turn in public policy. Nor has growing support for harsher sentences interrupted the trends of increasing support for social tolerance and civil liberties, and generally declining support for violent responses to crime (questions of perceived self-defense aside). It thus seems to reflect public frustration with a manifest policy failure, but not a more general lurch to the right.[27]

Tax attitudes, on the other hand, were surprisingly muted and lenient, given the background facts. As discussed in more detail below, the unfairness of the tax system, and the burden it placed on average-income Americans, increased substantially in the 1960s and 1970s. Between the mid-1950s and 1980 the tax burden of the average American family nearly doubled, and between the mid-1960s and 1980 the federal tax system became significantly less progressive, as the corporate share of federal tax revenues dropped sharply and the share provided by regressive payroll taxes dramatically increased. Given this background, it is not surprising that by the late 1970s overwhelming numbers of Americans thought the tax system was unfair. In 1977, near the high point of the much-publicized "tax revolt," Harris reported that 89 percent of Americans thought that "the big tax burden falls on the little man in this country"; in 1978, Harris reported that 80 percent thought taxes were "unreasonable." The same year, H. & R. Block reported that 74 percent believed middle-income families were paying too much in taxes, while 76 percent thought high-income families, and 72 percent thought large corporations, were paying too little.

Despite this very widespread perception of unfairness, however, the *increase* in the (always large) share of the population thinking their own taxes were too high was negligible. In Harris polls, it rose only one percentage point over the 1969–78 period. Public opinion on trading off services and taxes also showed stability in the late 1970s. The percentage favoring keeping "taxes and services about where they are" (45%) was the same in 1975 and 1980; so was the percentage (38%) favoring a decrease in services and taxes. Finally, it is important to emphasize that among the general public (as opposed to business elites) the salience of the tax issue has never been great; only tiny percentages have ever named "high taxes" as the country's most important problem, and the 1970s were no exception.[28]

On balance, then, it seems reasonable to conclude that increased burdens on average Americans, and especially increased unfairness in the tax system, made the public more resistant to tax hikes and more receptive to promises to cut taxes. It did not, however, set off a ground swell of public clamor for the reduction of taxes. And it certainly did not provide a mandate for the regressive revisions of the tax system inaugurated during Reagan's first term. As of January 1985, 75 percent of Americans still thought the tax system was "unfair to the ordinary working man or woman." Here again, then, movements in public opinion have a highly imperfect, or even negative, relation to movements in public policy.[29]

And then there is foreign policy. Here, it should be said, there *is* evidence, particularly in the late 1970s and early 1980s, of a conservative turn in public attitudes on the important issue of military spending. According to the Gallup Poll, between 1976 and 1981 the percentage of Americans believing the United States spent too much on military spending declined from 36 percent to 15 percent, while the share thinking the United States spent too little grew from 22 percent to 51 percent. This shift is by far the strongest piece of evidence for the more general claim that American public opinion has moved right, and is commonly cited as a mandate, delivered to and acted upon by both the Carter and the Reagan Administrations, to sharply increase U.S. military outlays. That it is the *only* case of strong convergence between public views and public policy changes should give pause in making a revisionist claim. Its exceptionalism aside, however, several other aspects of this "mandate" qualify its usefulness for the revisionist case.[30]

First, the largest part of the shift occurred very late in the period, in 1979 and 1980, after military authorizations had already begun rising dramatically. As late as December 1978, NBC News/Associated Press showed 50 percent of the population actually favored a *decrease* in military spending, as against an increase in outlays or a decision to keep spending at current levels. Since popular consensus on the need for a military buildup only followed that buildup, it cannot be readily identified as its cause.[31]

Second, even admitting this exceptional congruence between public opinion and policy change, there is good reason to believe that the shift in public opinion was itself caused by elite action. The public does not form its opinions in a vacuum, and by the late 1970s, as we will discuss below, anxious elites were mobilizing a massive campaign to increase military spending. Careful studies of media views of military spending, for example, show increasing hawkish sentiments expressed throughout the period and, importantly, show the public's opinions consistently following, not leading, the views of elites. This campaign reached a crescendo in 1979–80, when the fall of the Pahlevi regime in Iran, the seizure of the American Embassy in Teheran, and the Soviet invasion of Afghanistan were repeatedly cited as proof that U.S. military capabilities were in serious decline. By 1980, with both parties calling for enormous increases in military spending, Democratic candidate Carter denouncing the Soviet invasion of Afghanistan as "the worst threat to world peace since World War II," and Republican candidate Reagan repeatedly insisting that the United States had "unilaterally disarmed" during the previous decade, opposition to increased military spending simply ceased to be a respectable political position. In this context, it is not surprising that large sections of the public expressed concern about American military readiness. But this picture contrasts sharply with familiar claims that the public simply "woke up" to the need for a military buildup.[32]

Third, the "mandate" for increased spending, as it turned out, was fragile and short-lived. After peaking in 1980 and early 1981, support for increasing military outlays dropped sharply. Harris reported that the percentage of Americans in favor of "increasing . . . the present defense budget" plummeted from 71 percent in 1980 to 14 percent by early 1983. The ABC News/*Washington Post* poll found that those who thought the Reagan buildup was "going too far" rose from 28 percent in 1981 to 51 percent in 1983, while NORC found that those who favored reductions in military spending rose from 11 to 32 percent over 1980–83. By that time, indeed, the general distribution of attitudes on military spending resembled the situation in the early 1970s, close to the height of domestic opposition to the Vietnam War. Once again, however, the movement in public opinion bore little relation to the movement in public policy. Even as public support eroded, the military buildup continued.[33]

Fourth and finally, the strength of public support for any given spending initiative is best assessed in the context of other spending priorities. Public perception of trade-offs between military and social outlays clearly played an important role in diminishing support for the buildup, and does not help the revisionist case. ABC News/*Washington Post* polls over the period between early 1981 and late 1983 showed support for increased domestic spending grew from 49 percent to 67 percent for programs directed to the poor, from 43 percent to 75 percent for education programs, and from 49 percent to 66 percent for health programs—all while support for military spending declined. The Harris Survey provided even more direct evidence on this point by asking respondents to choose, for particular social programs, between cutting back those programs and cutting back military outlays. On federal aid to cities, those preferring cuts in military spending to cuts in the programs grew from 41 percent to 54 percent between 1981 and 1984; for federal aid to education, from 60 percent to 71 percent; for federal health programs, from 58 percent to 67 percent. For unemployment compensation, they grew from 46 percent to 70 percent over 1981–82 alone. Here, too, it is very difficult to reconcile changes in public opinion with the changes in public policy inaugurated during Reagan's first term.[34]

For all these reasons, then, the increased support for military spending is a weak peg on which to rest the revisionist case.

Even granting a brief increase in support for additional military spending, however, what about public support for the use of force abroad? Once again, there is a split between Americans' professed ideological positions and their willingness to support specific, especially costly, acts of intervention. As Richard Lugar, Republican chair of the Senate Foreign Relations Committee, summarized this state of affairs in January 1985:

In poll after poll, Americans express their concern about hostile governments which imperiled our interests in Latin America and elsewhere. But in the same polls, Americans display an equal and overwhelming opposition to any course of action which might actually frustrate governments which are harmful to us.[35]

More concretely, while short-term military operations against tiny opponents are sometimes (briefly) applauded, as in the case of the Grenada invasion, Americans are generally opposed to sustained military interventions abroad. During Reagan's first term, for example, early majority support in 1982 for a U.S. Marine presence in Lebanon turned to solid opposition by late 1983. By September, Harris reported 61 percent approving and 35 percent disapproving of Reagan's handling of the situation there. The bombing of the Marine barracks in late October produced a brief "rally round" (as in "rally round the flag") boost in public support for a continued military presence, with Gallup reporting support for that policy increasing from 28 percent to 34 percent between October and late November, but by mid-January 1984 it was back down to 28 percent. Disapproval of Reagan's general handling of the situation, on the other hand, rose from 52 percent in November 1983 to 60 percent by early February 1984.[36]

In other areas of U.S. intervention, similar results were reported. Over the 1982–84 period, Harris reported general disapproval of Administration policies in El Salvador running consistently at around 65 percent. Opposition to sending troops to El Salvador was even higher; in major network surveys conducted over 1982–83, it averaged more than 80 percent. Government policies toward Nicaragua were also unpopular. Opposition to the U.S. mining of Nicaragua's harbors, according to an April 1984 CBS News/New York Times poll, ran at 67 percent; the same poll reported two-to-one majorities opposed to Contra aid, even when asked if the United States should "help people in Nicaragua who are trying to overthrow the pro-Soviet government there."[37]

Finally, in what is arguably the most important single area of foreign and military policy—U.S. strategic policy and relations with the Soviet Union—recent polls do indicate a profound shift in public sentiment. Here again, however, the change runs in a direction exactly opposite to the direction of policy change during Reagan's first term. Despite the talk among Administration officials of winnable nuclear war, and Reagan's own bellicose rhetoric against the "evil force," the survey data indicate that public aversion to nuclear weapons is strong and growing, that arms control meets with wide public approval, and that overwhelming majorities of Americans, while continuing to disapprove of the Soviet Union, are more reluctant than ever to prompt a showdown with the U.S.S.R. and urgently wish to live more peacefully with it. A late 1984 survey of public attitudes toward the U.S.S.R., co-authored by the noted pollster Daniel Yankelovich, summed up the American mood as one of " 'live-and-let-live' pragmatism." Some 67 percent of Americans believe that the United States should let the Soviets have their system of government while we retain ours, since "there's room in the world for both"; 53 percent think the United States would actually be safer if it stopped trying to halt the spread of Communism to other countries (only 22 percent disagreed).[38]

Fear of nuclear war and widespread skepticism about the possibility of "winning" the arms race provide the foundations for this new pragmatic approach to U.S.–Soviet relations. On the perils of nuclear war, some 96 percent of Americans believe that "picking a fight with the Soviet Union is too dangerous in a nuclear world"; 89 percent believe "there can be no winner in an all-out nuclear war; both the United States and the Soviet Union would be completely destroyed"; 68 percent (and 78 percent of those under thirty) think that if both sides keep building nuclear weapons, instead of negotiating their elimination, it is only a matter of time before they are used; and 38 percent (50 percent of those under thirty) think a full-scale nuclear war is likely to occur in the next ten years. In light of these views, it is striking that 50 percent of Americans think the Reagan Administration is playing nuclear "chicken" with the Soviet Union.

Regarding arms, Americans certainly do not want to "lose" the arms race (57 percent, for example, think the United States should continue to build new and "better" nuclear weapons), but equally certainly they do not think it can be "won." Some 84 percent of Americans believe the United States no longer has nuclear superiority; 90 percent think both the United States and the Soviet Union already have an "overkill" capacity; and 92 percent believe that if the United States developed a bigger nuclear arsenal than the Soviets, the U.S.S.R. would simply keep building until it matched the United States.

Concern about nuclear weapons and the current state of U.S.– Soviet relations, indeed, leads strong majorities of Americans to favor substantial revisions of U.S. nuclear strategy and positions on arms control. Some 77 percent believe that the United States should soon have a policy of not using nuclear weapons to respond to a conventional Soviet attack; 74 percent believe the United States should now have a policy of never using nuclear weapons in a battlefield situation; upwards of 75 percent have for years favored a bilateral nuclear freeze; 61 percent favor a unilateral six-month freeze on nuclear-weapons development to see if the Soviets respond in kind, even if they take advantage of the gesture; 56 percent support signing an arms-control agreement even if foolproof verification is impossible; and 84 percent are opposed to using new weapons as "bargaining chips" in arms-control negotiations.[39]

Reagan's Popularity

But if public opinion has generally run against the right turn in public policy, why was Reagan so spectacularly popular during his first term, and especially during the first two years of that term, when most of his Administration's major programs were put in place? The answer is simple: he was not.

Press claims that Reagan's first term marked him as the most popular President of the postwar period are simply false. Over all of that term, his approval rating averaged 50 percent, lower than the averages for Eisenhower (69%), Kennedy (71%), Johnson (52%), and Nixon (56%), and not far above that of Carter (47%). Reagan's high point was reached shortly after taking office, when in May 1981 he recorded a 68 percent approval rating. Four out of the five other elected postwar Presidents had higher peaks—Eisenhower (79%), Kennedy (83%), Johnson (80%), and Carter (75%)—while Nixon's 67 percent approval peak was not significantly lower. Reagan's low point of 35 percent, on the other hand, reached in January 1983, was significantly lower than those of Eisenhower and Kennedy, matched the level Johnson sank to just before he withdrew from national politics in 1968, and came close to the 24 percent approval rating that Nixon received in July and August of 1974, just before he resigned the Presidency in disgrace.[40]

During the first two years of Reagan's Presidency, when his Administration made its greatest advances, his approval ratings were particularly unimpressive. The average approval ratings for Reagan's first and second years were 54 percent and 44 percent, respectively. The

TABLE 1.2
"Nice-Guy Effects" for Reagan and Predecessors

President	Personal Appeal (1)	Performance Approval (2)	"Nice-Guy Effect" (1)/(2)
Reagan, August 1982	60%	41%	1.46
Carter, April 1980	66	40	1.65
Ford, October 1975	69	44	1.57
Nixon, August 1973	56	36	1.55
Johnson, July 1968	76	40	1.90

Source: The Gallup Poll: Public Opinion 1982 *(Wilmington, Del.:*
Scholarly Resources Inc., 1983), 243

first- and second-year average approval ratings for Carter (62 and 47%),
Nixon (61 and 57%), Kennedy (75 and 72%), and Eisenhower (69
and 65%) were all substantially higher.[41]

As Reagan's approval rating—which measures satisfaction with job
performance—plummeted in the polls over the 1981–82 period, the
press began emphasizing his enormous personal popularity. Readers
were told that while the public did not like what Reagan was doing
to them, they loved the man who was doing it. There is some measure of truth in this. Reagan's ratings for personal appeal always remained well above his ratings for job performance. But press accounts commonly did not go on to point out that significant differentials
between performance and personal approval ratings of Presidents are
utterly routine, that they always show greater personal approval than
performance approval (since Americans, for whatever reason, want to
believe their Presidents are nice guys), and that in fact the differential
Reagan enjoyed was proportionately smaller than those of most of his
predecessors, not larger. We can indicate this by taking personal appeal ratings for various Presidents at a time when their performance
approval ratings were all about the same, and then dividing personal
appeal by performance approval to get a rough measure of the "nice-
guy effect" different Presidents have enjoyed (Table 1.2).

Of course, Reagan's approval ratings rose spectacularly over the
1983–84 period, climbing from their low of 35 percent in early 1983
to a strong, though hardly unprecedented, 61 percent by the time of

FIGURE 1.1

Unemployment and Approval of Reagan

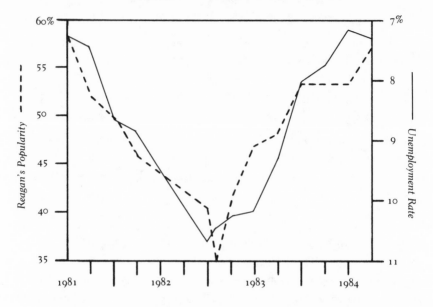

Source: Civilian unemployment rate from Bureau of Labor Statistics;
Reagan approval ratings from Gallup poll (all data quarterly, except
the January 1983 Gallup readings)

the election. They have continued strong ever since. Reagan's average approval ratings for his third and fourth years were 44 and 56 percent, respectively, as compared to Carter's 38 and 40 percent, Nixon's 50 and 56 percent, Eisenhower's 71 and 73 percent, and Kennedy's 1963 rating of 64 percent. But as virtually all careful analyses of the trends in Reagan approval ratings conclude, this upward swing, like the downward one before it, seems to have been caused almost entirely by changes in economic conditions in the country. It gives no evidence of a magic bond between Reagan and the public. Indeed, if one controls for economic conditions, Reagan's popularity does not differ significantly from Jimmy Carter's.[42]

Polls leading up to the election also fail to support the myth of the Great Persuader. ABC News/*Washington Post* surveys, for example, repeatedly asked voters if they liked the President personally, irrespective of his politics, and then asked if they intended to vote for him.

TABLE 1.3
Doing Well Financially

"I will do better financially under Reagan, but . . . ."

	Prefer Reagan	Prefer Mondale	Undecided
Disapprove of Reagan's handling of the economy	63%	35%	2%
Disapprove of his handling of foreign policy	66	32	2
Have the same views as Democrats on most issues	79	19	4
Feel the Republicans are more conservative than themselves on most issues	76	22	2
Feel Reagan sides with special interests	81	16	3
Feel Mondale sides with average citizen	86	13	1
Feel Mondale programs will be fairer to all people	71	27	2
Feel Mondale will reduce the threat of nuclear war more than Reagan will	68	31	1
Feel blacks have been hurt, not helped, by Reagan	77	21	2

Source: ABC News/Washington Post *poll, September 6–11, 1984, as in note 44.*

What emerged consistently from these polls was that personal approval was far less important than policy approval in determining policy choice. In a survey in May 1984, a huge 70 percent of those who said they like Reagan personally but disapproved of his policies reported that they would not vote for him.[43]

Finally, it is important to stress that the policy approval Reagan did receive in the 1984 vote was almost entirely confined to judgments on recent economic performance and on hopes that the economy would continue to boom along. With economic considerations swamping other policy concerns, this led to anomalous results, with vast numbers of voters voting for Reagan even if they disagreed with his position on a host of issues. This was particularly striking among voters who thought they would be better off under a Reagan second term. An ABC News/*Washington Post* poll in September 1984 found that 53 percent of registered voters thought they would be personally better off. Many of this group disagreed with Reagan on a range of issues; nonetheless, they said overwhelmingly that they would vote for him (Table 1.3).

Exit polls, as already indicated, confirmed such results. On virtually all the important issues identified with the "Reagan revolution" in public policy, public opinion ran against the President. Moreover, of those voting for Reagan, only a vanishingly small 6 percent (as compared with an already low 11 percent in 1980) directly identified his conservatism as one of the key things that mattered to them, and only 5 percent offered agreement with his views as their chief reason for support.[44]

The conclusion is inescapable. With the exception of the rise in support for increased military spending, which was rapidly reversed, there is little or nothing in the public-opinion data to support the claim that the American public moved to the right in the years preceding Reagan's 1980 victory. If American public opinion drifted anywhere over Reagan's first term, it was toward the left, not the right, just the opposite of the turn in public policy. And there is nothing in the data to support the claim that Reagan's first term marked him as the most popular President in modern times or that he has a magical hold over the electorate.

Voting Behavior and Partisan Identification

Most studies of American voting behavior also fail to find evidence of a major realignment of voter allegiances toward the Republicans. The most carefully conducted studies of policy voting in 1980, for example, conclude that the vote was more a negative referendum on Carter than an endorsement of Reagan's policies. Similarly, most analysts who have looked at the results of the 1980 and 1984 elections in the light of long-term voting trends find little evidence for the durable shift in voting allegiances that is usually considered characteristic of major political realignments. Instead, they find signs of confusion and turmoil without any clear new pattern.[45]

Reagan's personal victory in 1984 was very impressive. He took 59.2 percent of the two-party vote, and won every state except Mondale's home state of Minnesota, which he lost by fewer than four thousand votes. This translated into the second-greatest electoral-college landslide in modern American history (exceeded only by Roosevelt's percentage in 1936). It was also the fourth Republican victory in the last five Presidential elections. In those five elections, Republicans have garnered 55 percent of the two-party vote and won three land-slide victories; twenty-three states (with a total of 202 electoral votes, 68 short of a majority) have gone Republican *every* time; no state has done that for the Democrats.[46]

Below the Presidential level, however, the gains were unimpres-sive. In 1980, in a less sweeping national victory, Reagan brought thirty-three representatives and twelve new senators with him. In 1984, by contrast, the Democrats posted a net gain of two seats in the Sen-ate and a net loss of only fourteen seats in the House. In state elec-tions, they dropped one governorship and control over five of the ninety-nine state legislative houses. These minor losses did not erase the gains made during the 1982 midterm elections. Indeed, the Re-publicans now have slightly fewer seats in the Senate and House, and half a dozen fewer governorships, than when Reagan first took of-fice.[47]

If anything, the 1984 election gave evidence of further electoral *dealignment*, with voting defined ever less sharply along partisan lines, and a continued decline in the capacity of conventional politics to organize and integrate electoral demand. On such basic dimensions of electoral vitality as overall participation rates and competition in congressional races, for example, the election results again suggested continued decay. As a percentage of the potential electorate, voter turnout stagnated, rising only 0.7 percent from its 1980 level to run at 55 percent. Some 76 million eligible Americans—21 million more than voted for Reagan—abstained. Thus, while Reagan's 59.2 per-cent share of the two-party vote was a certifiable landslide, his share of the potential electorate, as in 1980, was certifiably not. In 1980, Reagan had garnered only 27.6 percent of the potential electorate, a smaller share than Wendell Willkie won in his decisive 1940 loss to Roosevelt. In 1984 he garnered 32.3 percent, or a smaller share than that gained by Eisenhower in both his elections, by either Kennedy or Nixon in 1960, by Johnson in 1964, or by Nixon in 1972. To put this in comparative perspective, Reagan's share was about eight per-centage points less than the share of the French potential electorate won by Giscard d'Estaing in his 1981 loss to François Mitterand.[48]

Congressional competition reached an all-time low. Both the number (408) and the percentage (93.8) of congressional races contested by incumbents reached historic highs, as did the number (392) and percentage (96.1) of races won by incumbents. There were relatively few close races. A stunning 74.9 percent of winning candidates took 60 percent or more of the vote—the highest such figure on record, with records going back to 1824. More immediately, as the divergent results at the Presidential and subnational levels reported above indicate, there was very little *partisan* channeling of the vote that Reagan got. Despite sharp differences in the general political climate in 1982 and 1984, in the 340 House races where candidates from both parties faced each other both times, the net swing toward the GOP over the 1982–84 period was a paltry 3.7 percentage points. To win, of course, local Democrats had to run well ahead of the national ticket. In the thirteen states with gubernatorial elections, the Democratic candidates ran, on average, 10.6 percentage points ahead of the national ticket; in the thirty-two states with Senate elections, they ran 8 points ahead; and in non-Southern congressional elections (in the South many Democratic seats still go uncontested, not permitting meaningful comparison), 9.4 points ahead. In individual races, these spreads could be enormous. Incumbent Democratic senators Claiborne Pell (R.I.) and Bill Bradley (N.J.) both ran 25 points ahead of Mondale; in North Dakota, the lone House member from that state, Byron Dorgan, ran 44 points ahead. Even more striking, perhaps, were the victories of quite liberal Democratic senatorial candidates, such as Tom Harkin in Iowa or Paul Simon in Illinois, against incumbents in states that Reagan won decisively. None of these results suggests a broad electoral realignment.[49]

Some recent analysts of trends in party identification nevertheless point to a rise in the percentage of Americans identifying with the Republicans, and particularly in the percentage of young people identifying with the party, as evidence of an electoral realignment toward the GOP. At first glance, again, the evidence looks very suggestive. In the last quarter of 1984, Gallup and other polls reported that the ratio of Democratic "identifiers" to Republican ones was about 1.1/1, closer to statistical parity than at any time in the past forty years. And a 15-percentage-point swing toward the GOP among younger voters (eighteen to twenty-nine years old) in the 1984 election, meanwhile, led all other age groups. Unfortunately for the revisionists, however, this proves next to nothing.[50]

First, public affection for the two parties is volatile. Public opinion on which party is best able to handle "the most important problem" facing the country, for example, which is commonly used as an indicator of public support for the different parties, has zigzagged repeatedly over the past four Presidential elections. In October 1972, on the eve of Richard Nixon's landslide victory over McGovern, Republicans led Democrats by 39–29 percent on this question. By February–March 1975, in the wake of Watergate, the Democrats led 42–14. Slowly, Republicans gained and Democrats declined over the next few years, reaching a 30–20 split—still favoring the Democrats—in August 1979. Then over the next year the Republican share doubled, with party divisions reflecting a 40–31 Republican lead by October 1980. Within two and a half years, by April 1983, this Republican position had been halved, and the Democrats had regained a commanding 41–20 lead. From there the Republicans began gaining again, reaching a standoff of 30–32 with the Democrats by February 1984, and 39–37 percent by August 1985.[51]

Explicit identification with the major parties showed less volatility in the late 1970s, but significant shifting around during the past few years. Over 1975–79, the Gallup Poll reported Republican identifiers comprising 21–23 percent of the electorate, with Democratic identifiers taking a 45–48 percent share. Then, as the economy declined under Jimmy Carter, Reagan won the 1980 election, and the Republicans moved aggressively in 1981 on their tax and spending proposals, the number of Republican identifiers increased dramatically, rising from 21 percent of the electorate in the first quarter of 1980 to 28 percent in the third quarter of 1981; Democratic identifiers dropped from 47 to 41 percent. At the time, there was excited talk of a new realignment in American politics. But just as quickly as the Republicans had narrowed the gap to 13 points, it widened once again. Over the next seven quarters Republican identifiers fell to 23 percent of the electorate; Democratic identifiers increased to 46 percent. Finally, as the recovery took hold, the Democrats ran a campaign that promised higher taxes but not economic growth, and Reagan won another election, the Republicans surged forward again in party identification to a fourth quarter 1984 split of 38 percent Democratic, 35 percent Republican.[52]

Of course, such short-term volatility in party identification could be consistent with a long-term trend toward the GOP. Particularly when used to support a claim that what we are witnessing is an electoral realignment away from the New Deal, however, the data on party identification over time do not support such an argument.

The virtual parity between the major parties reported in late 1984–85, for example, is not unprecedented in the post-New Deal period. During the 1940s, just when revisionists claim the "New Deal coalition of groups" was at its peak, comparable or even closer conditions of parity obtained. In 1940 and 1944, the ratios were the same as in late 1984 (1.1/1); in 1946, the parties were perfectly balanced at 1/1; and after an uptick in the late 1940s, they returned to roughly the same level (1.2/1) in 1952 and bounced around considerably afterward. Given the ups and downs in the ratio, if one takes the whole post-New Deal period as a point of reference, different trends in party identification can be shown depending on what year one begins with. If one begins in 1937, 1949, or 1952, the trend (albeit slight) in party identification has actually been toward the Democrats. If one begins in 1964, the high point of Democratic identification, the trend (again slight) has been toward the Republicans. Since the data can be used to show different things, the real question is where it is most appropriate to begin the observations. But the data alone, of course, do not answer that.[53]

All these ambiguities, in turn, suggest deeper problems in such identification data. Party identification is chiefly interesting as a predictor of how people will vote once they get inside a polling booth and how they can be expected to continue to vote in the future. But both the election results reported earlier and the volatility and inconclusiveness of trends in party sentiment emphasized here give reason to doubt the usefulness of identification data in making such predictions. The absence of partisan channeling of the vote in 1984, after all, was not a new phenomenon. It was only a very striking case of what has long been observed of American voters—that they seem to resort less and less to parties as a key to their vote at all.

While direct evidence of this is hard to come by, it is suggestive that over the past five national elections, the percentage of voters reporting having voted a "straight ticket" (all-Republican or all-Democratic) has been a consistent minority, ranging between 37 and 44 percent of the electorate. The percentage of congressional districts choosing representatives of one party and a President of another has also risen sharply since the mid-1960s, climbing from just over 26 percent in 1960 to close to 44 percent in 1984. Clearly, most voters do not feel bound by party labels. On the second ground for taking party identification seriously—the stability of that identification—the recent volatility of identification speaks for itself. More and more, it seems, voter responses to questions about "identification" record little more than the party identity of the candidate they voted for in the last election or intend to vote for in the next.[54]

Against the argument that party identification among the young has shown a sharp trend toward the Republicans, all of the above can be noted again, with the additional caveat that the political sentiments of young people seem even more volatile than those of the rest of the electorate. One reason why the swing toward the Republicans among the young was so great in 1984 is that it was swinging back from being the age cohort that most strongly endorsed Jimmy Carter in the election of 1980. Such short-term swings aside, the voting behavior of young people does not appear to be a very good predictor of political realignment. Recent research suggests that in the 1920s young people also voted disproportionately Republican, just prior to the upsurge in Democratic support during the New Deal.[55]

Finally, if the GOP was really making serious strides in identification among voters, weak Democratic identifiers would be likely, especially if specifically invited, to join the GOP. But a recent Republican effort to persuade 100,000 Democrats to register Republican, based on just that premise, fizzled embarrassingly; the Republican National Committee had to cover its very expensive failure with a blanket of juggled statistics. And as we will discuss in some detail, despite an enormous expenditure of resources, Republican registration efforts among nonvoters in 1983–84 were not particularly impressive.[56]

Reagan's Election

To maintain the view that Reagan's policies do not reflect a new popular consensus on policy, of course, one needs an alternative explanation of just how he has managed to win two elections by landslides. But this question has an entirely plausible answer that leads to none of the sensational conclusions drawn by the revisionist Democrats: *the economy.*

We have already noted that Reagan's approval rating moved in close tandem with the economy, and in this he is not exceptional. A

TABLE 1.4

Electionomics: Percent Change in Real Per Capita Disposable Income (1972 Dollars) from Year Previous, Select Election Years

Year	% Change	Year	% Change
1932	−14.2	1960	0.0
1936	+11.4	1964	+5.6
1940	+5.3	1968	+3.1
1944	+2.2	1972	+2.9
1948	+3.5	1976	+2.6
1952	+1.1	1980	−0.6
1956	+2.7	1984	+5.8

Source: Economic Report of the President, 1985 (Washington, D.C.: GPO, 1985), Table B-24; Survey of Current Business, July 1984, Table 8.2

huge amount of research confirms the general importance of economic performance in voter approval of elected officials, not only in the United States but throughout most capitalist democracies. Indeed, quite reasonable predictions of Reagan's percentage of the two-party vote in both 1980 and 1984 can be derived from a very simple model that considers only changes in real disposable income per capita shortly before an election and a measure of Presidential popularity (which correlates closely with economic performance). One widely disseminated model of this type fits the 1984 case almost perfectly, predicting a Reagan percentage of 59.4 percent, only 0.2 percent off the final result.[57]

Such "political business cycle" models suggest that the recent problems of the Democrats are more cyclical than secular. Above all, they are matters of timing. Jimmy Carter pumped up the economy in 1977 and the beginning of 1978, but then drove it into recession just in time for the 1980 election. He thus became the first President since Herbert Hoover to run for reelection at a moment when the national income was actually shrinking, and the first elected incumbent since Hoover to lose a bid for reelection. Ronald Reagan did not make this mistake. His Administration chose to have a long and exceptionally deep recession early in its term, and then (helped along by the collapse of OPEC and other factors) staged one of the greatest political business cycles in modern history, producing a 5.8 percent increase in real per capita disposable income in 1984—the largest election-year increase since 1936. Though one can argue to infinity whether the last 2 or 3 percent of Reagan's vote was or was not produced by this boom, the point is that income growth of this size cannot fail to produce a smashing victory for an incumbent no matter what the other party does. It is not a reason for the opposition to agonize.

That the economy was the key issue in 1980 and 1984 is also confirmed by survey data. Most studies of the 1980 election see it principally as a referendum on Carter's bad economic performance. In 1984, every major election poll found economic issues dominant in voters' minds. More immediately, and of considerable relevance to current plans to move the party to the right, a lack of confidence in the Democrats' program for the economy was the single most important reason, at the level of voting behavior, for the Democrats' defeat.

Consider voter opinion on the "New Deal issues" cited earlier. Contrary to revisionist claims, such issues continued to preoccupy voters in the 1980 and 1984 elections. In 1980, New Deal issues were salient among 76 percent of the electorate; in 1984 their salience actually increased to 84 percent. In 1980, however, the Democratic bias on the composite of New Deal issues fell to 47 percent, some 16 points below its 1976 level, and in 1984 it recovered only to 53 percent. Thus if those elections had turned solely on New Deal issues, the Democrats would have lost resoundingly in 1980 and won only a narrow victory in 1984.

This drop-off in Democratic bias on New Deal issues had nothing to do with changed public perceptions of Democratic positions on such issues as social security, worker protection, assistance to the aged, medical care, or labor unions. On all those issues, in fact, the Democratic bias actually *increased* between 1976 and 1984. What changed was voter perception of the Democrats as macroeconomic managers.

Of concern to voters in all Presidential elections during the 1952–84 period was the election's expected impact on the economy (including the impact on employment, wages, salaries, working conditions, and inflation). This classic New Deal issue had an average salience of 25 percent over the 1952–76 period, and during that period the Democratic bias on the issue averaged an impressive 72 percent. In 1980 and 1984, however, two things happened. First, the issue became even more salient, rising to 32 percent in 1980 and 33 percent in 1984. Second, and most dramatically, the Democratic bias plunged to 20 percent in 1980 and recovered to only 29 percent in 1984. This whopping 47 percent drop between the average bias during the 1952–76 period and that during 1980–84, more than any other factor, explains voter rejection of Democrats at the polls. Significantly, it coincided with the party's move *away* from its traditional commitments to promoting employment gains and growth.[58]

Such data point up the implausibility of the revisionist case as an electoral strategy. They suggest, indeed, that a move to the right may be the *worst* possible electoral move the Democrats could make, and that the mistake the Democrats made in 1984 was not their alleged "reaching down" but the fact that they did not "reach down" nearly enough. On economic issues, the Democrats offered voters almost nothing in 1984. Though Mondale spoke incessantly about the values of work and self-discipline, he became the first Democratic nominee in many years to fail even to put forward a major jobs program. Nor did he couple his call for tax increases with a program of popular economic revitalization. Faced with a choice between someone who promised them little besides a rise in taxes and a candidate who at least verbally championed economic growth and lower taxes, there may be no particular mystery about why voters deserted Mondale for Reagan or declined to vote at all. Looking to 1988, the data suggest that a revisionist Democrat even more grimly committed to lowering expectations will be abandoned by the voters in even greater numbers.

Conversely, the overwhelming importance of economic issues undermines revisionist arguments about the need to make conservative ideological appeals to parts of the old New Deal base. Even accepting the proposition that Southern white males need to be attracted back to the party, for example, the evidence suggests that the surest way to do that is not by abandoning Southern blacks but by running hard on economic issues that unite low-income groups across racial lines. Nor is this suggestion mere speculation. The success of several Southern "populists," including Alabama governor George Wallace, point up the appeal of such a strategy. Nothing in the evidence suggests the need for, or electoral desirability of, merely aping conservative Republicans.

Which Special Interests?

The claims revisionist Democrats make about public opinion and electoral strategies are not the only vulnerable points in their argument. A major problem is presented by their single-minded focus on "special interests" and general refusal to consider alternative explanations of Democratic decline. Some of these alternative accounts focus on an apparent increase in the power of the mass media, others on the growth of the religious right, or on the rise of business organizations in national politics, or, in different ways, on the political imperatives of declining U.S. economic performance. Their conclusions are often sharply at odds with those drawn by the revisionists, who rarely bother even to consider them. [59]

This indifference is most evident where it is most damaging—in the accounts revisionists put forward of the structure of power and decision-making within the Democratic Party since the time of the New Deal. In the past two decades, a vast literature on the New Deal has grown up. Drawing on many new primary sources, this work substantially revises many conclusions of the old classic histories, particularly regarding Roosevelt's relationship with the business community. By establishing a far more complex and discriminating account of the role business (especially certain sectors of big business) played in the formulation of major New Deal initiatives, and the support key business groups extended to FDR, this literature makes it impossible to credit accounts, like Huntington's, that define the New Deal coalition strictly in electoral terms. [60]

Neglect of the role business interests play in the party also raises major questions about the revisionists' efforts to pin responsibility for the party's current troubles on the "New Politics" of labor, blacks, women, or the poor. Reading Huntington, for example, one might think that the major fund-raisers for George McGovern's Presidential bid were college students, Black Panthers, and the leadership of the National Organization for Women, instead of the chair of the executive committee of Xerox and Max Factor III. One might think, too, that the Democratic slate in 1984 was determined by groups of women, blacks, and Hispanics, who flew Democratic presidential hopefuls around to their respective headquarters to decide whom they would name to head the ticket. Such conclusions bear little relation to reality.

More immediately, the revisionists' inability to come to terms with the role played by business and other elites within the party from Roosevelt onward results in a peculiar inconsistency in their argument—one which raises major questions about their general understanding of political change in America. On one hand, they clearly share the general conviction—held by American liberals and conservatives alike—that political power in America derives essentially from voters. Thus they agree with most historians of the 1950s that the New Deal expressed the policy desires of a dominant coalition of groups within the electorate. In the next breath, however, they rail at the influence they claim that special-interest groups, without an electoral base and unconcerned with electoral success, have exercised within the party since 1968.

Though Huntington offers a brief, unconvincing effort to reconcile these views, it is not immediately apparent how they can be reconciled. What exactly is the role elites play in political parties in modern America? Do they, or do they not, dominate parties and party systems? Under what circumstances, and in particular under what conditions of popular pressure from below, will competition among elites result in control by the electorate? The absence of systematic answers to these questions probably has more than a little to do with the fact that revisionist Democrats rarely offer *any* systematic evidence for their claim of "special interest" domination. Most commonly, they simply assert it.

This list of weaknesses in the revisionist Democratic case could be extended further, but the essential point should already be clear. Before the United States wrecks its cities, shrinks its education system, abandons the regulation of business, turns back the clock on rights for women, blacks, and Hispanic Americans, reverses the progressive income tax, heats up the arms race, invades another Third World country, or simply eliminates unions, we need to take a hard look at the recent history of the American political system. How and why did the New Deal political system decline? If, as the poll data suggest, public attitudes toward major policy questions have remained programmatically liberal, how does one account for America's right turn in the 1970s? Why did leaders of the major parties keep trying to jettison more and more of the New Deal's programs, including domestic programs that are popular with vast numbers of voters? Why did they repeatedly insist on pursuing sharply deflationary monetary policies, often at great electoral cost?

Of even greater importance for assessing the future, why, in 1981–82, did the Democrats respond so feebly to Reagan's initiatives? What motivated the party, despite widespread private doubts, to unify around Walter Mondale (and, until he withdrew, Edward Kennedy) in 1981–82? Why, once this very moderate coalition crystallized, did it break down so rapidly in the Democratic primaries, as first John Glenn and then Gary Hart and finally Jesse Jackson challenged the apparently invincible Mondale? And what explains the bizarre course of Mondale's Presidential campaign? Facing an uphill struggle against an incumbent, why did he settle on the suicidal course of campaigning on a promise to raise taxes? Why, with signs of disaster mounting all around him, did he persist with his single-minded focus on deficit reduction, without offering any positive economic program? Finally, how does one assess the party's future prospects? Is a general party realignment in progress, one that will bring a generation of Republican dominance in national politics, or can the Democrats recover? If they can recover, what sort of Democratic Party is likely to emerge, and what difference will that make to the well-being of ordinary Americans?

These are the questions we seek to answer in this book.

2/

The Life of the Party:

From the New Deal

to Nixon

As we have just seen, a crucial part of the revisionist Democrats' case rests on the contrast they allege between the way the Democratic Party functions today and the way it operated in the halcyon days of the high New Deal. But this contrast is more commonly asserted than demonstrated, and no detailed account of the differences in party policymaking in the two periods has been offered. As a result, the revisionists beg important issues both about the nature of the New Deal itself and about the more general nature of political change in America. To begin our own account of America's right turn, these issues need to be addressed.

What defined the New Deal, and what produces massive policy changes of the sort now occurring in American politics? In most conventional accounts, the answer to *both* questions is obvious—American voters. The advent of the New Deal (if not the Great Society and its aftermath) is "explained" as the direct result of the emergence of a new coalition within the American electorate—a coalition that united the sometimes overlapping ranks of Southern whites, Northern city dwellers, immigrants, blacks, and millions of ordinary workers. The interests of this electoral coalition, it is argued, defined the New Deal's range of policy initiatives, while the stable voting patterns of its members assured those policies of longevity. It follows that the current turn away from New Deal policies follows from voter rejection of those policies.

This view of the origins and maintenance of the New Deal, more-over, is usually offered as more than a claim about that particular case. To revisionists and most other commentators, it also (if, in the case of the revisionists, somewhat inconsistently) provides a frame-work for understanding how political power is generally acquired and lost in American life. Specifically, the New Deal is thought of as an instance of the phenomenon, and evidence for the theory, of "critical realignment."

Party Systems and the Theory of Critical Realignment

According to the theory of critical realignment, most American elec-tions are settled by marginal shifts within relatively well-defined and stable blocs of voters, such as Roman Catholics, blue-collar workers, rural Protestants, and Southern whites. "Standing alignments" of such blocs define "party systems" that persist over many elections—in the way, for example, that Huntington and most other analysts recognize the "New Deal party system" as lasting from at least 1936 on into the 1960s. Over the course of several elections, all sorts of short-term influences—foreign-policy crises, idiosyncrasies of particular candi-dates, swings in the business cycle, and so on—can temporarily alter the balance of power between the political parties. Long-run ("secu-lar") changes in partisan strength may also occur. Still, so long as the basic alignment of these voting blocs survives, only marginal altera-tions take place within the party system they define. Characteristic patterns of voter turnout, political competition, party symbols, public policies, and other institutional expressions of the distribution of power survive from election to election.[1]

At times, however, as during the New Deal itself, this pattern of "normal politics" is broken, and one or a few closely spaced "critical" or "realigning" elections occur. Associated with the rise of new polit-ical issues, intense social conflict, acute factional infighting within parties, and the rise of strong third-party movements, such "realign-ing elections" sweep away the old party system. Triggering a burst of new legislation, and setting off or facilitating other changes that may take years to complete, these elections fix the new pattern of politics that characterizes the next party system. As a leading scholar defined such periods:

. . . eras of critical realignment are marked by short, sharp reorganizations of the mass coalition bases of the major parties which occur at periodic intervals on the national level; are often preceded by major third-party revolts which reveal the incapacity of "politics as usual" to integrate, much less aggregate, emergent political demand; are closely associated with abnormal stress in the socioeconomic system; are marked by ideological polarizations and issue-distances between the major parties which are exceptionally large by normal standards; and have durable consequences as constituent acts which determine the outer boundaries of policy in general, though not necessarily of policies in detail.[2]

This view of political change has much to recommend it. A great many electoral studies once appeared to confirm it, and certain features of political history that it highlights—notably the dramatic indications of vast upheavals within the electorate during certain crucial periods like the New Deal—must be taken seriously by any theory of American politics. At present, indeed, the realignment perspective is the consensus popular view of political change, regularly espoused not only by revisionists but by Democrats of all stripes, by leading Republicans anxious to install the GOP as a new majority party of a post-New Deal party system, and by much of the press.

But even as the realignment perspective has penetrated most popular commentary on American politics, recent scholarly writings have become increasingly skeptical. Even those who remain committed to some version of the theory often express misgivings.

All sorts of objections have been raised. Some stem from the confusion that marks the realignment literature over whether one or a handful of concatenated elections constitute realignments; whether realignments at the national level require more than the accumulation of changes, at different times, within particular states or regions; and whether Presidential, congressional, or even local elections are the ones that should be analyzed for evidence of basic shifts within the electorate. While these objections may be the least serious for the basic structure of the theory, even they raise critical difficulties for the broadly psychological explanations of changes in party allegiance that advocates of the view have commonly relied upon.[3]

There is also the blunt fact, which after more than twenty years of work is becoming acutely embarrassing, that all efforts to date realigning elections precisely have so far ended in confusion. Despite a broad consensus that the Jacksonian period, the Civil War, the 1890s, and the New Deal all witnessed realignment, no one has succeeded in identifying patterns of voting behavior unique to those few periods. As a consequence, all efforts to specify realignments end up either over- or underpredicting them. Either the Civil War, or the Jacksonian era, or some other "consensus" realignment is omitted from the list, or Warren G. Harding's brief, unhappy, overwhelmingly Republican Administration ends up qualifying as one, or some other clearly unacceptable outcome emerges.[4]

For present purposes, the most important objections to the realignment theories stem from the growing doubts about the integrity of the basic voting blocs that are supposed to be the major protagonists in the realignment story. Stimulated by the negative results of the attempts to date realignments precisely, analysts have begun to look more closely at the other literature's claims about how those voting blocs behave. The results of this recent work are lethal.

Where virtually all realignment theorists have emphasized the existence and durability of voting blocs of distinct groups whose "standing alignment" remains stable throughout the course of any given party system, then changes abruptly with the advent of an era of critical realignment, the most recent literature suggests other patterns. Depending on how one configures the data, either the blocs that earlier analysts claimed to find simply do not exist; or they do exist sometimes, but are not stable over the life of the party systems they were thought to define; or they exist, and are stable, but individual voters in each group fade mysteriously in and out of the group's constant aggregate percentage (so that, for example, 60 percent of Group X consistently votes Republican, but not the same 60 percent each election); and so on. Correlatively, some work finds relative stability in voting patterns across periods of realignment; that is, what voting blocs do exist are not decisively scrambled.[5]

The variations and anomalies are endless, but the main implications of this recent work are clear—that the durable voter coalitions that are supposed to define party systems are often mirages, and that critical realignments are not only difficult to define, but often were simply not occasions during which massive, lasting shifts in voter sentiment occurred. In the words of three analysts highly sympathetic to the realignment perspective:

. . . electoral change during the historical periods usually identified as realignment was not in every case either as sharp or as pervasive, nor was lasting change as narrowly confined to a few periods, as the literature suggests. Although these periods were marked by both deviating and realigning electoral change, which shifted the balance of partisan strength within the electorate toward one or the other of the parties, these shifts did not involve the massive reshuffling of the electorate that some formulations of the realignment perspective describe. Moreover, indications of substantial continuity of the alignment of electoral forces across virtually the whole sweep of American electoral history can be observed. . . . Electoral patterns do not, by themselves, clearly and unequivocally point to the occurrence of partisan realignment.[6]

Such views, it should be emphasized again, do not imply that voting patterns never change. Nor do they exclude the possibility that members of a particular social group might align more with one political party than another during some period (as many groups, including blue-collar workers, did in the 1930s). They do suggest, however, that movements of or within voting blocs are simply too diffuse and variable to be used to define party systems, and that something other than a shifting and friable electoral base must be used to identify them.

An Alternative Approach
At least in part because they cannot think of any other criteria of identification, many analysts of American voting behavior have concluded that the whole realignment approach must be jettisoned; but this conclusion is even less satisfying than the original theory. Whatever its defects, the theory of critical realignment does have the immense virtue of focusing attention on the problem of qualitative change in U.S. politics. Work done within the framework of the theory has also made any number of illuminating suggestions about the ways in which policy changes relate to institutional transformations in American society. Rejecting the theory altogether risks neglect of these problems and insights, and other analysts have therefore sought different approaches to the question of party systems and realignment.[7]

This study follows one of them—the suggestion that what properly defines American party systems is not blocs of voters but patterns of interest-group alignment and coalitions among major investors.[8]

In sharp contrast to the voter-centered analysis that lies behind older realignment theories, this "investment" approach to the analysis of partisan conflict attempts to incorporate into social-science theory a fact which most election analysis only rarely comes to grips with—that efforts to control the state, by voters or anyone else, cost heavily in time and money. Merely developing views about major issues of public policy, and evaluating the candidates who compete for electoral affections, costs a great deal. Formulating and implementing particular policy initiatives costs even more. Given the background inequalities in wealth, income, information, and access to key decision-makers characteristic of most advanced industrial states, as well as the host of "collective action" problems that proliferate within them, these costs weigh particularly heavily on those with modest means. And while organization can compensate for background material inequalities, it itself requires major investments of time and money, and cannot be presumed. As a result, voter control of the state, while not zero, is likely to be uncertain and variable.

In the United States such control is even more problematic. By constitutional design, the U.S. political system is intensely fragmented, and its structure poses great obstacles to the aggregation and coordination of voter demands. The major parties, which are among the oldest in the world, are relatively undisciplined "constituency" organizations, rather than programmatic vehicles for defined ideologies. Particularly given the absence of proportional representation, barriers to third-party entry into the political system are high. Popular secondary institutions, such as unions and cooperatives, claim a relatively small share of the population as active members. The low-involvement political system imposes many costs on voters that other countries do not, and voter turnout is among the lowest and most decisively class-skewed in the industrialized world. These many differed aspects of the American case both reflect and prolong its "exceptionalism." Voters here, by comparison to most other advanced industrial states, are especially disorganized, and this disorganization further raises the costs to individual voters of attempting to control the state.[9]

As a practical matter, then, the fundamental "market" for political parties in the United States is not individual voters. The real market for political parties is defined by major "investors"—groups of business firms, industrial sectors, or, in some (rare) cases, groups of voters organized collectively. In contrast to most individual voters, such investors generally have good and clear reasons for investing to control the state, and the resources necessary to sustain the costs of such an effort. These major investors define the core of the major parties, and are responsible for sending most of the signals to which the rest of the electorate responds.[10]

From the standpoint of such an "investment" theory, the rise and fall of American party systems is thus best analyzed by examining the rise and fall of investor blocs. In considering the rise and fall of the New Deal, for example, the approach does not recommend spending time, as do many revisionists and the older generation of liberal historians, speculating endlessly (and usually unverifiably) on the mysteries of charismatic domination by great Democratic Presidents. Rather, it recommends first identifying the investors that originally constituted the New Deal coalition, then tracing how and why they left the coalition, and where they went.

This is what we shall attempt to do in this and the next chapter, in a discussion that ranges from the origins of the New Deal to the election of Ronald Reagan. Before we begin, however, one vital caveat is in order: What follows covers a great deal of ground in very little space. Of necessity, many important issues and events cannot be addressed at all, and even those that are addressed cannot be analyzed exhaustively. Instead, we are guided by the questions raised in the previous chapter. The discussion concentrates, severely, on providing the material to answer them.

The New Deal Coalition

To understand the collapse of the New Deal as the organizing principle of American politics, one must first define the original investor coalition that came together around Roosevelt in the Great Depression. At the center of that coalition were not the millions of farmers, blacks, and poor that have preoccupied liberal commentators, nor even the masses of employed or striking workers who pressured the government from below (and later helped implement some of the New Deal's achievements), but something else—a new power bloc of capital-intensive industries, investment banks, and internationally oriented commercial banks.[11]

This bloc constituted the basis of the New Deal's great and virtually unique achievement—its ability to accommodate millions of mobilized workers amidst world depression. Because they were capital-intensive, firms in the bloc were less threatened by labor turbulence and organization. They could thus "afford" a coalition with labor, at a time when the costs of that coalition were, at least by American standards, high. Because most large capital-intensive firms (with the important exception of the heavily protectionist chemical industry, which did not belong to the bloc) were world, as well as U.S., pace-setters, they stood to gain from global free trade. They therefore allied themselves with leading international financiers, whose own minus-cule work force presented few sources of tension, and who had sup-ported a more broadly internationalist foreign policy and lower tariffs since the end of World War I. Together, members of this bloc pro-vided the needed business support for the two broad policy commit-ments—liberalism at home, internationalism abroad—centrally iden-tified with the New Deal.

Although this bloc represented only a small part of the business community in the 1930s, it was immensely powerful. It included many of the largest and most rapidly growing corporations in the economy—including such firms as General Electric, IBM, Pan Am, and R. J. Reynolds; many major oil concerns, including Standard Oil of New Jersey, Standard Oil of California, Cities Service, and Shell; and major commercial and investment banks, including Bank of America, Chase National Bank, Brown Brothers Harriman, Gold-man Sachs, Lehman Brothers, and Dillon Read. Its members were recognized industry leaders with the best and most sophisticated man-agements. No less importantly, firms in this bloc embodied the norms of professionalism and scientific advance which fired the imagination of large parts of American society in this period. The controlling interests in the largest of these enterprises also dominated the leading American foundations, which in the previous several decades had come to exercise major influence on both the general climate of po-litical opinion and the specific content of American public policy. And while the point cannot be pursued here, what might be termed the "multinational liberalism" of the internationalists was also aided significantly by the spread of liberal Protestantism; by a process of newspaper stratification that brought *the* free-trade organ of interna-tional finance, *The New York Times*, to the top; by the growth of capital-intensive network radio; and by the rise of major newsmaga-zines. These last promised, as Raymond Moley himself commented while taking over at what became *Newsweek*, to provide "Averell [Harriman] and Vincent [Astor] . . . with a means for influencing public opinion generally outside of both parties."[12]

In the darkest moment of the New Deal, as Roosevelt's initial response to the Depression, the "First New Deal," collapsed in 1935 amid rising public criticism and turmoil, this bloc came dramatically together. Broadly supported by the heads of such firms as General Electric, Standard Oil of New Jersey, the Chase National Bank, and IBM, a host of prominent investment bankers (such as Sidney Weinberg of Goldman Sachs, Averell Harriman of Brown Brothers Harriman, and James Forrestal of Dillon Read), and many oil companies and independents in Texas and elsewhere (including Royal Dutch Shell, Cities Service, Standard Oil of California, and such legendary oilmen as Sid Richardson and Clint Murchison), the Roosevelt Administration instituted another sweeping package of social reforms. This "Second New Deal" included the landmark Social Security and Wagner acts, the Public Utilities Holding Company Act, several tax bills, and the Interstate Oil and Gas Compact legislation, which established the mechanism that regulated the price of oil for a generation. Breaking sharply with the traditional Republican policy of high tariffs, the Administration also embarked on a historic program of trade liberalization and efforts at currency stabilization.[13]

By intervening in support of the Second New Deal's meliorative social policies, this bloc spared Roosevelt the choice—then being forced on leaders of other countries with fewer capital-intensive and internationally oriented big businesses—between socialism and the termination of a constitutional regime. Their support permitted Roosevelt to emerge as the guardian of all the millions, and to initiate a set of policies that delivered unprecedented benefits to the general population while satisfying a leading segment of American business.

For ordinary Americans, the merits of the New Deal system were obvious. After passage of the Wagner Act, unions grew by leaps and bounds, rising from a membership of fewer than 4 million in 1935 to 8 million by 1940, and 14 million by 1945, and becoming a significant investor in the Democratic Party in their own right. Wage and price controls during World War II shored up the purchasing power of American workers, while the institution of "pattern bargaining" that became prominent after the war helped generalize the wage gains won in unionized sectors. Coupled with those wage gains, new strategies of Keynesian macroeconomic management kept effective demand well above earlier levels and helped drive the economy along. Even after the tremendous expansion of the economy in World War II, growth and employment performances were strong. Despite many recessions along the way, between 1947 and 1972 the real value of gross, fixed, nonresidential investment increased about 150 percent, and output per worker more than doubled. Unemployment, which had averaged close to 15 percent between 1920 and 1939, averaged less than 5 percent from the end of World War II on into the early 1970s. At the bottom line, over the 1947–73 period, real per capita disposable income increased 84 percent, and real median family income doubled. There was no question about it: most Americans were living better.[14]

These domestic gains were coupled with a U.S.-led expansion and opening of the world economy. By the close of World War II, the United States alone produced 60 percent of the total manufactures in the industrialized West, and 40 percent of total goods and services. It dominated the international oil business, enjoyed supremacy in most of the key industries that would shape the postwar world (aircraft, automobiles, computers, and electronics among them), and had consolidated an enormous financial sector that permitted it to replace England as the world's banker.

From such a position of strength, large sections of U.S. business profited enormously from the New Deal commitment to free trade. Pursued during the 1930s in a series of trade and currency agreements negotiated by the Roosevelt Administration, this commitment was institutionalized in the postwar period in the "Bretton Woods system," which provided the framework for international economic relations for the next generation. Bretton Woods established the dollar as the "vehicle" currency to be used in the conduct and financing of international trade, and brought order to foreign-exchange markets by establishing a system of fixed exchange rates among the world's currencies, tied to the dollar; the dollar, in turn, was convertible to gold. In addition to these monetary arrangements, the postwar system featured several other institutions aimed at integrating the world economy, including the International Monetary Fund, chartered to provide short-term loans to countries experiencing balance-of-payments difficulties; the International Bank for Reconstruction and Development (World Bank), which made low-interest loans to developing regions; and the General Agreement on Tariffs and Trade (GATT), which provided a framework for international negotiations to manage trade disputes and lower tariff barriers.

Here, too, the results were impressive. During the 1938–67 period, in an expanding system of "multilateralism," international trade volume grew at an annual cumulative rate of 4.8 percent, 12 times the rate of increase during the 1913–37 period. The real value of U.S. direct foreign investment doubled during the 1950s, and doubled again in the 1960s. Overseas assets of leading international American banks grew steadily in the postwar period, then exploded during the boom years of the 1960s, rising from $3.5 to $52.6 billion by decade's end.[15]

Considering the wars, strikes, trade struggles, and political infighting that disrupted U.S. politics in the generation after Roosevelt's reelection in 1936, the new Democratic coalition chiefly responsible for these policies can hardly be described as having lived happily ever after. Commitments to free trade, government assistance to the poor, the protection of workers, and income redistribution were often sharply contested, and quarrels raged between the major parties over the precise extent and direction of government intervention in the economy. After World War II, voter turnout, which had increased dramatically at the height of the New Deal, leveled off, and after 1960, it began declining precipitously outside the South. Depending on the strike rate and the internecine conflicts that usually raged in the Republican Party over trade policy, many business Democrats often preferred to think of themselves as liberal Republicans.

Still, for more than a generation, the basic political formula fashioned during the Heroic Age of the New Deal—social welfare, trade unionism, minority rights, expanded popular participation in government, the concept (and more equivocally, the reality) of a progressive income tax, and free trade—scarcely varied. Republicans, when in power, did not dare stray too far from it. And since even imperial America could not provide enough victorious generals to keep the GOP competitive forever, the long-run position of the Democratic Party looked secure.

The process by which this New Deal system fell apart was complex and drawn out. Leads and lags in its consolidation and decay abound, and elements of its eventual disintegration were apparent almost from the time of its first emergence. As early as the mid-1940s, for example, sharp internal conflicts were sapping the labor movement's organizational strength and momentum. Within a few years, "Operation Dixie"—the much-vaunted union effort to organize the South—failed disastrously; employers in the West, including Hollywood, began their largely successful attempts to roll back unionization in that region; and Congress passed the sharply anti-labor Taft-Hartley Act. Faced with increased employer and state resistance, and preoccupied with the task of destroying its own radical wing, the labor movement turned inward. It largely ceased to make aggressive and explicitly political appeals to the rest of the work force, and its own organization and leadership changed in ways that weakened the popular base of the New Deal. The Cold War that went on outside the labor movement, and in particular the purge of the universities and the media in the late 1940s, also contributed importantly to this decline, not least by forging a powerful ideological consensus that desperately constrained public debate about the ends of government. Throughout the late 1940s and 1950s, many of the staunchest supporters of the New Deal's most democratic impulses were driven from the scene, with incalculable consequences, in the long run, for the stability of the Democratic coalition.

New Frontiers and the Great Society

For this study, however, the story of the Democrats' decline can most conveniently begin in the late 1950s, at a time when the party was about to receive a renewed boost of business support. At the time, dissatisfaction with the Republicans' austere fiscal policy and stop-go management of the economy ran rife among American multinational businesses. In 1957–58, as what struck observers then as a particularly disastrous recession commenced, that discontent boiled over.

Led, not by women, blacks, unions, or even Lyndon B. Johnson, but by the Rockefeller brothers, a powerful group of multinational business figures began a public campaign to raise the American economy's rate of growth. First in Nelson Rockefeller's political speeches during the late 1950s and then in a series of Rockefeller Brothers Fund studies that involved leading Democrats, this bloc argued that a more consistent application of Keynesian economic principles and strategic reductions in taxes could raise the American economy's growth rate significantly above the anemic levels of the Eisenhower years.

They also argued explicitly that higher growth rates would permit an expansion of public-sector spending.[16]

Echoed in other studies of the period by the multinationally oriented Committee for Economic Development and much research sponsored by the Ford and other foundations, these proposals found scant favor among Republicans. But after Rockefeller lost the first of his several tries for the GOP nomination, the Democrats happily appropriated them. Attracted by the promise "to get America moving again," many multinational business figures turned once again to the Democrats as John F. Kennedy was elected.

Reflecting this constituency, Kennedy appointed a host of multinationally oriented figures to top slots in his Administration. In the Cabinet itself (after offering all three positions to Robert Lovett, the legendary Brown Brothers Harriman partner who had served under Roosevelt and Truman), he gave Treasury to Douglas Dillon, State to Dean Rusk, and Defense to Robert McNamara. Dillon was longtime head of Dillon Read, Rusk came from several years of service as the president of the Rockefeller Foundation, while McNamara, one of the early Harvard Business School "whiz kids," joined the Cabinet only weeks after his promotion to the presidency of Ford.

With such appointments in place, and advised by economists who had worked for the various business organizations that were promoting the new (that is, the old New Deal) growth strategy, the Administration moved forward on its economic program. At the Treasury, Dillon, Robert Roosa, and other leading Democratic financiers implemented "Operation Twist" and other programs to ease balance-of-payments problems that had to be surmounted before the economy could be stimulated. Together with Henry Ford II, David Rockefeller, and the Committee for Economic Development, Kennedy cosponsored the famous "supply side" investment tax credit (along with liberalized depreciation allowances) in 1962, and laid the foundations for the Revenue Act of 1964, which would cut individual income tax rates an average of 20 percent (dropping the top rate from 91 to 70 percent), and cut the general corporation tax rate 8 percent. Urged on by the same groups, the Administration made clear its commitment to freer trade with its passage of the Trade Expansion Act of 1962; it also began preparation for the historic "Kennedy Round" of GATT talks on tariff reductions.[17]

By mid-1963, the new strategy appeared to be working. Though the balance of payments and other problems intermittently created anxiety, the economy showed signs of taking off. As GNP started to race ahead, however, two new developments began to attract attention that had major implications for Democratic Party elites.

First, the always tenuous position of the liberal Republicans within the GOP was disintegrating completely. With the growing boom, imports exploded, threatening many traditional, labor-intensive Republican manufacturers, as well as some primary producers and national oil concerns. Joined by many agricultural interests and smaller businesses who received little or no benefit from the investment-oriented tax cuts and who often feared the effects of rising social spending on their supplies of low-wage, unskilled labor; copper companies, whose prices were collapsing; some defense contractors; and many leftover opponents of the New Deal—these groups went on the offensive. Though at the time they represented a minority of Americans, they constituted a majority of Republicans. After a series of bitter primaries, this coalition seized complete control of the party. Party elites wrote an import-restriction clause right into the party platform. They also denounced the U.N., internationalism, and (memorably) the Rockefellers, as they nominated Barry Goldwater for President.[18]

The other striking development was the growing wave of grass-roots protest rising from communities that had previously held marginal status in the New Deal coalition, particularly black Americans. While Roosevelt had, under pressure, pioneered sufficient civil-rights protections to lead black voters, en masse, to abandon the "party of Lincoln," and Truman's efforts were enough to provoke the famous "Dixiecrat" challenge to the Democrats in 1948, the civil-rights movement, and its relationship to the Democratic Party, was entering a qualitatively new phase. Spurred on by the mechanization of Southern agriculture and wartime manpower shortages in the great industrial centers, millions of Southern blacks had migrated to the North during the 1940s. In the 1950s, the push out of the South continued, but urban labor markets failed to absorb the infusion of new workers. Especially as inner-city unemployment soared, the newly nationalized black population increased its demands for racial equality. The fact that the population was nationalized, in turn, added resonance to the cutting-edge protests of Southern blacks, who were then beginning to mobilize against the "Jim Crow" segregationism of that region.

In the 1950s, dramatic protests of segregated municipal services, as in the Montgomery bus boycott, and sharp struggles over the integration of public schools provided a focus for the new protest movement. In 1960, with actions like the student sit-in at a segregated lunch counter in Greensboro, North Carolina, the movement's scope and tactics widened further. Centered in black churches, but assisted by numerous white activists and students and a handful of New Deal-oriented liberal foundations (including the Stern, Taconic, and Field foundations) with helpful connections to the media and organizations like Atlanta's Southern Regional Council, the movement sharply gained momentum after Kennedy's election. The spring of 1961 saw well-publicized "Freedom Rides" into segregated bus terminals in Alabama and Mississippi, where the freedom riders were attacked by angry mobs (eventually compelling the dispatch of federal marshals to quell them); 1962 was punctuated by riots at the University of Mississippi (again compelling federal intervention) in response to James Meredith's matriculation as a student. These protests reached a peak in 1963, the year that saw Birmingham police commissioner "Bull" Connor turn fire hoses on demonstrators, George Wallace block the doorway to blacks at the University of Alabama, and, in August, the massive March on Washington, where 250,000 demonstrators at the Lincoln Memorial, and a television audience of millions, listened to Martin Luther King say "I have a dream." By this point, the scope of civil-rights protests was truly massive. In 1963 alone, in only eleven Southern states, an estimated 20,000 people were arrested in 930 protest actions in 115 different cities.[19]

In most periods of American history protests on the scale of the civil-rights struggle have led to wholesale repression. But for multinational elites in the 1960s the logic of the situation was quite different. Already in the midst of a program to raise both growth rates and civilian-sector spending, they would hardly be put off by the thought of new social programs. In addition, because they were losing what remained of their position in the GOP, they had a powerful incentive to secure the position of the Democratic Party for a generation. Solidifying the loyalties of one major segment of the population (while finally permitting them the right to vote) would help achieve that goal. Accordingly, as economic growth boomed ahead, many decided to aid the civil-rights movement instead of attempting to crush it. Liberal foundation trustees and distinguished members of the New

FIGURE 2.1

Foundation Grants to Black and Civil-Rights Movement Organizations

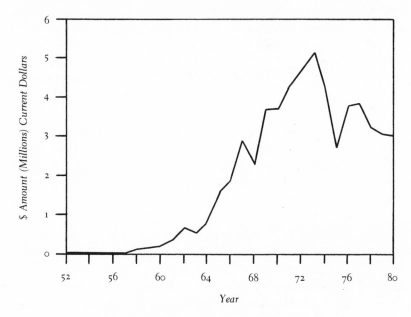

Source: J. Craig Jenkins, Patrons of Social Reform, *in progress*

York and Washington, D.C., bars assisted the efforts of the freedom riders and voting-rights groups. The elite media were sympathetic, while Kennedy Administration officials—who, unlike many of the private groups, definitely hoped that the movement would proceed at a more deliberate pace—arranged a tax exemption for wealthy elites anxious to donate funds to the movement.[20]

After Kennedy's assassination, the same bloc of multinationally oriented, capital-intensive business figures massed behind Lyndon Johnson. Because the point is so important in assessing claims about exactly which set of "special interests" was running the party, it is worth noting explicitly that it was leaders of these business groups— and not blacks, women, or union members—who arrayed in almost wall-to-wall support of LBJ's prodigious fund-raising efforts in the 1964 elections and his promotion of a "Great Society." They also staffed the upper tier of LBJ's Administration, dominated most of the important commissions, panels, and informal circles around the President, and approved the controversial grants Ford and other large foundations made during this period to help organize the unorganized and to register blacks in the South and the cities to vote. It was they who made the pivotal decision to admit women to many exclusive previously all-male colleges; it was their attorneys, in the leading law firms of New York and Washington, who encouraged their younger associates to practice a certain amount of *pro bono* legal work to support the protests. From this group also came the directors of the network broadcasting companies and other major pillars of the Eastern liberal media. [21]

So long as an expanding economy provided sufficient revenues (as it did over the 1961–68 period, when real GNP grew 40 percent), the political program this coalition pursued was, like the original New Deal program, almost irresistible. Multinational firms received trade liberalization and tax cuts. The Kennedy Round of GATT negotiations, for example, yielded an average cut of 30 percent in trade barriers, while Kennedy's supply-side investment tax credit, along with the major 1964 tax reforms, offered big corporations major tax relief. [22]

Multinationals were also primary beneficiaries of the massive Kennedy-Johnson military budgets. Despite the much-publicized "welfare shift" of the New Frontier and Great Society years, annual military spending over FY 1962–65 averaged $80 billion (FY 1972 dollars), the same level maintained over FY 1958–61. It then rose dramatically during the Vietnam buildup to average more than $96 billion over FY 1966–69. Such high levels of spending often provided an important subsidy to the multinationals' domestic production. More importantly, however, they permitted the repeated application of U.S. force abroad to secure their overseas investments. [23]

At the same time, workers were provided with jobs and rising wages. Civilian unemployment averaged only 4.9 percent over the 1961–68 period, and only 3.9 percent between 1965 and 1968, while real average gross weekly earnings for private nonagricultural workers rose more than 12 percent over 1961–68. [24]

Social welfare spending also rose dramatically, with immense broadening of health, income-security, and education benefits for the middle class as well as the poor. Federal spending on "human resources" (a "superfunction" budget category including education, training, employment, social services, health, social security, medicare, income security, and veterans benefits and services) grew from $32 billion to $66 billion (current dollars) over the FY 1962–69, increasing as a share of total federal outlays from 30 to 36 percent.[25]

There was, in short, something for almost everyone. Indeed, in the golden afterglow of Johnson's landslide defeat of Goldwater, the Democrats seemed, for a brief moment, on the verge of consolidating a permanent hold on American politics. But this, of course, was not to be.

Democratic Difficulties

Within just a few years of Johnson's landslide election, the smoothly functioning Democratic political machine was already breaking down. Many of the multinational business figures who had so strongly backed Johnson were going over to Nixon. Sentiment within the business community for a recession was strong. Resistance to taxes and social-welfare spending was rising. Blue-collar support for the Democrats was shaky, and Democrats were bitterly divided over the Vietnam War. Commentators who had only a few years before looked forward to a long period of Democratic dominance now eyed the possibility of a realignment in favor of the Republicans.

While the predicted realignment proved to be a mirage, the middle and late 1960s did see secular changes in the position of the Democrats. Identifying these changes, however, requires a careful look at the truly significant trends among the many contradictory currents in American politics at that time.

If, as the investment perspective suggests, one looks first of all to switches in allegiances of organized groups and elites, then the New Deal party system could break down in only a limited number of ways. The peculiar coalition of the Democrats—multinational, capital-intensive industry and finance, organized labor, and now increasingly well-organized minorities—could disintegrate either because labor and the minorities disappeared or because the multinationals left the party. Alternatively, the firms in the Republican ranks could become more powerful relative to those willing to support the Democrats.

We consider business first. As discussed below, both sunbelt growth and the subsequent surges in world commodity prices did disproportionately advantage some large fortunes and sectors of big business traditionally hostile to the New Deal. Yet, as a glance at the top 50 or 100 firms in the various *Fortune* lists during the 1960s will demonstrate, growth among the large firms and fortunes of America in the 1960s was widely dispersed. As a consequence, it is primarily to a substantial reshuffling among formerly Democratic–inclining firms and fortunes (rather than a takeover by new "sunbelt" elites) that one should look to explain the Democratic decline.[26]

In evaluating this possibility, however, one must attempt to sort out factors that would drive lasting wedges within the Democratic coalition from disruptions that, while dramatic, were transitory and without much importance for long-run party realignment. Viewed in this light, many factors commonly adduced to explain the party's decline probably did not matter much.

Less Than Meets the Eye

The most commonly cited cause of Democratic decline, Vietnam, probably did very little lasting harm to the party. At the time, it assuredly divided business interests within the Johnson coalition. Especially after the Administration failed to raise taxes in 1966, the fabulous dollar outflow that the war entailed exacerbated the already shaky U.S. balance of payments. As pressure mounted on U.S. gold reserves, the dollar itself came increasingly into question, threatening its key role in the Bretton Woods financial system. Left unchecked, this threat, as David Rockefeller himself once explained, would almost certainly cost U.S. banks heavily. Foreign deposits would leave and the banks' own position in the world economy would decline. Many other multinationals figured to lose also, as the ability of the United States to pay for other important overseas commitments disintegrated.[27]

By early 1968, many prominent multinational spokesmen were questioning the war, and the elite media, themselves major multinational enterprises, were increasingly skeptical. André Meyer, the legendary Lazard Frères investment wizard, was encouraging Robert Kennedy to speak out against the war, and other figures from Wall Street were pouring money into the Presidential campaign of Minnesota senator Eugene McCarthy.[28]

But while the elite criticism and growing popular protests against the war embittered hawks in the party, and drove many weapons producers briefly over to the Republicans, the war could divide the party only as long as it lasted. Once it ended, the way would be open to reunite most of the party elites—as eventually happened in 1976, when James Schlesinger and other superhawks came dramatically over to Carter after working against Ford in the Republican primaries.

Similarly, oil producers no doubt had good grounds for suspecting that a bitterly divided, inevitably inwardly-looking Democratic Party would be less likely to move boldly to fill the void looming in their most vital area, the Middle East, as the British prepared to pull back their forces east of Suez. Accordingly, once Nixon made his famous volte-face, and accepted Nelson Rockefeller's foreign-policy adviser, Henry Kissinger, as his own, they swung massively to him in 1968— yet they, too, had no reason permanently to burn their bridges to the Democrats.[29]

Had it been confined to the symptoms then visible, it is equally unlikely that the more general deterioration of economic performance that marked the American economy after the mid-1960s would have led to many permanent changes in party alliances. What one can assert with confidence is that late 1960s run-up in wages, compared to productivity, would not have broken up the party in the long run. While it briefly drove many panicked big businesses over to the GOP, in the expectation that Nixon would promptly tighten the money supply and jolt wage growth, almost no one appears to have foreseen the disaster that lay in store for the American economy. The wage correction envisaged after the 1968 election was cyclical, not secular. Business, especially multinational business, thought the interruption in real growth would be temporary. For the same reasons, although many multinational business figures wanted to cap the rate of increase in social spending, very few contemplated rolling back social security or other major programs. That was something for cranks— like Goldwater.[30]

Nor do most of the other commonly cited factors in the decline of the party in this period account for its long-run decline. Some recent analysts have emphasized the importance of the increasingly dense organization of business evident during this period as a central cause of Democratic difficulties. But unless one assumes, as one should not, that business is monolithically Republican, increased business organization *per se* explains virtually nothing. Many of the businessmen who were indeed organizing then—such as John Connor (chair of Allied Chemical, controlled then by the same Graham family that owned *The Washington Post*) or Sidney Weinberg—supported Humphrey in 1968. Others did the same, or threw support to alternative Democratic candidates. And many others among those mobilizing, of course, had supported Democrats in previous elections.[31]

Another popular explanation for the Democrats' troubles—the increasing role played by TV in American politics and culture—is similarly unhelpful. According to one version of this argument, since TV is expensive and since the Democrats have less money than the Republicans, greater reliance on TV tends to hurt the Democrats. This is not an argument about TV, but about money, and greater or lesser reliance on TV advertising does not itself explain why the Democrats get more or less money from investors. Lyndon Johnson, it will be recalled, got a great deal more money than Barry Goldwater in 1964, and spent a great deal more (very effectively) on TV spots. That Jimmy Carter and Walter Mondale were not able to repeat this performance against Ronald Reagan is not a result of the medium, but of their financing.

A second and more subtle version of the TV argument emphasizes that TV cuts across many different audiences. This is said to disadvantage the Democrats in their use of the medium, because their party features a more heterogeneous mix of constituencies than the GOP. Each time the Democrats use TV to appeal to one group, the argument goes, they risk alienating another. Because the GOP is more homogeneous it suffers less from this trade-off problem, and can use TV more efficiently as a political medium. As the role of TV has grown, this difference in efficiency has become more important.

This second TV argument is almost impossible to falsify, but seems weak for at least two reasons. First, both major parties are coalitions of diverse groups (the Democrats have no monopoly on that status), and diversity is a precondition of growth in American politics. The bigger the party, the greater the diversity, and, presumably, the greater the problem of trade-offs among diverse constituencies. It should not be limited to the Democrats. Second, even during the Democrats' heydays of heterogeneity they repeatedly demonstrated their ability to use modern media to speak across, and unite, diverse constituencies. Consider Roosevelt's "Fireside Chats," or Kennedy's famous press conferences, or Johnson's State of the Union addresses. As in many other areas of public debate, the alleged "trade-off" does not exist.

But even if either or both of the two versions of the TV hypothesis are credited in their substance, there are serious problems in timing. The great rise in the influence of TV did not come in the 1960s and 1970s, but during the 1950s, when the percentage of American households owning the new medium jumped from 9 to 87 percent; since then, of course, the growth has been much less dramatic. If increased TV penetration works against the Democrats, the most dramatic decline in Democratic successes would thus most plausibly be expected in the early or middle sixties. Instead, Lyndon Johnson defeated his Republican opponent by a landslide.[32]

The Decline of Organized Labor

The role of the chief nonbusiness investor in the party—organized labor—was somewhat different. The long boom of the middle and late 1960s tightened labor markets and increased labor's bargaining power with business. Because the boom was pulling wages up, and the unionized percentage of the work force was drifting down only slowly, indices of the "strength of labor" (such as the pattern of wage settlements) that primarily reflect changes in labor-market conditions show labor's fortunes actually improving until at least 1971.[33] Thus labor, which surely did not abandon the Democrats during the 1960s, did not "disappear" during that decade either. Indeed, in the context of the wage gains won by union members during the long sixties boom, it might be asked if wage pressures destabilized the Democrats in a different way, by driving firms out of the party. That question, which we think is best addressed in the context of the drastically different economic conditions of the middle and late 1970s, is considered in the next chapter. For reasons explored there, we think, on the whole, that it did not. But if labor cannot be looked to (either in the 1960s or in the 1970s) as a primary source of decline in the New Deal coalition, its political fortunes within the party, and the decisions it made in the 1960s, nevertheless invite attention. They do so because they illuminate the range of constraints on elite business responses (including those of Democratic business figures) to the later situation. And here what should be emphasized is that those constraints were weakened during the 1960s.

Considered in political terms, labor's strength within the Democratic Party was deteriorating rapidly. In the mid-1960s, despite the most one-sidedly Democratic Congress since the New Deal, and the ritual commitment to labor in the Democratic Party platform, labor failed to secure its long-sought abolition or amendment of the Taft-Hartley Act's infamous "14(b)" provision, which was used by Southern and Western state legislatures to outlaw union shops, thus posing significant barriers to union organization in those regions.[34]

Instead, on labor-law reform and other aspects of domestic labor regulation, Johnson listened to the pleas of such business groups as the Labor Law Study Group (LLSG), an elite association of some fifty of the nation's top firms (including AT&T, Ford, General Dynamics, GE, Humble Oil, 3M, and U.S. Steel) and some forty of its leading trade associations (including the reviving National Association of Manufacturers and the U.S. Chamber of Commerce), formed in anticipation of labor's offensive on Taft-Hartley. Staging an elaborately choreographed fandango with Senate Republican leader Everett Dirksen, LBJ allowed the move to repeal 14(b) to die in filibuster, thus squandering the greatest opportunity the postwar period ever provided his party to help labor. And while the Administration dallied, the LLSG and other new business organizations that emerged in response to the 1960s boom's run-up in wages flailed away at existing legal protections for workers. Among the most significant of these other business associations was the Construction Users Anti-Inflation Roundtable—boasting a membership that included top officers from General Electric, Exxon, Kennecott Copper, General Motors, U.S. Steel, and Du Pont—which began a coordinated, and eventually almost nationwide, attack on the construction unions at the heart of the AFL. Later, in the 1970s, the Anti-Inflation Roundtable would metamorphose into the Business Roundtable, the preeminent lobbying arm of big business throughout the decade.[35]

Nor did the Democrats assist unions on the other great issue of growing concern to them—the devastating impact that ever freer trade was having on union jobs. Imports fell with particular force on older, less competitive, and more heavily unionized sectors of American manufacturing—including shoes, textiles, and steel—and union membership losses attributable to imports mounted throughout the decade. But Johnson, like Kennedy before him, turned aside labor's pleas for import protection. He pressed forward with the deep tariff cuts of the GATT's Kennedy Round and helped block efforts labor made in Congress to increase trade protection.

Organized labor's response to the labor-law and trade setbacks was less than rousing. Unwilling to press either issue to the breaking point, it did very little to reverse the course of its own decline.

At its base, labor failed in the 1960s to broaden and consolidate its power through the organization of unorganized workers. Between 1953 and 1960 wage-deflated union organizing expenditures per nonunion worker had already dropped 9 percent; over 1961–71, they dropped another 21 percent. The number of organizing drives in the private sector stagnated, and the annual percentage of private nonagricultural wage and salary workers organized into unions through NLRB elections declined, dropping from about 0.8 percent of that work force in 1955 to 0.6 percent in 1960, 0.5 percent in 1970, and 0.3 percent by 1975. Rather than conduct these costly organizing drives, labor accepted the Democratic Administrations' invitation to organize government workers. The gains made there, however, were not enough to reverse the continued decline of organized workers as a percentage of the civilian work force, which dropped from 26 to 21 percent over 1970–80. Private-sector unionization declined even in absolute terms, with 320,000 members lost in the AFL–CIO over 1969–79.[36]

Perhaps even more seriously, thanks to Johnson's alliance with (part of) big business, unions failed throughout the 1960s to expand significantly in the South and West. Because these were the fastest-growing regions in the country, failure to secure organizational gains there guaranteed the decline of labor's national political strength. In a political system beset by sharp regional disparities, where the basis of most legislative politics is logrolling and the swapping of favors, organized labor repeatedly suffered from its status as an almost purely regional phenomenon. In many parts of the country, it simply had very little with which to deal.

But the leadership of the movement remained unconcerned about this deterioration. As longtime AFL–CIO president George Meany commented in the early 1970s, when the deep rot in labor's organized base was already clearly visible: "Frankly I used to worry about the membership, about the size of the membership. But quite a few years ago, I just stopped worrying about it, because to me it doesn't make any difference."[37]

Nor did AFL–CIO leadership do much to ally itself with the great protest and social movements which rocked the 1960s. While parts of labor supported parts of the civil-rights movement, especially in its early stages, relations between the two were never easy and became increasingly troubled through the decade, which ended with ugly (and generally completely successful) attempts by entrenched union leaders to crush black worker organizations. The labor leadership's attitude toward the emerging women's movement was less ambiguous: it was openly hostile. Later, after a period of tepid support, it turned against the environmental movement too.[38]

Labor's leadership thus passed up yet another golden opportunity to expand the dwindling number of private-sector workers in unions. Even worse from a long-run standpoint, its divergence from these movements virtually guaranteed that their leadership structure would eventually be heavily weighted toward business—both in the direct sense that the many "natural" advantages black business groups and corporate-career-oriented women enjoyed would eventually bring them to the top of these organizations and in the equally fundamental sense that liberal corporate-dominated foundations and media became the only places these groups could hope to obtain resources to organize.

The consequence of this was to make the movements more conservative, less oriented toward the welfare of average workers, and much more vulnerable to business/foundation decisions on what, where, and how much to fund. They were, for example, ill prepared for the foundations' later decision, in the 1970s, to pull back on their support for social action. In the meantime, besieged for funds by many different organizations, the liberal business groups could play endless games of divide and conquer. Labor unions would continue to lose members, and millions of blacks, women, and Hispanics fail to get the unions they needed. Having abandoned most efforts to reach (increasingly Southern and Western) white male blue-collar workers who were not organized, as well as most blacks and women, the movement that could most sensibly claim to represent almost every ordinary American's general interest could hardly avoid looking more and more like the "special interest" of a lucky few.[39]

Continuous with these responses on the domestic front were labor's actions in foreign arenas. Here, too, the positions of the AFL–CIO leadership helped alienate labor from many of its natural domestic allies—as in the case of its tireless boosting of the Vietnam War. Not uncommonly, the AFL–CIO also contributed directly to U.S. military adventures and covert actions abroad, as with its longtime activities in support of "free trade unionism" abroad. Channeling funds from

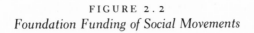

FIGURE 2.2
Foundation Funding of Social Movements

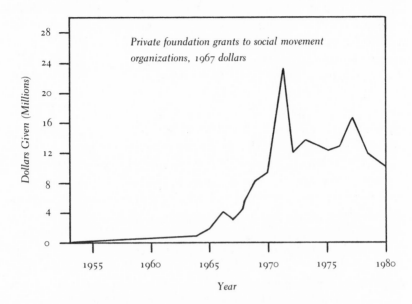

Private foundation grants to social movement organizations, 1967 dollars

Source: J. Craig Jenkins, "Foundation Funding of Social Movements," in The Grantseekers Guide, ed. Jill Shellow, 2nd ed. (Mt. Kisco, N.Y.: Moyer Bell, Ltd., 1985), 13.

the CIA and other U.S. government agencies, such AFL–CIO affiliates as the American Institute for Free Labor Development (AIFLD), which operated extensively in Latin and Central America, helped subvert opposition movements in repressive regimes and topple left-leaning or nationalist governments.

In the 1960s AIFLD played supportive roles in undermining the Jagan government in British Guiana, in the Brazilian coup of 1964, in the overthrow of the Bosch government in the Dominican Republic in 1965, and in a long campaign to undermine the labor movements of Uruguay and Argentina. Later, after the election of socialist Salvador Allende to the presidency of Chile, it would play an instrumental role (aided, of course, by many other U.S. interests) in destabilizing and finally toppling that regime. At AIFLD, as in other labor ventures during that period, representatives of what Meany described as "enlightened American Business" were welcomed on board as advisers for labor's activities. AIFLD's board was long chaired by

W. R. Grace's J. Peter Grace, who would later emerge as a key Reagan supporter, and the organization drew the early participation of other prominent Latin and Central American investors, including Juan Trippe of Pan American World Airways, Charles Brinkerhoff of Anaconda Copper, William H. Hickey of United Fruit, Robert C. Hill of Merck & Co., and the ubiquitous Nelson Rockefeller.

For their own part, top labor statesmen eagerly accepted the token positions (usually comprising less than 1 percent of the membership) they were offered in elite private foreign-policy organizations like the Council on Foreign Relations, a sort of private patronage that complemented the government patronage, and trips to the White House provided by the Johnson Administration.[40]

Coupled with their inability to stop imports, the union leaders' enthusiastic support of American foreign-policy objectives also worked directly to hurt their members' economic position. Much American military and foreign aid is used to prop up regimes that repress their own citizens and their wages. Such aid in effect subsidizes multinational expansion abroad by lowering the costs of that expansion— either by lowering wages or by reducing risks of popular (and investment-threatening) social upheaval in repressive regimes. Particularly as new developments in transportation, communications, and production-process design further facilitated the segmentation of world production chains and the "outsourcing" of all manner of products, the labor leadership's role in promoting multinational expansion abroad came back to haunt American workers in the form of business relocations to other countries and a tidal wave of low-cost imports. In the case of Vietnam, of course, labor's boosting of U.S. aggression had more immediate and visible costs for union members: body bags containing the remains of their sons.

In addition to all this, the labor leadership's unwillingness to challenge the Democrats and their corporate supporters on the financing and design of the new social programs inaugurated during the 1960s also served to divide the New Deal system's popular constituencies. The problem at its starkest was this: In their haste to demonstrate their wholehearted commitment to "free enterprise," AFL–CIO leaders had enthusiastically endorsed the "investment tax credit" concepts that lay behind the early Kennedy tax initiatives and the major 1964 tax act, and essentially abandoned the fight for the expansion of the progressive income tax. When coupled with the peculiar structure of the new social programs that Kennedy and Johnson were promoting, this decision produced two disastrous results.

First, while Kennedy, Johnson, and their multinational supporters had no intention of moving directly against the income tax, they also had no desire to pay for the social programs they were supporting. Accordingly, to finance most of the social programs, they simply borrowed a leaf from the high New Deal. Like Franklin Roosevelt before them, they arranged to have most of the benefits financed by a rise in the social security tax—the most directly regressive of all American federal taxes. Especially when combined with the cuts in corporate tax rates, and the proliferation of corporate credits, this step made the tax system significantly less progressive than it had been, while sharply increasing tax burdens on those who could least afford it. Between 1965 and 1975, corporation income taxes declined as a percentage of gross federal receipts from 21.8 to 14.6 percent. Over the same period, social security taxes and contributions rose from 19 to 30.3 percent. The effects were felt most keenly at the bottom of the American income pyramid. For those in the bottom (first) decile, the effective rate of payroll taxes nearly tripled between 1966 and 1975; for those in the second decile, it more than doubled.[41]

Second, Johnson and his multinational constituency were businessmen first, last, and always. Though they were committed to the idea that state action could prop up the free-enterprise system, they had no intention of bringing socialism to America. They looked, accordingly, to advisory groups and task forces of businessmen (and conservative professionals and bureaucrats dependent on the business groups for patronage and bureaucratic support) to define how those programs would work. Put baldly, they wanted urban programs designed on the advice of mortgage bankers, downtown merchants, real-estate magnates and developers; crime programs directed by what one sociologist called "the police industrial complex"; and medical programs that reflected the uncertain balance of power struck by the often warring segments of the business and professional community concerned with medical care: drug and pharmaceutical companies; large foundations interested in health; medical instrument companies; the American Medical Association; various types of hospitals; and insurance companies. Encouraged by some large foundations and the example of the New Deal, they also built into virtually all these programs an emphasis on litigation as a means of resolving conflicts, rather than mediation or conciliation. [42]

These features of the programs ensured several results. First, save for social security itself, which continued to be administered by a tiny, centralized staff, they would be inefficient, delivering a relatively low level of service for the money. Second, they would be difficult to reform, because many of the programs would have developed powerful support not simply among citizens (who were regularly denied unions and many other services they could benefit from) but from many businesses. Third, as the programs became more expensive, corporate tax rates fell, and the highly regressive social security tax structure collected more and more revenues, the burden on the average taxpayer would grow. It was a system that could hardly avoid inflaming tensions between different groups of middle- and lower-income Americans. Several Republican analysts noted this, although they ascribed the result mostly to "demography." [43]

The Nixon Transition

At the time Nixon took office, predictions of a new political realignment based largely on these "demographic" shifts and "value" conflicts ran rife. And, indeed, had the Nixon Administration represented a coherent power bloc with a clear interest in making such an appeal, such a coalition might have come to life. But the regime was in fact highly fragmented. The product of elaborate compromises among different and commonly competing groups (including a formal pre-nomination commitment by Nixon to the textile producers to guard their tariffs), the Administration is best thought of as a typical transition product of a party system in disintegration. Spokespersons for the old opposition to the New Deal (textiles, steel, and other protectionist concerns and some independent oil companies), represented in the Cabinet by men like Frederick Dent or Howard Callaway, jumbled uneasily together under one roof with an odd assortment of multinationally oriented figures including Elliot Richardson, William Rogers, and, of course, Kissinger. [44]

As a consequence, until the catastrophic 1973–75 recession convinced most American elites that they were facing a true long-run crisis, the Administration did not pursue a consistent policy toward the heritage of the New Deal.

On some occasions, Nixon and some of his advisers talked like people who wanted to roll back most of what had occurred since 1935, or at least since the Great Society. Through revenue sharing, block grants, and a program advertised as "New Federalism," the Nixon Administration moved to undermine the categorical programs that Johnson and other Democratic Presidents had used to solidify their constituencies. The Administration also made some low-key efforts to inhibit the progress of the civil-rights movement and (encouraged, according to John Ehrlichman, by Secretary of Labor George Shultz) to play blacks and labor off against one another. It also responded more repressively than the Johnson Administration to the rising level of mass protest, which by the late 1960s included substantial popular protest against the Vietnam War. Aggressively implementing the Crime Control and Safe Streets Act (1968), and gaining additional federal crime legislation in 1970 (and later, in 1973), the Administration vastly increased federal funding of state and local police officials through the Law Enforcement Assistance Administration (LEAA). LEAA funding for "technical assistance," weapons acquisition, and other programs to assist local police rose from $100 million in FY 1968–69 to $300 million in 1970, and increased substantially each year after that; by 1976, reflecting the commitments of the Nixon Administration, LEAA had spent $5 billion on various crime programs. Combined with sweeping violations of civil liberties and a variety of illegal espionage and intelligence programs, this signaled a "tougher" attitude toward domestic protest.[45]

But the limited nature of these initiatives is striking. As a number of analysts have already noted, in many key policy areas the Nixon Administration continued along the same general lines as Johnson. Social spending increased substantially, not only because of already established commitments to Great Society programs, but also because of the Administration's own spending initiatives. During Nixon's first term, for example, social security benefits were repeatedly raised—by 15 percent in 1970, another 10 percent in 1971, and another 15 percent in 1972. In addition, in a major reform of the program, the 1972 Social Security Amendments moved to secure such hikes by mandating automatic inflation adjustments in benefit levels beginning in 1975. And in some areas, most notably in its famous guaranteed-income family-assistance plan, the Administration demonstrated a willingness to engage in major liberal reform.[46]

The reason is straightforward. As Nixon himself clearly sensed, the part of his bloc that was tied to the "Eastern liberal establishment" largely retained its commitment to the policy formulas of the New Deal. Though many of these business and foundation types were concerned about wage pressures, lagging productivity, and the weakening U.S. terms of trade (itself a product partly of increasing Third World nationalism, but mostly of boom-induced competition among producers in the advanced economies that bid up the prices of inputs to production), their concerns generally remained short-term. The problems they saw were correctable in economic theory by a short period of austerity, which would lower both wages and prices of imports from the Third World. They did not necessitate an all-out attack on the welfare state.[47]

Holding back the rising pressure from traditional Republican manufacturing for a major assault on labor, Shultz and his successor as Secretary of Labor, John Dunlop (the Harvard professor and eventual GTE director who actually joined AFL–CIO chiefs in Caribbean investments), along with other multinationally oriented economic-policy makers, sought to continue the traditional accommodative relations between labor and big business. As the withdrawal of troops from Vietnam, the coming of détente, and the Administration's famous policy of building up regional surrogates for the United States in areas of vital interest (such as Iran in the Middle East) reduced the need for defense spending, the same elements in the Administration were quite willing to let social programs expand.[48]

Environmental Legislation

Even more striking than the pattern of social spending and labor relations during Nixon's first term was the virtual explosion of "social" regulation that took place then—in particular, regulation concerning the environment. Because these regulations figure later in our story of Democratic decline, and because the political pressures that produced them have not generally been understood, this sudden burst of legislation merits more than a moment's notice.

Since all production in any economy involves transforming nature, there is a special, limited sense in which virtually all economic activities place the environment at risk. "Free enterprise" economies have, however, an inherent tendency toward substantial environmental deterioration, since without affirmative state action of some sort, profit-maximizing producers have every incentive to throw as many of their costs as possible on someone else. Factory owners, for example, add to their profits by discharging their wastes into neighboring rivers and venting smoke into scenic valleys. Were they compelled to clean these discharges up—or, in the terminology of modern welfare economics, if they were forced to "internalize" the costs they were transferring to other citizens—their own costs of production would rise. Though industry spokesmen often gloss over the fact, most debates over environmental regulation are arguments about who will bear costs, not about whether they will be paid at all.

It is apparent that some cases of environmental damage involve head-on collisions of the interests of "business as a whole" with that of the public. Virtually all profit-maximizing producers, for example, have an interest in concealing hazardous workplace conditions from their employees. But few other environmental issues are so clear-cut. While almost everyone enjoys their once-in-a-lifetime visit to the Grand Canyon, appreciation of the environment, like most other good things in a market economy, is often a form of luxury consumption. Accordingly, what is at issue in many environmental disputes is not (or not only) the distribution of costs between "business" and a broad "public," but between certain businesses and other firms and members of the upper classes.[49]

It is possible, as some accounts of early-nineteenth-century Manchester suggest, that the sources of wealth for an upper class could be so concentrated that few if any of its members would find it in their interest to try to limit such externalities. But in a complex and diverse business community, this is quite unlikely. Costs are costs, and the same keen self-interest that leads enterprises to pollute will lead to resistance by at least larger economic actors.[50]

Were there sufficient space, one could trace in detail the ties of the coastal rich, such as the Rockefellers, to the creation of the National Park System and other monuments of the early environmental movement. For the present, however, it must be enough to notice that an economy dominated increasingly by services (themselves less dependent, in general, on environmental degradation) could hardly fail to produce increasing numbers of bankers, brokers, insurers, and real-estate magnates, as well as many other upper-income people who enjoy the environment and who, in contrast to most Americans, have the means to protect it.

In the 1960s, as revolutionary technologies in plastics and other petrochemically based products took hold, and rapid growth in the South and West led utilities to look increasingly to ecologically fragile hinterlands for additional sources of power and water, it was inevitable that large numbers of such people would resist strongly. Other groups with an interest in the "environment" also became embroiled. The Oil, Chemical and Atomic Workers, for example, helped promote the ill-fated Occupational Health and Safety legislation. Makers of catalytic converters helped finance the fight for clean-air legislation. The Southern Railway located the "snail darter" and brought to a halt a major waterway project sponsored by competing barge interests. Eastern coal producers attempted to use "clean-air requirements" to cripple Western producers. The insurance industry promoted the air bag and other safety measures. Developers, fisheries, and tourist-oriented businesses rose up against oil spills off their coasts that threatened their livelihood. And interests in heavily industrialized (and thus heavily polluted) Northeastern and Midwestern cities promoted stringent national standards for the protection of air and water quality. This increased the operating costs of firms doing business in relatively less polluted areas in the South and West and in rural America, and thereby worked to slow the rush of business to those regions. Overjoyed to discover fertile new areas for expensive litigation, lawyers also rushed to file suits.[51]

The prevalence of litigation and lobbying is, indeed, a clue to the direction the environmental movement gradually took. Though small, locally rooted, and poorly budgeted radical groups remained on its fringes, the organizational center of the new environmentalism rested in a handful of major foundation and litigation groups, the most aggressive of which—such as the Environmental Defense Fund and the National Resources Defense Council—had strong ties to multinational finance. In the case of those two groups, international lawyers and leading business figures make up more than three-quarters of the board, while major foundations and prominent financiers donate funds or, in the case of the National Resources Defense Council (which Laurance Rockefeller helped incorporate), actually founded them. Without the support of their affluent board members and continuing infusions of grant money, these groups could not possibly have mustered the resources their vast litigation programs required. They also had excellent contacts with (if indeed their trustees did not own) the major media, which, as another service industry whose owners and managers feared and resented the costs other industries dumped on them, figured to be a natural ally in any event.[52]

Why the Johnson Administration, which drew most of its top personnel entirely from such circles, should therefore have encouraged the initial stages of this movement is therefore no mystery. Nor, with Russell Petersen (the future president of the Audubon Society) and a good many other multinational environmentalists holding major positions in its ranks, should it be surprising that the Nixon Administration did.

Nixon's NEP and the 1972 Election

There was, however, one area where the Nixon Administration did depart from the policy framework of the New Deal. In August 1971, Nixon unveiled his notorious New Economic Policy (NEP) for the United States. In addition to instituting a regime of wage-price controls to curb continuing pressures to inflation, the NEP suspended the dollar's convertibility to gold—a decision that set the dollar free to "float" against other currencies, and thus lose value; and imposed a 10 percent surcharge on all dutiable imports. It thus broke sharply with the Bretton Woods commitments to expanding multilateralism and free trade.

The pressures that finally led to the NEP took a long time to build, and their source is deeply rooted in the structure of the Bretton Woods system itself. By relying on the dollar as the world's reserve currency, Bretton Woods required that the United States continually supply the rest of the world with dollars to use in the conduct and financing of international trade. For a while after World War II, the need for additional dollars was met mostly by direct transfers—foreign aid, the Marshall Plan, and America's huge overseas expenditures for military and other purposes. Later, private capital outflows helped swell the total. During the 1950s and 1960s, as the world economy recovered from World War II and vastly expanded its production and trade, the U.S. "capital account"—the account of investment and other capital flows between the United States and the rest of the world—was nearly continuously in the red.[53]

As Robert Triffin and other critics eventually pointed out, however, this "dollar standard" had a severe drawback. Confidence in the dollar depended ultimately on the belief that the United States stood ready to redeem all those dollars in gold. In the long run, however, billions of dollars flowing abroad threatened to accumulate into a massive "dollar overhang" beyond any possibility of redemption. At that point, instead of holding dollars, other countries might seek to convert them to gold, leading to a run on the gold reserve and causing a collapse of the dollar standard.[54]

During the 1960s, the United States debated with France and other countries over the costs and benefits of this dollar standard. By the late 1960s, however, the argument was becoming academic. U.S. trade performance was declining, private capital flows abroad were increasing, and the Vietnam War escalation was in full swing. By the late 1960s, the annual U.S. capital account deficit was running in the $10–$15 billion range. The stream of dollars flowing abroad had become a roaring torrent, and foreign confidence in the dollar was ebbing rapidly. In 1971, after declining for several years, the U.S. merchandise trade balance also turned negative—for the first time since 1893.

A feeling akin to panic gripped many sectors of American business. The clamor from import-threatened sectors for trade restrictions became deafening, while multinational free-traders voiced fears that the entire postwar system of multilateralism might unravel. As the Nixon Administration desperately sought some sort of accommodation between the groups, a special Presidential commission on international economics (known as the Williams Commission, after its chair, an executive of IBM), whose members included executives from both successful multinationals and import-threatened sectors, came forward with a proposal that the United States aggressively pursue a general revaluation of other currencies.

Because it promised to lower the value of the now badly overvalued dollar, this suggestion attracted support from both free-traders and protectionists. Many of the latter, particularly the bigger ones that could still afford to retrench, could hope that a revaluation of other currencies would again make them competitive. Many free-traders, on the other hand, were well aware that the existing degree of dollar overvaluation was unsustainable in the long run. It would ultimately have to be corrected. In August, with calls for action rising (including pressures from the Business Council), imports continuing to flood in, and no prospect in sight for international agreement on new exchange rates, Nixon acted unilaterally and declared his NEP.[55]

The move triggered a firestorm of agitation. The allies—especially the Japanese—were alarmed. And while nearly everyone in the business community agreed that some sort of action had been necessary, many business groups were upset with the way the Administration had acted. Protectionists had cause for alarm, since the NEP's 10 percent import surcharge was announced as temporary, and viewed by free-traders merely as an expedient to force the currency realignment. Extreme free-traders, however, opposed even temporary import barriers, while many more internationalists feared the spasm of economic nationalism might trigger a trade war.

The deepening anxiety among multinational business groups led to action on several fronts. Leading business figures and free-trading economists sharply criticized the NEP and agitated for trade liberalization. Organizations like the OECD, the Atlantic Council, and (eventually) the new Trilateral Commission mounted major campaigns to increase international coordination of economic policies and shore up domestic support for free trade and internationalism. And while domestic firms (often in alliance with labor) complained bitterly about illegal trade actions by other countries and promoted hundreds of trade-restriction bills in an increasingly protectionist Congress, multinationals pressed to control the damage, and downplayed what in retrospect do indeed seem to have been flat violations of the GATT rules by the Japanese.[56]

Some multinational business figures went further. They began lining up behind Democrats—a few behind George McGovern, but most behind Senator Edwin Muskie, a rather clearly favored candidate of traditional Democratic internationalists. For a brief moment, indeed, it appeared that divisions along the trade issue might govern business alliances in the 1972 election.[57]

But this was not to be. Just as Muskie's campaign was getting under way, the infamous "plumbers" associated with CREEP (Committee to Re-Elect the President) began their campaign of "dirty tricks" against him, introducing all manner of logistical and other problems in his effort, and surely contributing to the frustration evidenced by his famous crying jag during the New Hampshire primary. As Nixon hastily withdrew the 10 percent import surcharge, Muskie's campaign sagged, and then disintegrated.[58]

In the meantime, Nixon was moving to placate the international-ists. In late 1971 his Administration entered into a series of bilateral and multilateral negotiations on exchange rates, which by December issued in the so-called Smithsonian Agreement on exchange-rate management (and, eventually, the transition to floating exchange rates). Once the Smithsonian Agreement was in place, the Administration withdrew the import surcharge. And as 1972 began, the Administra-tion made clear its opposition to protectionist legislation pending in Congress (most prominently, the famous Burke-Hartke bill), while pressuring, eventually successfully, for a new round of GATT tariff-reduction talks in Tokyo.

Nixon's moves on the trade issue interacted with developments among the Democrats to bring many internationalists into his cam-paign. In Democratic ranks, Muskie's collapse had opened the way for McGovern, who had been waging an obscure campaign for the Democratic nomination for the past two years. Backed by a small bloc of prominent antiwar multinationalists—including Max Palev-sky, then chair of Xerox's executive committee; Michel Fribourg, head of Continental Grain; and Max Factor III, a name familiar to at least half the American population—McGovern had also won the alle-giance of many academics and other professionals.[59]

For most American business, however, even "liberal" multina-tional business, McGovern's aggressive anti-Pentagon stance and openness to progressive redistribution marked him as beyond the pale. Once he appeared headed for the nomination, accordingly, most multinationalists accepted the overtures the Nixon Administration was making, and helped swell his campaign war chest to enormous (and, as it turned out, quite illegal) proportions. With the class enemy run-ning, multinational bankers and financiers also departed sharply from their customary practice, and sat by almost mutely while Nixon and the Fed turned on the monetary spigot for one of the greatest political business cycles in all U.S. history.[60]

As they waited for the post-election downturn that everyone but the voters saw coming, most business leaders undoubtedly expected it would be a replay of Nixon's 1969–70 recession, which had man-aged a successful "correction" to overheated wages. By 1971, wage growth had been reduced to 1.9 percent, while productivity growth had increased to 3.6 percent, and profits were rebounding sharply. When the Fed again tightened up after the 1972 election, however, the business community received a stunning surprise. Predictably, the economy slid into recession, and the huge rise in unemployment drove wages down. But this time the economy did not bounce back. Wages went down, and down, as the American economy, and most of the developed world, entered its worst period since the Great Depression. Even after the recession ended, U.S. wages kept dropping. Profits, productivity growth, and export shares also declined; only inflation and imports rose.[61]

The recession that began at the end of 1973, and stretched through the beginning of 1975, was a watershed event in American political economy. It marked the end of the long period of growth that had been sustained since World War II, underscored the changed position of the United States in the world economy, and ushered in a sustained period of domestic stagflation. It was then that American politics finally made its decisive turn to the right.

3/

Right Turn:

The Dismal 1970s

In a community as fragmented and decentralized as American big business, truly profound reversals of opinion usually require considerable time. Because such changes are as much processes as events, assigning a single date to them almost inevitably courts misunderstanding. But insofar as such an effort ever makes sense, it does for the terrible recession of the early 1970s. Lasting seventeen months, from November 1973 to March 1975, it was by far the longest and deepest economic downturn the United States had experienced since the Great Depression. It was then that the great developments that eventually drove American politics to the right became dramatically evident. And it was then that basic doubts about the whole New Deal began to spread throughout the American business community, including its multinational wing.

Deteriorating U.S. economic performance in an increasingly competitive and integrated world economy is the analytic key to the Democrats' decline. In a variety of ways, sagging growth and profits at home, and increased competition abroad, made the business community much more cost-sensitive. This stiffened business opposition to the growth of social spending and forced the Democrats to work within tighter fiscal constraints on their domestic programs. Pressures on the social side of the budget increased as growing U.S. involvement in the international economy, and in particular in the Third World, widened demands within the business community for increased military spending. Moreover, these competing demands on the budget could not be easily reconciled by simply raising taxes, for as profit margins sagged and intensified competition from abroad made it more difficult for corporations to pass taxes through to consumers, much of the business community was mobilizing in support of further tax reductions. Over the course of the decade, the convergence of these different pressures and demands produced a growing budget crisis in the United States, in effect forcing a choice between social and military spending.

For the Republicans, pressures to make this choice presented an enormous political opportunity. Unencumbered by a mass base, and devoted, as Office of Management and Budget (OMB) director David Stockman would later put it, to the principle that "government doesn't owe anyone anything," the Republicans were quite prepared to serve as a vehicle for tax and domestic-spending cuts and increased military outlays. For the Democrats, however, the growing trade-off between guns and butter forced the party to walk a political tightrope between the demands of its elite constituency and the needs of its mass base. Even as the Democrats moved to the right over the course of the decade and the center of American party politics shifted, the tensions within the Democrats' ranks made them a less efficient vehicle for business aspirations than the Republicans. The GOP was thus the first beneficiary of America's right turn.[1]

Economic Decline

While it was highlighted by the 1973–75 recession, the economic deterioration that drove this process began before, and continued after, that catastrophic event. In sketching some of its dimensions here, accordingly, we will refer back and forth in time. At the bottom line, profits of U.S. firms declined after 1965 and failed throughout the next fifteen years to regain their early 1960s levels (Figure 3.1). Annual net investment in plant and equipment followed suit, falling from an average 4 percent of GNP during 1966–70 to 3.1 over 1971–75 and 2.9 percent over 1976–80. As the baby-boom generation moved into the job market in the 1970s, the average annual growth rate of net fixed investment per worker dropped even more sharply, falling from 3.9 percent during 1966–70 to a bare 0.4 percent over 1976–80. Productivity suffered in turn, as the annual growth of output per worker employed in nonresidential business fell from 2.45 percent

FIGURE 3.1

Rate of Return on Capital for Nonfinancial Corporations

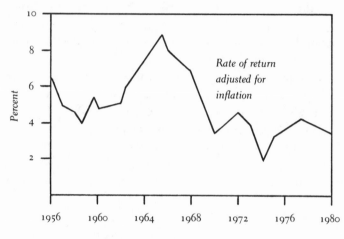

Rate of return
adjusted for
inflation

NOTE: *Rate of return* = $\dfrac{\textit{Corporate profit after taxes}}{\textit{Net capital stock (including inventory)}}$

valued at current (replacement) costs

Source: Scott, "Competitiveness," 30

over 1948–73 to 0.08 percent over 1973–79. Not surprisingly, over-all growth rates tumbled. Average annual growth in real GNP also tumbled, from 4.1 percent over 1960–73 to 2.3 percent over 1973–80.[2]

For workers, the picture became particularly gloomy. After averaging 3.8 percent over 1965–69, unemployment rose to 5.4 percent over 1970–74 and 7 percent over 1975–79. Average real gross weekly earnings for private nonagricultural workers moved erratically in the late 1960s and early 1970s, rising 3 percent between 1965 and 1969, then dropping in 1970 below their 1968 level, then rising again to a postwar peak in 1972. After that they trended sharply downward, and by 1980 reached their lowest level since 1962. Real median family income also stagnated: after doubling between 1947 and 1973, it dropped 6 percent over 1973–80.[3]

The international picture looked even worse. In the immediate postwar period, the United States had stood unrivaled as the world's hegemonic economic power. As the economies of Western Europe and Japan rebuilt, however, and parts of the Third World were more tightly integrated into the world capitalist system, the relative position of the United States declined. Between 1950 and 1960, the U.S. share of world GNP dropped from 40 to 26 percent, and its share of world trade fell from 20 to 16 percent. Over the next two decades, both shares continued to fall, dropping to 23 and 14 percent, respectively, by 1970, and to 21.5 and 11 percent, respectively, by 1980. America's largest firms were not excepted from this trend. In 1956, 42 of the world's top 50 industrial companies were U.S. firms. By 1970, the number had dropped to 32; by 1980, it was 23.[4]

It should be noted that much of the early decline in the U.S. share of world GNP and trade simply reflected a correction of the peculiar situation that obtained at the close of World War II, when the economies of other major countries were still in ruins. At least after 1960, however, the gradual decline in the relative size of the U.S. economy was outpaced by the decline in trade. In dropping from 26 to 21.5 percent over 1960–80, the U.S. share of world GNP declined 17 percent. During the same period, the U.S. share of world trade dropped much faster, falling 31 percent. Quite apart from the growth of other economies, U.S. competitiveness was in decline.[5]

This decline in competitive position was particularly evident in U.S. manufacturing. Overall, the U.S. market share of manufactures fell from 26 to 18 percent over 1960–80, and the trade balance on non-R&D-intensive manufactures grew increasingly negative from the early 1960s on. Positive trade balances in R&D-intensive manufactures grew over the same period, but even here the U.S. lost its world market share in most of the top categories. As noted already, declining U.S. competitiveness eventually showed up in a negative balance on the merchandise trade account in 1971. With a brief interruption in the mid-1970s, the trade balance grew increasingly negative through the rest of the decade.[6]

Even as it lost out in international competition, however, the United States became increasingly *integrated* into the world economy, a development that marked a virtual revolution in U.S. international economic relations. Together, exports and imports comprised only 7 percent of U.S. GNP in 1960, and as late as 1970 they comprised only 8.3 percent, or roughly the same share they had claimed forty years before. By 1980, however, their combined share had more than dou-

TABLE 3.1

The Internationalization of the U.S. Economy

	1960	1970	1980
Exports as % GNP	4.0	4.3	8.2
Imports as % GNP	3.0	4.0	9.2
Export of Manufacturers as % Manufactured Goods GDP	8.8	11.6	24.3
Import of Manufacturers as % Manufactured Goods GDP	4.8	10.3	21.3
U.S. Foreign Investment Abroad	$30.4b	$75.6b	$215.5b
Profit on Investment Abroad as % Total Corporate Profits	12.2	21.8	23.0
Direct Foreign Investment in U.S.	—	$13.2b	$68.4b
Foreign Assets U.S. Banks as % Total Assets U.S. Banks	1.5	12.2	26.0

Source: James M. Cypher, "Monetarism, Militarism and Markets: Reagan's Response
to the Structural Crisis," MERIP Reports 14 (November–December 1984): 10.
See references cited therein.

bled, to 17.4 percent. Once again U.S. manufacturing provides the most dramatic evidence for this change, with both the exports and the imports of manufactures rising, by 1980, to more than 20 percent of domestic production. These, of course, are aggregate figures. In particular cases and sectors, import penetration and export dependence were considerably greater.[7]

Even more important, such general measures of import and export flows can only suggest what may have been the single most important consequence of this convergence of declining competitiveness *and* increasing U.S. integration in the world economy—the fact that most U.S. firms (accounting for perhaps 70 percent or more of goods and services in the U.S.) now felt sharper competitive pressures from abroad, which in turn affected their own pricing policies. To a rapidly expanding degree, even big firms, including some of those that were maintaining market share, now operated in an environment in which prices were affected by international market forces beyond their immediate control. As a consequence, they tended to become "price takers" rather than "price makers," and were less capable of simply passing increased costs along to consumers.[8]

The precise sources of the decline in U.S. domestic and international economic performance are matters of continuing dispute. There are many analyses, each with its (usually subsidized) proponents, and each with its favorite causal factor: the decline of the work ethic, a slowdown in innovation, new foreign strategies of international competition, a long-term crisis in work relations, excessive government regulation, increasing state or federal deficits, changes in relative prices resulting from the energy crisis, poor management. The list could easily go on.

Some of these explanations, such as the alleged slowdown in innovation or the popularly diagnosed decline of the Protestant ethic, rest on evidence so slender that they are hardly worth taking seriously. Others, which center on an alleged capital shortage in the 1970s or the "short-run" focus of U.S. managers, are almost equally implausible. More probably, in our view, the basic problem was a complex failure of investment, deeply rooted in the social organization of production in the United States, that was exacerbated by the emergence of the Third World as a major actor in the international economy. But we will not explore these matters here. No great agreement on the sources of U.S. economic difficulties is needed to recognize that those difficulties had profound political consequences in the United States, as domestic actors struggled to adjust to a radically altered environment. And it is those political responses, rather than the economic troubles that provoked them, that provide our focus here.[9]

The Attack on Labor

As the extent of U.S. economic deterioration became evident during the 1973–75 recession, business responded in predictable ways. Firms under pressure sought to cut costs, and while wages were already falling dramatically (so dramatically, indeed, that even many business spokespersons eventually conceded that wage costs were not the source of their continuing difficulties), for most firms the most natural place to begin cost cutting was with the price of labor.

These efforts took different forms. Continuing the pattern of the 1960s, many businesses operating in the Northeast and Midwest simply relocated production on a massive scale to areas where labor was cheaper and less organized. In some cases, firms located in the older industrial cities of those regions merely moved a few miles, from highly unionized central cities to less densely unionized, more hospitable neighboring suburbs. In many other instances, modern techniques for decentralized production made it possible to move operations (and, much more rarely, headquarters) to sites in the South and West or abroad.[10]

Businesses also employed an arsenal of different strategies to improve their bargaining position with particular workers. In nonunion environments, flexible work schedules, elaborate individualized incentive schemes, and other attempts to forge a more "cooperative" system of industrial relations for the regulation of internal labor markets proliferated. Where workers persisted in attempts to form unions, a whole new class of labor-management consultants, skilled in the evasion or prudent violation of national labor law, found an expanding market among employers. Having risen in the mid-1960s after the downturn in profits, employer unfair labor practices against unions skyrocketed in the 1970s. The number of charges of employer violation of section 8(a)(3) of the Labor Management Relations Act, for example, which forbids employers to fire workers for engaging in union activity, doubled from 9,000 to 18,000 over the 1970–80 period. The number of workers awarded reinstatement or back pay by the NLRB rose from 10,000 to 25,000. By 1980, the number of illegal discharges for union activity had risen to about 5 percent of the total number of pro-union votes in representation elections before the Board. Put otherwise, by that time American workers faced a 1 in 20 chance of being fired for merely favoring unionization. Activists and in-shop organizers, of course, faced even greater risks.[11]

The small minority of workers who were already unionized were better able to resist the general downward push on wages. As a result, the "union premium," or average differential between union and nonunion wages for comparable jobs, increased from 19 percent in the 1970–75 period to 30 percent during the second half of the decade. Again, however, such average figures disguise radically different particulars. In many cases union members suffered severe reductions in wages and benefits during the period. And many did not enjoy high wages to begin with.[12]

More importantly, as emphasized in our discussion of the 1960s, wages alone do not tell the full story of union strength. Throughout the 1970s, as during much of the 1960s, labor continued to divide itself from its natural allies at home, while promoting aggressive U.S.

foreign policies abroad. It failed to rejuvenate itself through aggressive organizing: the number of workers organized each year through NLRB elections declined 43 percent over 1970–80; the number lost through "decertification" elections more than doubled; the organized share of the civilian work force dropped from 25.7 to 20.9 percent. And its political influence waned. The decade began with Meany's successful move to block any Federation endorsement of George McGovern, the most liberal Presidential candidate in recent memory. It continued with labor twice (once under Ford, once under Carter) losing its fight to legalize "common situs" picketing, an issue of grave concern to embattled construction unions. And in what may have been its most spectacular postwar defeat, union leadership failed even to secure the modest changes in labor law and administration proposed in the Labor Law Reform Bill of 1977–78. There, in a replay of the fight over Taft-Hartley 14(b), a Republican-led filibuster killed the bill in the Senate, while another Democratic Administration looked on.[13]

But while virtually all of American business pressed for wage reductions in the 1970s, and the employer offensive against unions and unionization hurt a major investor in the Democratic Party, the significance of the wage and unionization issues should not be overestimated in explaining America's right turn. By hurting labor, the employer offensive marginally hurt the Democrats' capacities of mobilization; it also weakened resistance within the party to the turn to the right. But the decline in labor's power in the 1970s only continued a long downward slide evident since at least the mid-1950s. It was not a new development, unique to the later period, that can be looked to as precipitating a general policy realignment.

Considered from the standpoint of the distribution of business "investment" between the two parties, moreover, the wage and labor issues look even less impressive as causal factors. As emphasized here repeatedly, the firms that provided the key support for the New Deal, and most of the major firms that later backed Kennedy and Johnson, were heavily capital-intensive. Labor costs for them were thus relatively less important than they were for labor-intensive firms. The latter, as a practical matter, had little choice but to become rock-ribbed Republicans, and had made this choice long before. Thus while the increased competitive pressures of the 1970s led virtually all firms to be more attentive to labor costs, and weighed especially heavily on labor-intensive firms already oriented toward the Republicans, the labor question alone probably squeezed comparatively few traditionally Democratic firms out of the party.[14]

The Attack on Regulation

What labor costs could not do by themselves, however, other features of the new world political economy the 1973–75 recession created could. Reeling from intense foreign competition, many sectors of big business, *including* several of the most capital-intensive multinational ones, such as pharmaceuticals, paper, and petrochemicals, lashed back at what they claimed were "unduly burdensome" government regulations—in particular "social" regulations of the environment and worker safety that fell particularly hard on these sectors. As one measure of business mobilization, statistical studies show that these regulated concerns were among those most likely to organize PACs during the period. They also launched major efforts to influence public opinion and attitudes of other elites. Many firms sponsored studies by academics and consultants that downplayed environmental risk. They cultivated ties with university researchers and scientists in the federal research laboratories. And they launched a broad campaign to influence the media. The pharmaceutical-related Smith Richardson foundation, the petrochemical-related Scaife funds, the chemical-related Olin foundation, and other lavishly funded institutions launched broad campaigns against government regulation and in support of "free enterprise." They supported "neoconservative" journals like *The Public Interest* or the American Enterprise Institute's anti-regulatory *Regulation*. They poured enormous sums into a variety of "research institutes" such as Accuracy in Media that campaigned against alleged anti-business bias in the mass media. They supported conservative legal groups that brought suit against actions by the government and private parties that conservatives disapproved of. And they funded many campus newspapers and other projects oriented toward influencing students and other young people.[15]

Contrary to myths of the spontaneous generation of conservative ideas, this effort was quite deliberate, and expensive. As prominent free-marketeer, former Nixon Treasury Secretary, and Olin Fund chair William Simon urged his corporate colleagues, business should provide funds "in exchange for books, books, and more books" extolling the merits of free markets:

> Funds generated by business (by which I mean profits, funds in business foundations and contributions from individual businessmen) must rush by multimillions to the aid of liberty . . . to funnel desperately needed funds to scholars, social scientists, writers, and journalists who understand the relationship between political and economic liberty.[16]

And rush they did. Olin provided major funding (on the order of $3 million a year by the end of the decade) to any number of free-market-oriented projects, ranging from the Law and Economics Center at Emory University, which emphasized the substitution of market incentives for legal controls in the "regulation" of business, to the New Coalition for Economic and Social Change, a conservative black alternative to the NAACP. Smith Richardson, also operating with a grants budget of about $3 million annually, provided support for the new movement of "supply-side" economics, which (among its other claims) emphasized the destructive effects of government regulation on savings and investment. The foundation was hailed by Jude Wanniski, a *Wall Street Journal* writer who promoted the movement, as "*the* source of financing in the supply-side revolution. . . . It's become the place to go if you have a project that needs money." Among the foundation's early grants in support of the supply-siders, offered on the advice of *Public Interest* editor Irving Kristol, was a $40,000 subsidy to Wanniski himself. It led to the publication of his *The Way the World Works*, a major popularization of supply-side thought. (Later the foundation would subsidize George Gilder's *Wealth and Poverty*, a book that emphasized the redemptive qualities of capitalist entrepreneurs, and that was widely described as the "bible" of the Reagan Administration.) Scaife, in addition to its many other conservative grants, also joined in the promotion of anti-regulatory fervor. Between 1973 and 1980, Scaife funds provided $3 million to the Law and Economics Center, close to $4 million to the new (founded in 1973) Heritage Foundation, $2 million to various conservative media projects (including $900,000 to *The American Spectator*, $150,000 to Accuracy in Media, and $500,000 to Erie, Pennsylvania, TV station WQLN to help underwrite Milton Friedman's TV series "Free to

Choose"), and close to $4 million to a variety of new "public interest" law firms attacking specific government regulations. (Between 1977 and 1982, Scaife would supply National Affairs, Inc., the publisher of *The Public Interest*, with $380,000.)[17]

Such foundation activities, while very important, were only the tip of a massive wave of corporate subsidy to attacks on regulation. By the mid-1970s, U.S. firms were spending more than $400 million a year on "advocacy advertising," much of it directed against government constraints on business. By the end of the 1970s, total estimated corporate spending on advocacy advertising and grass-roots lobbying, again with much of the effort devoted to attacks on regulation, ran to $1 billion annually.[18]

Though a few liberal, multinationally oriented Republicans remained committed to environmental and other regulation, the affinity of the Democrats for the environmentalists and other advocates of business regulation was stronger for both philosophical and financial reasons. Accordingly, the rising anti-regulatory, pro-"free enterprise" movement weakened the Democratic base in the business community and in the country at large. In addition, a range of regulatory restrictions—regarding the environment, pharmaceuticals, and dangerous (e.g., nuclear) technologies—specifically affected the Democrats' traditional base among firms doing large shares of business abroad. Particularly in the late 1970s, destructive competition among the major powers and the environmental perils of unrestrained Third World growth prompted some (very partial) multilateral efforts at environmental and other regulation—reflected in negotiations over the Law of the Sea Treaty, for example, or the Carter Administration's tightened policies on nuclear proliferation, or more aggressive enforcement by the Food and Drug Administration. As a result, companies that were anxious to sell untested drugs to the Third World, or export nuclear technologies, or engage in mammoth construction projects that degraded regional environments in other countries or offshore regions, sometimes found government in the way. Strongly identified with the Democrats, and backed by many of the same sectors (preeminently banking and other services) that promoted domestic environmental regulation, these international initiatives served to weaken support for the party among its other multinational supporters.[19]

International Factors

The most devastating blows to the position of the Democrats within the business community, however, came not from domestic actors, but from abroad. The first shock came from the great rise in oil prices in the middle of the recession. The second blow came as a consequence of the dramatic shift in world growth patterns that the recession highlighted.

OPEC

Though some analysts in the United States persist in trying to minimize the importance of the successive oil shocks of the 1970s, in fact the huge 1973 rise in oil prices (which followed the much smaller increase of 1971) was one of world history's truly momentous events. Like the great fall in the world price of grain that occurred in the 1870s and 1880s, the rise in the price of energy wrought sweeping changes in all sorts of basic social relations—in the social structure of the producing countries; the relative competitive positions of the United States and its major allies; and the distribution of income and industrial structure of the whole world.[20]

For the Democrats, the dramatic rise in oil prices had a number of immediate effects. One of these was obvious, if little noted. For more than a generation, the biggest and most powerful of America's capital-intensive industries, the oil industry, had been disproportionately Democratic. For all the many controversies that oilmen had fought out with individual Democrats and even Democratic Administrations, they remained the quintessential capital-intensive sector that could afford to be less intensely hostile to organized labor and long maintained a special relation to the party. In 1936, Franklin D. Roosevelt raised more money from Texas than any other state. Harry Truman's relations with various oil companies (if not the entire industry) were close enough to generate massive criticism, and they led to the resignation of a member of his Cabinet. And the legendary stories of Kennedy's and Johnson's dealings with oil are too well known to require comment. In the twinkling of an eye, however, OPEC did what a generation of Republicans, populist anti-oil Democrats, and even the old Tidelands Oil controversy were never able to do. It built a virtual Chinese Wall between oil and the Democrats.[21]

As OPEC raised its prices, world oil and gas prices soared, and the basis of an almost uncountable number of residential, locational, and business choices changed drastically. Responding to frantic pleas from some regional congressional delegations and many large industrial users, the government initially attempted to hold down domestic prices of oil and gas through a complex system of price controls. The astronomical sums involved made these programs some of the largest income-transfer programs in world history. Not surprisingly, most oil and gas companies ardently supported lifting the controls.

But while the ensuing debate on energy prices created turbulence in both parties, the discussion stirred especially vehement feelings within Democratic ranks. Because the lifting of controls struck so massively at labor, blacks, and the poor, most Democrats simply could not sponsor the move. As a consequence, and particularly after the strongly Democratic "Watergate Congress" of 1974 reduced the oil industry's depletion allowance, virtually the entire oil industry began going over to the Republicans.

In 1976, some (though far from all) of the industry did come back to the Democrats to support a candidate who had explicitly pledged to press for the deregulation of natural gas. Jimmy Carter, in a bid for support in the South and West, had made this promise in his quest for the party's Presidential nomination. He reiterated it shortly before the general election in a letter to then Governor (now Senator) David Boren of Oklahoma, who had been the very first governor to endorse Carter in a field of Democratic candidates that included staunch oil senator Lloyd Bentsen of Texas. Once in office, however, Carter changed his mind. Declining to press for natural-gas deregulation, he pushed instead for a "windfall profits" tax on the oil industry. Thereafter, in the wake of what many oil and gas Democrats still recall as the Carter Administration's Great Double Cross, the biggest of all America's capital-intensive industries increasingly concentrated on electing the candidates of a party that would let the "free" market set energy prices.[22]

The huge rise in the price of energy and (briefly) of many other primary commodities in the 1970s also hurt the Democrats in more subtle ways. Since U.S. deposits of oil, gas, and minerals are located disproportionately in the states of the South and West, these regions reaped windfall gains from the rise in commodity prices. This development was bound to weaken the Democrats, since the party was already weaker in those regions. But the commodity price rise had more specific effects as well.

For years, some very large fortunes in the South and West had strongly opposed the New Deal. Composed chiefly of growers and independent oilmen in Texas, Oklahoma, and California, this bloc had long patronized right-wing fundamentalist religious activities and spokespersons and other ultraconservative groups. As the boom in energy and commodity prices took off, the fortunes this bloc commanded received an automatic assist, with almost immediate political consequences. It stepped up support for various "New Right" spokespersons—including not only many political operatives associated with groups like NCPAC (National Conservative PAC) but also several leading evangelists.[23]

The Reverend W. A. Criswell, for example, whose downtown Dallas church is commonly reckoned among the largest and wealthiest fundamentalist churches anywhere, had long been supported by a virtual Who's Who of regional leaders of business and the professions, including several members of the Hunt family. In the seventies, as Criswell and other fundamentalists mounted a controversial campaign to capture control of the giant Southern Baptist Convention, oil billionaire and would-be Silver King Nelson Bunker Hunt began to support another well-known evangelist: the Reverend Jerry Falwell (whose board of directors at the "Old Time Gospel Hour" Bunker Hunt eventually joined). Cullen Davis, whose family commands a vast oil-and-minerals-based fortune, became a major backer of the Reverend James Robison, yet another prominent evangelist.[24]

Increased boosting of religious fundamentalism coincided, of course, with a sharp downturn in the well-being of most working- and lower-middle-class Americans. Threatened by imports, rising unemployment, and declining wages, and jostled by the entrance of millions of new women workers (and illegal immigrants) into slack labor markets, many of the most vulnerable members of American society were understandably disenchanted with the profane world (and the "secular humanism" that was said to be its organizing principle). Among at least some of them, inevitably, these religious appeals found wide resonance.[25]

And as the religious revivals of the 1970s gained steam, it became apparent that the commodity price boom was also leading to a broad renewal of a distinctly secular laissez-faire ideology in the South and

West. Elites in mineral-rich Western states stood to profit enormously from the price deregulation that the old-line Democratic constituencies in the East and environmentalists had to oppose. As a consequence, business communities in the West and parts of the South joined wholeheartedly in the broader movement for deregulation and also sought enhanced access to minerals on the vast tracts of Western land controlled by the federal government.

Soon, an organized "Sagebrush Rebellion" began in the West. Because the professed goal of this revolt was the recapture by locals of the resources controlled by out-of-state forces (the federal government), the movement often laid claims to the mantle of populism. If so, it was a populism akin to that of the Anaconda Copper Co. that backed Democrat William Jennings Bryan for President in 1896, rather than the poor farmers who organized the People's Party. Right-wing business interests, such as the Coors family, who helped bankroll James Watt's Mountain States Legal Foundation and any number of other conservative groups and causes, strongly promoted it. As the Sagebrush Rebellion roiled onward, it too served to undermine the Democratic Party's residual ties to major interests in those regions.[26]

By themselves, these far-ranging consequences of the world oil price might well have sufficed to wreck much of the Democratic Party's constituency within the multinationals. When they combined with a global shift in the pattern of economic growth that the 1973–74 recession heralded, however, they created a new condition that guaranteed its extinction, and the demise of the New Deal party system— a gigantic and ever-tightening budget crisis.

The Drive into the Third World

The story begins in the middle and late 1960s, when a widening gulf first became noticeable between rates of economic growth in the major Western "core" industrial economies of the OECD and more advanced economies of the Third World located on the so-called semi-periphery of the world economy.

After the 1973–75 recession, this phenomenon was too striking to be ignored. While the so-called Gang of Four countries of East Asia (South Korea, Taiwan, Singapore, and Hong Kong) and parts of Latin America, the Middle East, and Southern Europe boomed, growth rates in the United States and most of the other leading developed countries plunged. Overall, the average annual rate of growth in Gross

Domestic Product (GDP) among the developed countries dropped from 5 percent over 1960–73 to 2.4 percent over 1973–80. Among developing countries, by contrast, annual GDP growth averaged 5.8 percent over 1960–73 and 5.4 percent over 1973–80. The recession seemed to have passed them by. In particular developing-country cases, the contrast in performance was even more spectacular. The annual growth of "middle income" oil-importing developing countries in East Asia and the Pacific, for example, actually increased after 1973, rising from 8.2 percent over 1960–73 to 8.6 percent over 1973–79.[27]

Gradually in the early 1970s, and then with a rush during the Great Recession, elites in the industrialized West woke up to what was happening. Leading economists wondered aloud if a major turning point in the world economy had been reached. U.S. business groups and major foundations in the United States—including the prestigious Committee for Economic Development, the Business Council, and the Atlantic Council of the United States—began organizing study groups, issuing reports, and publishing manifestos about the crisis in the "West." It was commonly recognized that resolving this crisis would take many years of organizing and political struggle in the home states of the OECD. In the meantime, some way had to be found to deal with the persisting stagnation.[28]

For many of America's biggest and most successful enterprises, the preferred response was obvious. Having already expanded overseas in the 1960s, they were well positioned to move into the new high-profit centers of the Third World. And just as they were gearing up for this expansion, OPEC announced its price rises. This gave an even more powerful impetus to the move, for while in the long run OPEC's actions were to have conflicting, and even contradictory, consequences for the Third World as a whole, in the short run they had one unambiguous effect: they dramatically enhanced the importance of parts of the Third World to American business.

OPEC nations now flush with petrodollars suddenly emerged as major markets not only for investments but for all kinds of exports from the United States and other countries. Over the 1960–70 period, annual growth in imports among capital-surplus oil exporters had averaged a very strong 11 percent. Over 1970–81 this average growth rate nearly doubled, rising to a staggering 20.8 percent. Even more significantly, the oil-producing countries' vast cash flows qualified them as major depositors in international banks. As they accepted the deposits, however, the banks had to invest the money, at which point the relative growth rates of the First and Third Worlds again became crucial. With Third World countries growing two or three times as fast as the OECD, most of the money went right back out to the Third World, in a vast expansion of bank debt.[29]

A considerable percentage of this vast increase in debt probably came at the expense of equity investment in the Third World by other American multinationals. Since the banks preferred to make loans whose repayment was guaranteed by sovereign countries, Third World elites now could obtain financing for many more state-owned enterprises and go into business for themselves. But the sheer size of non-oil developing country debt, which grew from $130 billion in 1973 to $474 billion in 1980, was stupefying. An increasing share of it—about $280 billion by 1980—was owed to private Western banks, and among these, U.S. banks were preeminent. Rising rapidly after the mid-1970s, U.S. bank exposure to non-oil LDCs would top $100 billion by 1982. Along with the rapid increase in trade with the Third World, the deposits, all the direct investments that did occur (net direct investment flows to non-oil LDCs rose from $4.2 to $10.1 billion over 1973–80), and the expectation that growth and profit-rate differentials between the OECD and the developing nations would compound over time, this gave the commanding heights of American business a greater stake in the Third World than they had ever had before.[30]

The Collapse of Détente

By itself, of course, there was nothing about the deepening U.S. involvement with the Third World that was incognate with the New Deal. In the pivotal 1936 election, for example, Franklin D. Roosevelt's strongest backers from the oil industry included James A. Moffett, the man most responsible for the entry of the American oil companies into Saudi Arabia the year before. Nor would the troubles with America's allies that marked the seventies—over trade shares, macroeconomic policy, protection, conflicting objectives in the Middle East, China, and policy toward the U.S.S.R.—that naturally accompanied stagflation in the OECD have decisively altered the conditions under which the New Deal coalition could thrive.[31]

But the new American drive into the Third World coincided with a great debate in the United States over the wisdom of détente, and soon became an independent factor in the rationale of those who were agitating for a massive new military buildup.[32]

In an earlier essay on the 1980 election, we argued against the view that Soviet (mis)behavior, however egregious, triggered the collapse of détente. Since that essay appeared, President Reagan's own Scowcroft Commission has officially rejected the "window of vulnerability" theory (according to which Soviet abilities to target U.S. land-based missiles somehow infirmed an American deterrent that, after a Soviet first strike, would still include more than 4,000 warheads on submarine-launched ballistic missiles); the Reagan-controlled CIA has announced that previous estimates of 3 to 4 percent real annual rates of growth in Soviet military spending during the late 1970s and early 1980s were probably wrong, and that real annual increases were only about 2 percent; and a variety of U.S. intelligence sources, including the Defense Intelligence Agency, have admitted that over 1976–81 (at least) Soviet *investment* in new weapons did not grow at all. Other analysts have come forward with careful debunkings of the myth of U.S. "unilateral disarmament" during the 1970s, while a recent statistical study has shown that American military expenditures do not follow (or, in statistical terms, are "exogenous" to) trends in Soviet spending. We will not recapitulate our earlier argument, but only restate its central point.[33]

Détente did not come about because of a change in Soviet behavior abroad (the U.S.S.R. had just invaded Czechoslovakia) or because internal curbs on Soviet Jews and other dissidents were being relaxed. Détente occurred because it promised, briefly, to meet important needs of both Soviet and American elites. On the Soviet side, the need was for advanced technology and industrial processes. On the American side, the need was for precisely what the Third World and China ultimately provided on a more expansive scale: a new source of foreign investment opportunities and raw materials.

Enthusiasm for détente was far from universal, however. From the beginning a wide variety of business interests opposed it, including raw materials, chemical, and natural-gas concerns jealous of their rivals' successes in landing contracts with the Soviets; other American firms in sectors where the Soviets had, or eventually figured to have, a comparative advantage (e.g., many older labor-intensive industries that preferred that the United States trade with no one); and, naturally, much of the weapons industry. So did many groups and individuals, including many supporters of Israel, who were repelled by the Soviet state's often barbarous internal practices or who feared détente's effect on the balance of power in particular regions. Led by Senator Henry Jackson and many younger figures who would later assume high posts in the Reagan Administration, these groups helped block congressional approval of "most-favored nation" status for the U.S.S.R.

All this domestic opposition probably would not have succeeded if the key economic assumptions of détente had remained robust. Very soon, however, it became obvious that the Europeans were far better positioned to take advantage of trade with the U.S.S.R. than were the Americans. In addition, the Soviet market for finance quickly approached saturation (at about $60 billion), while major quality-control problems dampened Western demand for Soviet manufactures.[34]

The slowness with which Soviet-American trade developed only enhanced the attractiveness of the United States' rapidly developing ties with the Third World. Reciprocally, the growing U.S.–Third World connection served to reduce incentives to détente in the United States, since developing regions provided a massive and growing outlet for U.S. capital and goods.

Third World regimes, however, were notoriously unstable, and became even more so in the 1970s, particularly after 1973. In some poorer, less rapidly developing countries, the oil price rises themselves were a major destabilizing factor, as states struggling to pay their oil bills squeezed the public sector and the lower classes. In many rapidly growing areas, the notorious perils of headlong expansion and, perhaps, contagious examples of liberation movements in less prosperous neighbors also threatened to undermine regimes that (directly or indirectly) guaranteed payments on billions of dollars of development projects, commercial deals, and bank loans.[35]

Not surprisingly, the superpowers could hardly avoid being sucked deeply into regional alliances and local politics. Over the course of the seventies, both the United States and the U.S.S.R. became increasingly committed to various "regional surrogates," sought new bases, and beefed up their regional military presences, especially in the western Pacific and the newly important Indian Ocean. Attempts by both sides to advance their clients' fortunes led to more friction, which in turn made détente look even less plausible as a framework for U.S.–Soviet relations and added to pressures for a renewal of the Cold War.

In the U.S. case, the increasing commitment to regional surrogates and less direct forms of confrontation with the Soviet Union had earlier been codified in the "Nixon Doctrine," first outlined in Nixon's famous 1969 speech on Guam announcing his plan to gradually withdraw American troops from Vietnam and "Vietnamize" the war. Summing up the doctrine, then Secretary of Defense Melvin Laird declared that "America will no longer play policeman to the world. Instead we will expect other nations to provide more cops on the beat in their own neighborhood."[36]

As it turned out, these surrogate "cops" were unsatisfactory instruments of U.S. policy for several reasons. First, the regional allies of the United States were themselves unstable and often became more so with the massive infusions of military aid and other support that were part of the overall strategy. Second, close relations with surrogate powers often involved the United States in local disputes in which even Washington policymakers saw no important U.S. stake. Third, the surrogate powers, even when acting in compliance with U.S. wishes, were often unable to prevent political changes the United States regarded as inimical to its interests. Fourth, and not uncommonly, the surrogates simply did not do what the United States asked.[37]

The classic example of all these difficulties was Iran. There the United States encouraged the Shah's spending spree, amounting to $20 billion in orders and $9 billion in deliveries between 1970 and 1978, on American arms, ammunition, and military hardware. It provided a huge amount of technical assistance for the operation of these complex weapons (by 1978, some 10,000 American personnel were working on arms-related projects in Iran). And it regularly advised the Shah on his conduct of internal surveillance and repression. The eventual result was a revolution, which liquidated American assets and produced another heavily armed "unfriendly" regime in the Middle East. While Iran was a particularly dramatic instance of failure, however, it was not alone. And even as military assistance and arms sales rocketed upward in the 1970s (Figure 3.2), many American business figures pressed for an enhanced American capacity for direct intervention abroad.[38]

Growing disenchantment with the Nixon Doctrine contributed, throughout the decade, to growing support for increased U.S. mili-

FIGURE 3.2

U.S. Arms Export Trends: Fiscal 1970–83 (arms transfers through the Foreign Military Sales Program)

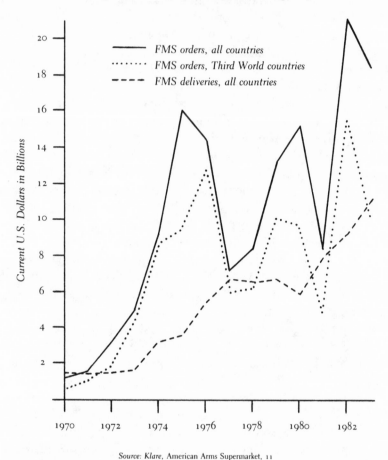

Source: *Klare,* American Arms Supermarket, 11

tary outlay. To an important degree, especially as it interacted with the increasingly sharp competition among the great OECD powers, it also contributed to the revival of more explicitly "unilateral" approaches to military questions. Heightening global competition revived the budgets and lobbying activity of a variety of old pressure groups from the high Cold War, including the American Security Council and the National Strategy Information Center. Other organizations, such as the Paris-based Atlantic Institute and the U.S. Atlantic Council, whose boards are heavily dominated by individuals with strong ties to U.S. and foreign multinationals, promoted more cooperative strategies, but also turned notably hawkish. Perhaps the most important of all the groups that led the push for rearmament, however, was the Committee on the Present Danger (CPD). This was launched right after Jimmy Carter's victory in 1976 by a broad cross section of leading businessmen and onetime military figures, and received a substantial start-up grant from David Packard, board chairman of Hewlett Packard.[39]

After the fall of Iran and the Soviet invasion of Afghanistan, it sometimes seemed that the entire American business community had been seized by a kind of frenzy. This in fact was not true, for while they supported an arms buildup, many financiers were nervous about the potential inflationary consequences of programs like the CPD's, which implied annual defense increases of 6–8 percent for many years, major new strategic systems, and a vast naval buildup. A few major American businesses whose leaders also held fast to the early 1970s logic of integrating the Soviets into the global economy, or still hoped to do business with the Soviets, continued to promote U.S.–U.S.S.R. trade. Pepsi-Cola chairman Donald Kendall, for example, whose company had signed a major contract with the Russians, served prominently on the Board of the Committee on East-West Accord, along with figures from a few other concerns, including Control Data, that also sought or enjoyed contracts with the Soviets. And when the leading critic of resurgent militarism within the Carter Administration, Secretary of State Cyrus Vance, resigned after the abortive attempt to rescue American hostages in Iran, he was promptly welcomed back onto the IBM and *New York Times* boards he had left four years before.[40]

By the late seventies, however, the whole tenor of the defense debate had shifted. Although survey data, as already noted, indicate little public support for increased military spending until the very end of the decade, virtually everyone quoted in newspapers, heard on radio, or seen on television agreed that military spending must rise. After Iran and Afghanistan, only the precise *rate* of increase remained open to debate.[41]

It is here that the deepest part of the New Deal's grave is to be found. Had economic growth continued in the 1970s at the same rate as in the 1960s, the arms buildup could have been financed with comparative ease. Though some domestic programs might have been squeezed, at least a limited war on poverty could still have been fought. Substantial sums would also have been available for cities, education, and other social-welfare programs. In the 1970s, however, economic growth was highly variable and uncertain. The money was not there.

The Campaign against Taxes

No less importantly, a crisis was brewing in the tax system. As already noted, Democratic Administrations in the 1960s had opted to cut corporate taxes, while dramatically increasing federal reliance on regressive social security payroll taxes to finance major social programs. As a result, between 1960 and 1970 the share of federal revenues provided by the corporate income tax dropped from 23.2 to 16.9 percent, while the share provided by individual income and social security taxes increased from 59.9 to 70.1 percent. During the 1970s these trends continued, with the corporate income tax share dropping to 12.4 percent of federal revenues by 1980, and the individual income and social security tax share increasing to 77.8 percent. Disaggregating individual income tax receipts and social security tax receipts shows an even more dramatic change during the decade. In real terms, while GNP grew 36 percent between 1969 and 1980, and total federal revenues grew 35 percent, individual income tax receipts grew 37 percent, roughly keeping pace. Social security taxes, on the other hand, grew a whopping 92 percent, while corporate income tax receipts actually declined by 14 percent.[42]

In addition to changes in nominal tax rates on corporations and enormous legislated increases in social security deductions, other factors conspired to produce these results. Inflation pushed taxpayers into higher brackets through "bracket creep," with particularly onerous effects on lower-income Americans. In addition, the massive system of "tax expenditures"—exclusions, deductions, and other loopholes, generally benefiting business—grew much faster than in earlier periods. Between 1969 and 1979, annual tax expenditures grew from $46.6 billion to $149.8 billion. By 1981, even before the enormous Reagan tax cuts for business enacted that year, better than 60 percent of all official tax expenditures directly beneficial to business derived from changes in the tax system during the 1970s.[43]

Such data suggest the material basis of what was later called the

FIGURE 3.3
Reasons to Revolt

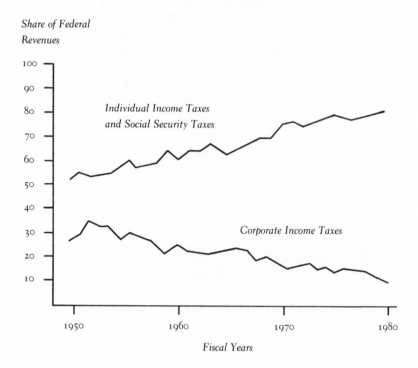

Source: McIntyre and Tipps, Inequity and Decline, 12

Great Tax Revolt of the late 1970s. By 1978, when all these trends were visibly apparent, Harris polls showed that 69 percent of the public felt they had "reached the breaking point" on the taxes they paid. As already noted, there was also widespread perception of unfairness in the tax system, with strong majorities favoring increased taxes for corporations and the rich. But as emphasized earlier, while this surely stiffened resistance to tax hikes, it did not generally lead the public to demand a reduction in their tax burden. Strong and continuing support for maintaining current levels of domestic spending intervened on that point.[44]

Instead, pressures for reducing taxes came overwhelmingly from those whose rates were already falling—the business community. The revolution in tax attitudes that did occur, as the title of one study of the period put it, was a "revolt of the haves," not the have-nots. And the chief reason for this, as emphasized earlier, was the increasing integration of the United States in the rest of the world economy. As that integration occurred, more firms found themselves competing in truly international markets, and an enormous section of the American business community was forced to be sensitive to foreign prices. This new exposure to international prices transformed the economics of taxation for many large corporations. Because they now faced prices set in world markets, they could no longer pass through corporate (and their portion of social security) taxes, as many probably could in a more closed economy. Almost inevitably, corporations began pressing for further reductions in their rates.[45]

This corporate tax campaign, in turn, fueled a similar drive to cut personal income taxes in the high brackets. Unless, as no one expected, total government spending was cut deeply at the same time corporate tax rates came down, a massive shortfall in revenues would result. Without a parallel cut in the top personal income tax rates, rich Americans could be expected to pick up part of this bill.

Particularly after the mid-1970s, a decentralized but powerful campaign to chop back both schedules soon got under way. Headed up by super-lobbyist Charls Walker, a former Treasury official in the Nixon Administration, the American Council for Capital Formation began a broad campaign of lobbying and "public education." With funds provided by a virtual cross section of the Fortune 500 (including many media companies, such as Time Inc. and *The New York Times*) and several large foundations, Walker commissioned studies by leading economists, briefed newspaper publishers and editors, and peppered Congress with propaganda for lower rates.[46]

At almost the same time, William Simon and other outspokenly conservative business leaders supported the National Tax Limitation Committee (NTLC), which was headed by a former member of the John Birch Society. Along with Walker and the National Taxpayers Union, the NTLC encouraged a movement for a constitutional amendment to mandate a balanced budget. Though many multinational business executives regarded that with great suspicion (the CED, for example, flatly opposed it and worked behind the scenes to kill it when it seemed likely to pass early in the Reagan Administration), the corporate-initiated movement to cut taxes became a powerful device to appeal to increasingly hard-pressed working Americans, who did not realize Walker and many of his supporters advocated replacing the income tax with even more regressive sales or consumption taxes.[47]

This tax campaign converged with other pressures to force the Democrats into a corner. In the context of slow and erratic growth, as the pressure grew for more military spending together with large cuts in taxes, a gigantic squeeze began to develop on social spending. This hurt the Democrats far more than the Republicans, since it constrained their ability to deliver the social benefits that had long secured them a real mass base. In the new political economy of the late 1970s, the party of Roosevelt, which had long been able to build and maintain its popular base by dolloping out discrete social benefits, no longer had the resources to do so. Indeed, the very existence of that base posed an important barrier to the Democrats' capacity to realize business objectives. For virtually all sections of the business community, the GOP appeared as a more efficient vehicle for realizing their aspirations.

Business Mobilization

By the mid-1970s the cumulative weight of all these factors—faltering domestic economic performance, lagging international competitiveness, the explosion of energy and other commodity prices, and pressures for increased military spending, along with a cost cutting in labor, regulation, social programs, and taxes—was immense. What might be termed the "old right" of the independent oil companies, protectionist sectors like textiles (whose leading spokesman was North Carolina senator Jesse Helms), and many raw-materials producers was on the march. Supplying millions of dollars of funds and other assistance to a wide variety of organizations—conservative publishing companies, foundations, think tanks, religious groups, and lobbying organizations—these groups vastly increased their national presence.

Simultaneously, in a process that was often mistaken for a "right-wing takeover" by the South and West, the center of gravity of American big business was also moving right. The Olin foundation—where William Simon was joined by the legendary John J. McCloy, a former backer of LBJ in 1964 and the recognized chairman of all things Eastern and established—several Scaife funds, Smith Richardson, Pew, Lilly, and other foundations, along with many corporations themselves, were spending hundreds of millions of dollars not only on promoting anti-regulatory fervor and the virtues of "free" markets but on hard-line national security studies, general attacks on the welfare state and social spending, assaults on the progressive income tax, and detailed criticisms of past excesses of the "liberal" media on Vietnam, foreign news reporting, and other issues.

To the unaided eye, these activities appeared indistinguishable from those of the traditional right wing. But in fact several important differences did remain. In contrast to the "old right" that wrote import restrictions into the 1964 Republican platform, most of the multinational sponsors of this new right turn remained strongly committed to free trade. They also still shied away from direct, public attacks on organized labor, preferring to wait for the mass flight to the sunbelt (and the resurgent National Right to Work Committee) to take its toll. And, while they were prepared to fund moderate "evangelical" groups, they did not share the fundamentalism of the far right.[48]

But the effect of this cultural turn was powerful all the same. Community organizations and liberal groups that had an easy time getting funds in the late 1960s and very early 1970s now struggled to find financing. Simultaneously the flock of conservative think tanks drawing vast business support—including the Heritage Foundation, American Enterprise Institute, Institute for Contemporary Studies, Hoover Institute, and National Bureau of Economic Research—were churning out the "books, books, and more books" that Simon called for, along with all manner of position papers, attacks on liberal "myths," and specific conservative policy suggestions. The network of "public interest" legal centers—including the Pacific, Capitol, Mountain States, Great Plains, Mid-America, and Southeastern legal foundations—were busy filing suits on issues ranging from welfare eligibility (to curb it) to environmental protection (to relax it). The boards of some of these newer groups, such as the San Francisco-based Institute of Contemporary Studies or the Washington, D.C.-based Heritage Foundation, mixed figures from multinationals that formerly bulwarked the older "liberal" establishment with representatives of far more conservative business interests.[49]

The budgets of all sorts of business lobbying organizations were reviving. By this time, the Business Roundtable had emerged from the old Labor Law Study Group and other antecedents and began flexing the power that came of being an association of the CEOs of

America's two hundred biggest firms. It was joined by a revitalized Chamber of Commerce, National Federation of Independent Business, National Association of Manufacturers, and scores of other trade associations. On a wide range of particular issues, these groups pressed forward with general business demands for tax relief, cuts in social outlays, and, in many cases, increases in military outlays.

The press also gradually shifted to the right. Though the TV networks and Eastern, multinationally oriented papers like *The New York Times* and *The Washington Post* remained well to the left of most nationally oriented conservative dailies and local TV stations in the South and West, they too came to reflect the new "mood." The shift at the *Times*, under new executive editor Abe Rosenthal, was later hailed by the Heritage Foundation's house journal, *Policy Review*:

[W]hat we are witnessing now is a distinctly American comeback. The *New York Times*, America's greatest newspaper, is reaffirming its greatness by retreating from the radicalism of the last two decades and once again taking up responsible journalism. It is the first liberal institution to identify the excesses of liberalism, mainly its flirtation with Communism, and to see to correct them. Many *Times* readers feared that the newspaper did not have such resilience. Abe Rosenthal is proving them wrong.

What this meant, more concretely, is that the greatest of American newspapers now featured less intensive and less critical coverage of U.S. interventionism abroad; far more tales of Soviet aggression and the well-known miseries of life in the Eastern bloc; far less concern, in coverage as well as on the editorial page, with the less well-known miseries of the poor and working populations at home; and less support for progressive domestic policies in taxing and spending.[50]

Carter

By the mid-1970s, then, all the basic forces that would eventually drive American politics to the right were already active. Real growth in the economy briefly revived in 1975–76, however, and the trade issue continued to divide business elites. As a consequence, despite the growing shift in business sentiment, there was still enough life in the New Deal coalition to elect one more Democrat. A sort of last hurrah to the New Deal, Jimmy Carter's campaign for the Presidency in 1976 received support from many multinational businessmen. They remembered the dramatic import surcharge the Nixon Administration slapped on in 1971 and, at a time of rising protectionist pressures, still valued the Democrats' continuing commitment to internationalism and free trade. The chairman of Coca-Cola took time out to help promote Carter's candidacy. *Time* magazine, Henry Ford II, and any number of members of the strongly free-trade-oriented Trilateral Commission (whose ubiquity in his Administration would eventually become a sort of joke) also aided him.[51]

Almost as soon as he gained office, however, Carter's efforts to maintain the old Democratic coalition were repeatedly undermined by the various forces just described. They became more and more powerful as the decade wore on, tightening the constraints under which his Administration operated. As a result, there was a discernible shift in policy during the Carter Administration, but not one which promised to be profound and lasting enough to satisfy the Democrats' traditional elite constituency. The tightrope the Democrats walked between elite demands and mass needs stretched further, and finally broke.

In the area of business regulation, for example, Carter began his term by appointing relatively liberal officials to a variety of regulatory agencies, stepping up their budgets, and moving aggressively on enforcement. For this the Administration was sharply attacked. Bowing to pressures, in early 1978 Carter issued an executive order mandating agency analysis of the economic impact of proposed regulations, a signal that "excessive" regulation would no longer be tolerated. Review of regulatory agencies was also centralized in the White House-based Office of Science and Technology Policy, the Office of Management and Budget, and, especially, a new Regulatory Analysis Review Group. Presiding over this new regulatory review apparatus was Charles L. Schultz, then chair of Carter's Council of Economic Advisers, who was a prominent critic of the irrationality of "command and control" regulation and a major booster of market-based alternatives to it.

At the time, this new effort at centralized control of agency rulings was advertised as merely a move to "rationalize" the process of regulation. Its rather clear effect, however, was to promote certain criteria of decision-making—preeminently highly manipulable "cost-benefit" analyses of regulation that cloaked real reductions in regulation—

while permitting discrete White House interventions in areas of particular concern to business. Those interventions came repeatedly in the next years of the Administration, sometimes—as in the fight over Carter's attempts to lower cotton-dust standards or loosen restrictions on strip mining—occasioning public notice, more often not. As far as Carter sought to dampen "regulatory zeal," however, for a growing portion of business he simply did not go far enough.[52]

Carter's attempts to broker among different regional interests were similarly unsuccessful, after again being marked by early attempts to press forward with a relatively liberal agenda. Early in his term, for example, the Administration sought to aid the Democrats' traditional urban constituencies by sharply increasing the flow of funds into the major cities of the Northeast and Midwest. But with the budget noose tightening, it soon became clear that a continuation of this support would require cuts elsewhere in the budget. Environmentalists with close ties to the same multinational business interests that were supporting Carter saw the impending trade-off as a great opportunity. For some time they had been identifying enormously expensive Western water projects as a good target for budget reduction. The Environmental Policy Center had even prepared a hit list of those projects that could still be canceled. Now that list was given to Carter, who endorsed it to widespread astonishment. He laid plans for the elimination of funding for nineteen water projects, along with a tightening of the criteria by which federal funds would be allocated to future projects.

The result was a political disaster that continues to trouble the party to this day. While environmentalists in Washington praised the move as a long-overdue correction to years of unplanned pork-barrel development, Carter's announcement of the proposed cuts set off a firestorm in the West, where water subsidies and funds for road construction were as important as urban-development aid or welfare were in the East. Democratic elites from the region joined Republicans to fiercely oppose them. In the end, Carter was forced to back down on much of the initiative, but by then he had hastened the departure of many Westerners from the national party. At the same time, his support in the East diminished, as funding to major cities was sharply reduced.[53]

On labor, Carter, in marked contrast to his successor, appointed highly competent and relatively liberal individuals to the NLRB. He

FIGURE 3.4

Urban Outlays as a Percent of Federal Outlays, 1967–84

Percent Urban
for All Federal
Budget

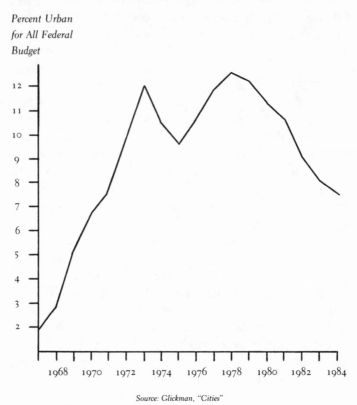

Source: Glickman, "Cities"

also backed (tepidly, to be sure) the Labor Law Reform Bill proposed in 1977. Labor Law Reform, however, as already noted, drowned under a tidal wave of business opposition. And employer unfair-labor practices skyrocketed at the Board.

On taxes, a similar story unfolded. After campaigning on a pledge to reform the federal tax system, which he had colorfully described as "a disgrace to the human race," Carter approached Congress in 1977 with a modest bundle of reform proposals. Only one of these was accepted (a revision of the "zero bracket," or income level below which individuals were not taxed), and it was regressively amended. The Administration approached Congress again in January 1978, with what was advertised as its major reform of the system. The measures proposed this second time around included at least some of the items that Carter had been promising since taking office—reductions in business-expense deductions and in taxes on middle-income Americans among them. But it also provided a variety of concessions to business, including reductions in the corporate tax rate and solidification and extension of a 10 percent investment tax credit. And it was also far more modest in its attacks on capital-gains tax exclusions than Carter had indicated it would be.[54]

Walker and other business representatives had anticipated a much more progressive reform package and were already lobbying against the bill. As a Washington insider described their actions after the proposal was unveiled, "They were braced for an attack; when the attack never came, they decided to invade!" The result of this invasion was a law which, along with a host of other regressive revisions, actually cut the top capital-gains rate by more than 40 percent (from 48 to 28 percent), while further raising the social security tax. When all was said and done, the top half of taxpayers received 79 percent of the tax savings provided in the law, obliterating any pretense of progressive reform.[55]

Even after these disasters, Carter continued trying to run a sort of limited, Eastern version of the New Deal under an ever-tightening set of constraints. He ratified the Panama Canal Treaty, pressured the NATO allies to assume a larger share of the alliance's military burden, and tried desperately to find new money for more social spending. Despite mounting protectionist pressures, the Administration also continued to push ahead on negotiations for another multilateral trade-liberalization agreement.

In late 1978, however, the bottom at last fell out of the Carter coalition. Anxious about both the pace of economic growth in the United States and the potential for a major downturn abroad, the Administration had for two years maintained a relatively easy monetary policy and allowed the exchange rate to fall. With the rate of unemployment dropping, however, imports rose, and in 1978 wage gains again briefly pulled ahead of productivity gains.[56]

Hoping to continue its expansionary policies, the Administration reviewed various methods of wage restraint. While labor leaders, top business figures, and economists at the Brookings Institution and elsewhere examined various proposals for a national "incomes policy" (such as the so-called TIP, or "tax-based incomes policy," that relied on the tax system rather than direct controls to secure wage restraint), the Administration sought international agreement for a multinationally coordinated expansion ("joint reflation") of the economies of Britain, Germany, and the United States. At the Bonn summit of the major industrial powers, however, the allies balked. The British refused to go along with the plan, and the German reflation was grudging. The failure of trilateral (in many senses) macroeconomic cooperation convinced many American multinational business executives that the United States could not count on allied cooperation and would have to make macroeconomic policy on a more unilateral basis for the time being. But it also left the Administration, which had entered office promising an expansion, out on a limb. With the U.S. rate of inflation racing ahead of that of its allies, anxiety about the dollar grew. In October 1978, the effects of the Administration's earlier reluctance to rein in the money supply became dramatically visible. A giant run on the dollar developed.[57]

Forced at last to choose between his constituencies, Carter did not hesitate. To restore confidence in the dollar, Carter promised in late October to reduce the growing budget deficit, cut government hiring, and eliminate additional regulations. He also announced a new series of wage-price standards, in another bid to get control of inflation. World financial markets responded negatively to this program, with international bankers voicing skepticism about Carter's ability to deliver. In November, the Administration moved directly to support the dollar, engineering a full percentage point jump in the Federal Reserve's discount rate, increasing reserve requirements on big time deposits, and pushing through a $30 billion package to support the dollar in international markets. In January 1979, Carter also unveiled what he described as a "lean" budget, aimed at reducing what were then projected as $40 billion budget deficits.

By then, however, the Shah of Iran had been driven from his throne, announcing a major disaster for many of America's largest industrial and service firms—including major banks, oil companies, construction firms, weapons suppliers, and any number of other exporters and service enterprises—that had been deeply involved in the Shah's regime. Stunned by its real and prospective losses, the business community's demands for increased military spending were reaching a crescendo. Compounding these problems was the oil shortage of early 1979, rising inflation, and another run on the dollar in the early summer. In July, Carter acted, in a complex rearrangement of his Cabinet and other top positions in the Administration. In the most important moves, Carter dismissed liberal HEW Secretary Joseph Califano and Treasury Secretary Michael Blumenthal; he then moved Fed Chairman G. William Miller to Blumenthal's old spot. Then, after David Rockefeller, Democratic investment banker Robert Roosa, and Bank of America chairman A. W. Clausen refused the post, he appointed Paul Volcker, a former Chase employee, to be Chairman of the Federal Reserve Board. Volcker immediately raised interest rates.[58]

From that point, everything went from bad to worse. Another dollar crisis led the Fed to pursue even more Draconian monetary policies, and interest rates approached lunar levels. Real growth in the economy ceased altogether, and for a couple of quarters was even negative. Almost simultaneously, the international economy nosedived. Adding to the pressures for increased military spending, the embassy hostages were seized in Iran and, at the end of the year, the Soviets invaded Afghanistan.

But the economic collapse gave Carter little room to maneuver. By early 1980, with Democratic investment bankers holding late-night meetings with the party's congressional leadership to demand budget cuts, the leader of the party of Roosevelt, Truman, Kennedy, and Johnson was forced to do the unthinkable. Only months before an oncoming election, he was forced to make massive cuts in funds for the poor, blacks, and the cities, and to further tighten the money supply. At the same time, Carter made clear his commitment to massive (5 percent in real terms) annual increases in military outlays.

Seeking to hedge his bets during the 1980 campaign, Carter shaded both the military buildup and the domestic cuts. As a consequence, he was attacked within the party from both his left, by Edward Kennedy, and his right, by the Democrats of the Committee on the Present Danger. Though he managed to secure renomination, after a difficult and exceptionally bitter fight, his political fate was sealed.

As Carter struggled with the new conundrums of Democratic leadership, Ronald Reagan was by slow degrees moving from the far right to the center right of the American political universe. Originally supported by ultraconservative entrepreneurs in California and elsewhere, some large fortunes inveterately hostile to the New Deal, parts of the armaments industry, many small businesses, and protectionist concerns in textiles and independent oil, Reagan failed to enlist many top business figures in support of his abortive 1976 run against Gerald Ford. But the rightward drift of the business community on taxes, defense, the environment, and labor had gradually added to his original core, and he was now willing to modify policy views that stood in the way of his acceptance by the multinationals, and particularly by what remained of the GOP's Eastern liberal establishment. Thus he gradually drew away from his longtime commitment to Taiwan (which interferes with the "China card" American foreign-policy elites regard as the pillar of American strategy in the western Pacific). He also signaled a willingness not only to cut personal tax rates, as Congressman Jack Kemp, Senator William Roth, and many entrepreneurs and some big-business executives with particularly handsome salaries advocated, but also to trim corporate rates, as most big business executives preferred (including the so-called Carlton Group, in which Charls Walker was a major player, which was then at work with congressional *Democrats* on a major tax-reduction bill of its own).[59]

Most importantly, Reagan sought a compromise on the GOP's most divisive issue—international trade. Backed by such prominent champions of the textile industry as Jesse Helms, and heavily supported in several primaries, after former Texas governor John Connally withdrew from the 1980 race, by U.S. Steel's protectionist David M. Roderick and other top western Pennsylvania business executives, the Reagan campaign also leveled a series of sensational public attacks on the famous free-trade-oriented Trilateral Commission. Nevertheless, as many of Reagan's original core supporters watched with mounting apprehension, in the spring of 1980 his campaign slowly struck an accommodation with the internationalist bloc. Eventually, it settled on a plan to initiate a broad new round of trade talks—but only after an indefinite number of years in which it would attempt to reshape both the U.S. and the world economy through a sweeping series of unilateral actions by the United States involving major changes in budgets, taxes, and interest rates.[60]

By putting off a showdown on trade into the indefinite future, the Reagan campaign opened the way for virtually all of American business to mass behind its candidate. And while occasional flaps about the Reagan program and personality persisted to the end, most of American business did gather round. With George Bush, who quickly forgot his earlier criticism of the Reagan program as "voodoo economics," on the ticket, the same media that had relentlessly picked at the arithmetic of George McGovern's proposals for income redistribution largely declined even to add up the numbers as Reagan promised simultaneously to cut taxes, balance the budget, preserve essential social spending, and vastly increase military outlays. Business groups' and the right's contributions to the Reagan campaign, the GOP, and "independent" political action committees that favored the Republicans broke all records. In one telling indication of the distribution of elite support, "independent" expenditures for Reagan were 382 times those for Carter. As all but a few investment bankers and a handful of multinational business figures deserted the hapless President, the West and even much of the East deserted the Democrats. The Republicans came to power.[61]

4/

"Reaganism"

During the 1970s, international economic disorder, foreign-policy reversals, and domestic stagflation generated intense conflicts within the American business community. Throughout the decade, and especially after the Great Recession, debates raged over trade, the role of the dollar, the terms of U.S. military relations, and any number of domestic issues. The increasing integration and competition of the world economy, and the drastically changed position of the United States within it, created vast pressures for a basic restructuring of American political and economic institutions. Those pressures were evident in the business community's shift to the right and the fracturing of the Democrats' old New Deal coalition. Yet the business community's main points of consensus—on wage and social-spending cuts, tax reductions, and increased military outlays—had distinct limits. Even as the right turn proceeded, persistent divisions made concerted action by business difficult, and therefore made coordinated restructuring impossible.[1]

The broad base of support Reagan attracted during the later stages of the 1980 election, and the dazzling legislative successes his Administration scored in the early months of his first term, convinced many observers that the Republicans had at last overcome these tendencies to fragmentation. On the right and in most of the center, commentators heralded the arrival of a class of "young intellectuals of a capacity Washington had not seen for years." On the left, many observers increasingly feared that Reagan would lead a united business community on a triumphant "new class war" to destroy both the New Deal and the Great Society.[2]

But while the Administration and its allies clearly hoped to bring about a lasting realignment of the political system that would secure a conservative Republican hegemony for a generation, the behavior (and occasional guarded statements) of the Reagan coalition's leading figures suggests that most were well aware of how fragile their bloc really was. Comprised of both nationalists *and* several species of internationalists; advocates of tight money *and* monetary ease; free-traders *and* protectionists; sponsors of a variety of contradictory tax plans; and many clashing foreign-policy interests—the coalition that brought Reagan to power was a mile wide but only an inch deep.

For all the temporary unity "free enterprise" or the idea of a right turn sometimes inspired, the members of the coalition could hardly expect for very long to bridge the conflicts that still threatened to divide them. With Jimmy Carter gone from the scene, there was every prospect that the group would soon shatter and thereby muff its historic opportunity. America might turn right, and the New Deal would disintegrate, but Republican dominance of the new, more conservative party system would not be assured. Accordingly, the Reagan camp deliberated long and hard on where to concentrate its energies.

Monetary Policy

Some decisions were easy. Fearing that action on the controversial "social agenda" promoted by far-right business groups and the evangelists they subsidized would distract attention from economic-policy initiatives, the Administration relegated these issues to a back burner. Some of their partisans were awarded posts that allowed them to promote ends that served the interests of the broader Reagan coalition—such as "defunding the left" or replacing lower-level liberal bureaucrats with officials more responsive to the new Reagan policies. They were, however, largely excluded from the highest positions within the Administration.[3]

Other choices were more difficult. For example, General Alexander Haig, the Chase director and former Kissinger aide whom Reagan named Secretary of State, relates in his memoirs how overriding economic policy concerns dashed the hopes he and others had entertained for decisive foreign policy initiatives at the start of the Administration. Even so, on what was probably the single most important economic policy issue at hand—the management of monetary policy—the Reagan coalition was unable to arrive at a consensus.[4]

Though the full story is likely to remain untold by its key participants for many years to come, it is clear that both big business and Administration officials were divided over whether to continue with the Carter Administration's tight-money policy as Reagan took office. One bloc of leading businessmen, which certainly included most financiers and many industrial firms (and was reportedly represented on the President's Economic Policy Board by Citibank's Walter Wriston), wanted to continue the Carter policy of sharply limiting growth in the money supply. Part of their reasoning, as laid out between the lines of an article in *Fortune* magazine by Herbert Stein (the former chairman of Nixon's Council of Economic Advisers), was utterly classic. As the money supply tightened, interest rates would rise and demand would drop. Falling demand would trigger a rise in unemployment, which would moderate wage demands and put downward pressure on prices. Price stability, in turn, would encourage foreigners to hold dollar deposits, and revive the bond market.[5]

Some members of this bloc appear to have hoped that the rise in unemployment could be brief. Advocates of what was then becoming known as the "credibility hypothesis" (originally put forward by William Fellner of the American Enterprise Institute), they claimed that a "credible" reversal of government policies would quickly induce workers to accept lower wages and employers to lower their prices. Most members, however, were far less sanguine: believing that the process of wringing inflation out of the economy might require years of austerity, they urged the President to abstain from the ritual promise not to fight inflation through unemployment. As Stein wrote, "it strengthens expectations that cannot be met and creates demands for actions that are unwise."[6]

A recent account by Henry Nau, the senior member of the Reagan Administration's National Security Council staff responsible for international economic affairs over 1981–83, reveals that internationally oriented members of the tight-money bloc favored austerity for a second reason as well. Convinced by the failure of efforts at international economic cooperation during the Carter Administration that negotiated approaches to world economic problems would not work, these business groups now wanted the U.S. government to use what was left of its hegemonic position in the world economy to impose a wide set of policies favoring private enterprise on the rest of the world. In this view, through tight money and related economic policies the United States could achieve what all political negotiations in the 1970s had failed to provide—a restructuring of the world economy that rolled back the rising tide of state involvement in enterprise and social protections for the work force.[7]

These efforts relied on the conviction that the United States "retains sufficient power to influence the international market significantly, even though it no longer has sufficient power to impose its will on that market through direct international bargaining." Their proponents therefore recommended "an assertive use of U.S. economic power in the marketplace . . . and a relatively passive U.S. economic diplomacy." More concretely: if the United States raised interest rates, other countries would eventually have to adopt austerity also; in due course, this would force adjustment by their labor forces and governments. Finally, the ensuing devastation might, at some later point, "help the United States apply its reduced political influence at the bargaining table to re-establish consensus and, if necessary, secure formal commitments to a revitalized international economic system." For the rest of the world, such an aggressive U.S. policy would be exceptionally costly and disruptive, but as Nau later put it:

If the president was prepared to accept pain and political risk at home, he had little reason to alleviate these costs abroad. . . . Admittedly, the unbuffered export of U.S. disinflation through high interest rates and recession would test the fabric of open international economic relationships, as well as the domestic political processes in some countries. But the administration ultimately concluded that disinflation without growth must be accomplished quickly or not at all.[8]

Since the world's poor and ordinary working people do not vote in American elections, their views about the wisdom of this course were not solicited. More immediately, while the strategy clearly had major business backing at home, and many employer organizations in Europe and elsewhere would eventually become enthusiasts (particularly after their exports took off in early 1983), at least some American business interests initially had doubts about it. Many of these dissenters simply feared that a steep downturn would seriously hurt their own concerns. Some multinationals also worried that a deep recession might aggravate pressures for protectionism and, as the chief economist of the CED observed, increase social unrest. Finally, Congressman Jack Kemp, drugstore magnate Lewis Lehrman, and a few other "supply side" advocates claimed that a return to the gold standard and big tax cuts would by themselves suffice to cure inflation, making unnecessary traditional policies of monetary restriction.[9]

These doubts initially impressed the Administration, and its early economic projections envisioned only a brief spell of tight money and high unemployment. There was also some talk about asking labor to restrain its wage demands in return for lower taxes and steadying the growth of the money supply. Very quickly, however, the Administration learned an elementary lesson in political economy: the Federal Reserve Board of Governors, and not the Administration, makes monetary policy. And the Fed already had a policy—tight money.

Because almost everything the Fed does is shrouded in mystery, it is impossible to say exactly what it thought it was doing in late 1980 and early 1981. In particular, it is hard to weigh claims that its Draconian credit policies may have been partly the result of a mistake—that the Fed did not realize how restrictive its policies were becoming. Suffice it to note that analysts are forever writing off famous instances where the Fed put the economy through a wringer as "mistakes" (no less a figure than Milton Friedman has made this claim even for the disastrous deflation of the Great Depression), while serious investigation almost always shows that pressure from big banks and other sources, and not some policy "error," was responsible.[10]

The case of the "Great Volcker Deflation" of 1980–82 is no exception. Appointed by Jimmy Carter at a time when the financial community was in an uproar over the decline of the dollar, Volcker, the former Chase employee, did exactly what his core constituency of international financiers wanted. Abandoning the Fed's longtime policy of targeting interest rates in favor of strict limits on the supply of money, he stopped the dollar's slide. Determined to wring inflation out of the system, Volcker and his supporters in the banks, insurance companies, and the rest of big business were perfectly prepared to confront the White House if they had to.[11]

In the end, they were never really forced to do so. While White

House supply-siders and the Secretary of the Treasury seethed in private and tried occasionally to deter the Fed from its deflationary course—even warning, as Treasury Secretary Donald Regan did in the summer of 1981, that the Fed was leading the economy back into a massive recession—most prominent figures of the Administration did not challenge the basic thrust of monetary policy. Instead, as the Fed tightened interest rates week after week, wages fell, and unemployment rose dramatically, they were pleased to see labor's bargaining position disintegrate almost completely. The gains for business that followed from this were enormous. With strike levels plunging to historic lows, and wages falling sharply, firms could afford to retrench: they could relocate, retool, and make major permanent reductions in the size of their work forces. As a consequence, until the catastrophic fall in national income finally bit seriously into business sales, most of the anxieties about tight money that had previously wracked the business community dissipated.[12]

As the shift in business sentiment became clear, the Reagan Administration settled down. Though some of its members continued to criticize the Fed, Reagan himself rarely said anything. When he did, it was usually either to confuse the question of responsibility or even, as happened a few days after his famous Valentine's Day 1982 "lovefest" meeting with Volcker, to endorse the Fed's policies. By March of that year David Stockman, who had only months before been promoting the wisdom of supply-side thought, assured a Chamber of Commerce breakfast group that the Administration saw a sustained period of unemployment as "part of the cure, not the problem," of American economic difficulties. Even at close to the bottom of the recession, when Volcker—concerned about slow growth in the world economy and the liquidity of the big banks during the debt crisis—finally eased off, Reagan supported a demand by the president of the U.S. Chamber of Commerce for tighter money. And for more than a year, Reagan's second chairman of the Council of Economic Advisers, Martin Feldstein, vocally cheered on the Fed.[13]

Taxes

The Administration's other major economic-policy initiatives—on taxes and spending—were the outcome of a more conscious and explicit policy-formation process. But they certainly did not result from the conscious design of any neoconservative intellectuals. They emerged in response to political pressures, which revealed quite clearly the internal tensions in Reagan's coalition.

As the previous chapter noted, several of Reagan's original core supporters (including William Simon, by then a leading portfolio manager for several large Arab business interests and a director of many companies) were known as strong advocates of the so-called Kemp-Roth approach to tax reduction. Emphasizing steep cuts in personal tax rates, advocates of this approach promised miraculous "supply side" effects on the lagging U.S. growth rates. In private, as all the world now knows thanks to David Stockman's "confessions" to *Washington Post* editor William Greider, many sponsors of this claim knew that it was false, but saw it as a "Trojan horse to bring down the top rate."[14]

The mass media, many of whose owners were then promoting lower taxation, puffed the concept and did not scrutinize the claims closely until long after the rates were lowered. This approach to cutting taxes did have important supporters within big business, particularly among some of the best-paid executives (for whom the drop in top rates would really add up to something), but most of its support came from entrepreneurs and rentiers, for whom reductions in personal tax rates mattered greatly. In the last years of the Carter Administration, however, big-business lobbyists represented in the Carlton Group had begun working with some members of the Democratically controlled House Ways and Means Committee on another approach, which emphasized slashes in *corporate* tax rates. Most centrally identified with their promotion of accelerated depreciation allowances for business, advocates of this strategy, in contrast to many prominent supporters of Kemp-Roth, were careful to emphasize the need for spending cuts to match their proposed corporate tax breaks.[15]

As more and more big, internationally oriented business figures drifted toward Reagan in the 1980 campaign, he gradually moved away from a pure Kemp-Roth strategy. Once it assumed power, however, the Administration was most reluctant to choose between its supporters. On the one hand, Reagan appointed the ubiquitous Charls Walker, the leader of the Carlton Group, as chair of his tax-policy transition team. On the other, he continued to promote the three years of Kemp-Roth cuts as a central Administration initiative. The Administration's first proposals for tax reform, issued in early 1981, reflected this political ambivalence by simply accepting both sets of proposals. The projected revenue losses were stupefyingly large (they would eventually total about $750 billion over the next five years), and with the Administration also announcing plans for vast new military outlays, many big businessmen were understandably dubious that compensating spending cuts of the required magnitude could pass. Fearing huge deficits, several big-business groups, including a majority of the Business Roundtable, urged scaling back the personal income tax cuts. Supply-siders, of course, were outraged.[16]

What followed taught David Stockman, early and forcefully, that "constituency-based politics," and not "idea-based policies," determined the Administration's agenda. With the White House in turmoil, the House Ways and Means Committee produced a bill modified generally in a direction the Roundtable desired. Then, fearful that the Democrats would run off with the tax issue, the White House issued its own proposal in June to cut back Kemp-Roth's three-year 10 percent personal income tax cuts and trim the depreciation provisions. Seeking to attract Southern Democrats, it added special tax provisions attractive to independent oilmen.[17]

Perceiving the threat to the depreciation allowances and other corporate tax breaks, big business mobilized rapidly. Immediately after the Administration's announcement, the Business Roundtable called an emergency meeting. Executives of America's top firms descended on Washington in droves, for an orgy of lobbying that became known as the "Lear Jet Weekend." The Roundtable then brought sharp pressure for yet another revision. Working with some White House officials and many other business groups—including Walker's American Council for Capital Formation, the American Business Council, the Chamber of Commerce, and the National Association of Manufacturers—its leaders went to the Ways and Means Committee with their request. The Democrats responded by proposing an even more expensive set of depreciation provisions than the Administration had and sweeping provisions for the "leaseback" of equipment that would drop corporate rates even more. Ways and Means also added additional provisions to appeal to independent oil companies.

With the party of Roosevelt and the New Deal now pushing a bill more finely geared to big business than the Republicans' own, the whole logic of the situation shifted. The Administration took over all the Democratic proposals and broadened the accelerated depreciation schedules (now dubbed the "Accelerated Cost Recovery System" or ACRS) still more by adding further "leaseback" provisions. Several more rounds of bidding followed, in which the Democrats tended to add tax breaks for big business while cutting back on the personal tax cuts. A huge number of separate deals were also struck: for special breaks for high-tech firms, for the drastic reduction of estate and inheritance taxes, and much more. As Stockman later put it: "The hogs were really feeding. The greed level, the level of opportunism, just got out of control."[18]

As it emerged from the Conference Committee, the final bill was a monstrosity bigger and wilder than probably anyone had envisioned early in the year. The business community naturally had to be pleased, but many executives in the Roundtable and the Administration still worried about the deficit. Though the bill postponed the effective date of the Kemp-Roth cuts, and cut the first-year tax reduction to 5 percent, it was certain to cause a major revenue shortfall, especially given the Administration's ambitious spending plans, and massive budget deficits. Yet the longer most big-business figures looked at the bill, the better they liked it. With the economy slowing down, and about to plunge, the need to get revenues to business was growing. In addition, as some principles in the negotiations leading to the final package have finally admitted, the Administration and many of its supporters calculated that growing hysteria over the ensuing deficit would create powerful pressures to cut federal spending, and thus, perhaps, enable the Administration to accomplish its goal of rolling back the New Deal.[19]

Thus reassured, the business community that had already panicked a Democratic President into cutting his own constituencies in advance of an election thought it could safely go ahead. The Chase Manhattan Bank took out huge ads supporting the Reagan program. The Roundtable also supported final passage, as did the Chamber, NAM, and NFIB.[20]

When the final dimensions of the Economic Recovery Tax Act (ERTA) of 1981 are considered, the reasons for business enthusiasm are obvious. While the corporate share of federal tax burdens had been dropping for some time, ERTA sharply accelerated the trend. Even after the "takeback" of some of the initial corporate benefits in 1982, effective tax rates for business were halved, dropping from 33 to 16 percent overall. By FY 1983, after averaging 15 percent during the 1970s (and 21.3 and 27.6 percent, respectively, during the 1960s and 1950s), the corporate income tax share of federal tax revenues dropped to 6.2 percent. Loopholes grew astronomically. Again taking the 1982 reforms into account, tax expenditures directly beneficial to corporations grew from $43 billion in FY 1980 to an estimated $120 billion in FY 1986.[21]

Big business had special reasons to be happy. A recent study of tax payments by 275 major, profitable corporations found that their effective rate of taxation over 1981–84 was only 15 percent, slightly below the overall effective corporate rate. More striking, 129 of the firms had managed to pay no income taxes, or receive rebates, in at least one of those four years. For this group, their real tax rate for the years they did not pay was −9.6 percent; on top of $66.5 billion in pre-tax domestic profits, they received $6.4 billion in tax rebates. Among them, 74 had paid nothing (or less) in federal income for at least two years, 26 had done this for at least three years, and 9 had achieved it each of the four years under review. Totaling tax payments and rebates, 50 of the firms had paid nothing or less over the whole 1981–84 period.[22]

Wealthy individuals were also pleased. An across-the-board cut of 23 percent in individual tax rates, coupled with a reduction in the top rate on unearned income from 70 to 50 percent (with the consequence that the top tax rate on capital gains dropped to 20 percent), complemented the corporate cuts with a massive subsidy to rich Americans. In 1984, for families in the bottom income quintile, the average reduction in tax liabilities attributable to the 1981 tax cuts was $3. For those in the top quintile, it was $2,429. As a percentage of disposable income, the reductions were less than 0.1 percent for families in the bottom quintile, rising to 1.4, 2.8, 4.0, and 5.9 percent for families in the second, third, fourth, and fifth quintiles, respectively. Taking inflation and the large 1981 and 1982 increases in social security tax into account, over the 1982–84 period taxes actually increased for all those making less than $30,000 a year (with a 22 percent increase for those making under $10,000). For those making over $200,000 a year, however, the Reagan cuts brought an average reduction in liability of 15 percent. Significantly, the Reagan tax initiatives also included the introduction, beginning in 1985, of income "indexation," or correction for inflation, thus making it extremely difficult to generate additional tax revenues without explicit tax increases. Given the historic difficulty of securing such increases in federal income taxation, at least in peacetime, ERTA's vast bailout to business and the wealthy would be very hard to reverse.[23]

Long before the bill finally passed, however, the Administration recognized that it had—almost inadvertently—stumbled on what looked then to be a surefire formula for holding on to its political support. In the golden glow of prospective tax reductions, and the drop in labor's bargaining position that the rise in interest rates was already inducing, the Administration had at least for a time found a way to square the circle. While withdrawing from traditional government obligations to working people and the poor, deflating the world economy, and introducing massively regressive revisions of the federal tax system, it could reward virtually all members of its highly diverse and rivalrous business coalition by simply giving them streams of cash.

Military and Social Spending

The Administration's major spending initiatives during 1981, passed as the Omnibus Budget Reconciliation Act even before the tax boondoggle was resolved, reflected this elemental perception. With virtually all of American business clamoring for an increase in military spending, the Administration responded by initiating the biggest sustained peacetime buildup in U.S. history. Over FY 1980–85, real military spending would increase 39 percent, while national defense budget authority would increase 53 percent. As a share of GNP, military outlays rose from 5.2 to 6.6 percent; as a share of the federal budget, they climbed from 23 to 27 percent.[24]

Significantly, the Reagan military budget was increasingly "weapons-driven," meaning that it devoted a larger and larger share of budget authority to "investment" (weapons procurement, research and development, military construction, warhead production), as opposed to "consumption" (operations and maintenance, personnel, and other miscellaneous) functions. In real terms, Department of Defense (DOD) budget authority for "investment" would increase 95 percent over the FY 1980–85 period, while authority for operations and maintenance increased "only" 37 percent and personnel 13 percent. As a consequence, investment rose from just over a third (38%) to just under a half (48%) of the vastly expanded total.[25]

The investment focus of the Reagan buildup immensely increased the share of DOD's budget that was "uncontrollable"—the area where funds are obligated to already existing contracts. Over FY 1980–85, as the government locked into a growing number of virtually uncuttable procurement contracts, uncontrollable outlays rose from 27 to 36 percent of the DOD budget. Counting in the additional 43 percent of overall defense outlays that went to salary and retirement benefits for military and civilian personnel, which are also very difficult to cut, this meant that by the end of Reagan's first term the "uncontrollable" share of the military budget was about 80 percent, and rising.[26]

The central purpose of the Reagan buildup, of course, was not the satisfaction of particular military contractors, but the satisfaction of more general business demands to enhance the U.S. capacity to project force abroad—to press and defend private American interests in an increasingly volatile world economy. Still, what may be thought of as a global subsidy to U.S. business was also a particular subsidy to sectors of that business. Significantly, the Reagan Administration never proposed extensive rethinking of American force structures. Instead, it mainly sought added missions and redundancy in weapons systems, piling contract on contract to domestic weapons producers in a rapid "modernization" of existing forces and in efforts advertised as increasing their "readiness."

A striking example of this was defense spending on strategic weapons. Contrary to Reagan's repeated claim that the United States had "unilaterally disarmed" during the 1970s, there had in fact been a substantial modernization and expansion of U.S. strategic forces during that period. In 1970, the United States had 4,000 strategic warheads. By the time Carter left office, it had 9,000, and the newer forces were substantially more accurate than the ones they replaced. Reagan inherited a strategic force capable of delivering, with a nearly 80 percent kill probability, more than 3,660 nuclear warheads against a wide range of "aiming points" in the Soviet Union, even *after* a massive Soviet first strike. Such forces provided an extremely high level of deterrence, and gave no evidence of "unilateral disarmament" by the United States. Nevertheless, the Reagan Administration came to office arguing that the U.S. strategic triad—the combination of air-, land-, and sea-based nuclear weapons—suffered from a "window of vulnerability," and even after its own Scowcroft Commission debunked this theory, and after agreement had been reached among the intelligence services that Soviet military spending during the previous decade was considerably less than previous estimates, it continued with a massive nuclear buildup.[27]

Over its first term, the Administration's nuclear buildup rose at nearly three times the rate of the overall defense program. Over fiscal 1980–85, budget authority for strategic weapons grew from $9.4 to $35.3 billion, an increase of 276 percent, while authority for major conventional and tactical weapons rose 111 percent. Such massive increases in the strategic program increased the share of the overall weapons budget held by strategic weapons; by 1984, for the first time in U.S. history, spending for strategic weapons exceeded spending on tactical and conventional weapons. Despite the huge sums spent, however, the Administration made no major change in the basic force structure. Instead, it engaged in unnecessary duplication of effort within or across different parts of the triad. By 1984, for example, the Air Force was at work on five different programs to penetrate Soviet air defenses: upgrading the B-52 bomber force, producing two new air-launched cruise missiles (the ALCM-B and ACM), and proceeding with acquisition of additional B-1B bombers as well as the Stealth. At the same time, the Air Force was moving along with the land-based MX missile, while the Navy was at work on the Trident D-5. The MX and D-5 missiles are also designed for the same purpose. Both are super-accurate hard target killers which, while MIRVed, "are designed to to have a high probability of destroying a Soviet missile silo with a single warhead."[28]

A similar irrationality seemed to pervade the massive naval buildup in conventional forces. Among the three services, the Navy got the largest share of budget authority over the 1980–85 period—$440 billion—although even this staggering commitment is misleadingly small, given potential stretch-out of costs for major systems and the commitment in support services over the lifetime of those systems that initial procurement entails. On one estimate a single carrier battle group, for example, costs $400 billion over the course of its (approximately thirty-year) working lifetime. It is not an investment one should enter into lightly. The reasons advanced by the Administration for building three new carrier battle groups, however, shifted repeatedly:

The reasons variously advanced have been to maintain a peacetime presence in the Mediterranean, the Western Pacific, and the Indian Ocean; because national policy requires stationing two carriers in the Mediterranean and three in the Western Pacific, which necessitates a total of fifteen for purposes of rotation; or because an attack on Murmansk or Vladivostok will be needed early in a conflict to give the president the option of escalating a conventional war "horizontally" in the event of a Soviet attack on an area of vital interest to the U.S.[29]

Such imprecise and shifting definitions of force missions, combined with the tremendous redundancy in Administration efforts and the sheer wastefulness of many of the spending programs, would eventually provide grounds for a limited attack on some of the more expensive components of the Reagan budget.

Dedicated to shifting the budget toward military spending, the Administration also moved aggressively to cut outlays to social programs. Part of this attack was directed to the big-ticket items in the social budget—the major social insurance programs. Worker eligibility under unemployment insurance programs was narrowed, and coverage would soon fall to record lows. The Administration also sought regressive reform of the medicare system in a series of proposals aimed at limiting program coverage and shifting the costs of health care onto its consumers. These proposals enjoyed only mixed success in Congress, which would itself initiate the most important single cost reduction reform in the health area—the change to a hospital reimbursement system based on flat-fee "Diagnostic Related Groups"—during Reagan's first term. Still, benefit reductions attributable to Reagan Administration programs amounted to $15 billion over FY 1982–85, and the Administration's general program of rationing care through increasing costs to consumers, along with the privatization of health care such an approach helps promote, gradually gathered steam.[30]

Administration efforts to gut social security were even more pointed, although here, too, the results were mixed. After securing congressional acquiescence in early 1981 to modest cuts in that program, it moved in May of that year to "reform" social security drastically. If enacted, its proposals—which included immediate 40 percent benefit reductions for early retirees, a roughly one-third reduction in disability benefits, and a variety of caps and changes in the calculation and adjustment of benefit levels—would have amounted to a 20 percent cut in the overall program, or about $200 billion over the 1982–90 period. But the proposals generated a storm of resistance (reflected in a 96–0 vote against them in the Senate), and the Administration backed away, with Reagan promising to hold off on any further suggestions until he received the report of the bipartisan National Commission on Social Security Reform due at the end of 1982. Nevertheless, in May 1982 the Administration endorsed a Senate proposal for $40 billion in benefits cuts over FY 1983–85. This too was beaten back.[31]

Eventually, the major cuts in social security would come through bipartisan action in Congress, which enacted a series of reforms of the system in early 1983 that closely followed the recommendations of the National Commission. These, too, were generally regressive. They included a delay in the July 1983 cost-of-living adjustments in the future if the trust funds fell too low, a gradual stretch-out in the retirement age from sixty-five to sixty-seven, a 33 percent increase in payroll taxes for the self-employed, the acceleration of scheduled general payroll tax increases, and an extension of coverage (and taxation) to new federal employees, for whom social security would replace more generous pension schemes, as well as all employees of nonprofit organizations. In the short term, the congressional reforms promised relatively small reductions in outlays (4.6 percent by 1985); in the long term their effect is much greater, amounting to as much as an 11 percent reduction in disposable income for recipients by 2030. And where congressional action was not required, the Administration moved forward without it to cut the scope of existing benefits, as in its reinterpretation of eligibility criteria for disability insurance.[32]

The deepest social spending cuts, however, came in low-income benefits and jobs and services programs. As with other aspects of the right turn in policy, the Administration's actions in this area sharply accelerated existing trends. Contrary to the common image of a steadily increasing population of means-tested benefit recipients throughout the 1970s, enrollment growth in virtually all means-tested assistance programs either slowed considerably or actually became negative after 1974. Moreover, the real value of many benefits had been declining for some time. By 1981, real average Aid to Families with Dependent Children (AFDC) benefits for a family of four had already declined more than 33 percent from their 1970 levels, while such familiar multiple-benefit packages as AFDC plus Food Stamps and AFDC,

Food Stamps, and Low Income Energy Assistance had dropped by 21.7 and 19.2 percent, respectively.[33]

Such benefit erosion aside, the scope and depth of the Reagan cutbacks in low-income assistance and services programs marked a qualitative change in social policy. Overall, the Administration sought 60 percent cuts in the discretionary grant programs closely associated with the Great Society, and roughly 30 percent cuts in low-income assistance payments. With most of the action taking place in 1981, Congress provided it with three-quarters of what was sought on the first group of programs and about a third of what was sought on the second. Among the most important individual program cuts were those in Food Stamps (14%), child nutrition (28%), Aid to Families with Dependent Children (14%), Supplemental Security Income (11%), Low Income Energy Assistance (11%), financial aid for needy students (16%), health block grants and other health services (33%), compensatory education (20%), social-services block grants (24%), community-services block grants (37%), general job-training programs (39%), and public-service employment (100%).[34]

That the low-income programs only comprised a small share of the total budget to begin with—and that the budgetary savings from their cutback was therefore slight—did not reduce the misery of those whose benefits were chopped. To take only a few examples: the reductions in Food Stamp benefits for some 20 million Americans hit the poor hardest, with 70 percent of the savings coming from families living below the poverty line; some 440,000 low-income working families (almost all headed by women) lost AFDC benefits, while several hundred thousand more had benefits reduced; Medicaid benefits, linked to AFDC, were therefore also scaled back, with the result that nearly a third of all children now living in poverty receive no Medicaid coverage; and as a direct result of cuts in low-income housing programs, an estimated 300,000 more families were pushed into substandard housing.[35]

Overall, by FY 1985 the various Reagan budget cuts in social programs reduced social spending by about 10 percent, below the levels projected under prior policy (roughly half of what the Administration initially sought); aggregate cuts on the nonmilitary side of the budget totaled about $175 billion over 1982–85. Especially given the emphasis on cuts in low-income programs (which, while accounting for only 10 percent of the budget, sustained one-third of all spending cuts during Reagan's first term), their impact was profoundly regressive. Approximately half the benefit reductions achieved during the Administration's first three years fell on households with annual incomes of less than $10,000; approximately 70 percent fell on households making less than $20,000. Households with incomes in excess of $80,000 carried only 1 percent of the burden.[36]

The combination of social-spending cuts, other budget initiatives, and the massively regressive tax bill produced a huge upward distribution of American income. Over the 1983–85 period the policies reduced the incomes of households making less than $20,000 a year by $20 billion, while increasing the incomes of households making more than $80,000 by $35 billion. For those at the very bottom of the income pyramid, making under $10,000 per year, the policies produced an average loss of $1,100 over 1983–85. For those at the top, making more than $200,000 a year, the average gain was $60,000. By the end of Reagan's first term, U.S. income distribution was more unequal than at any time since 1947, the year the Census Bureau first began collecting data on the subject. In 1983, the top 40 percent of the population received a larger share of income than at any time since 1947; both the bottom 40 percent and the middle 20 percent received smaller shares than at any time since then. On any reasonable measure (before or after transfer payments and taxes), poverty increased dramatically. By 1984 some 33 million Americans—one in seven—lived below the poverty line, 4.4 million more than in 1980, and 9 million more than in 1978. The plight of children was worse. In 1984, about one-quarter of all children under the age of six lived below the poverty line, and more than half of all black children under the age of six lived in poverty.[37]

Deregulation and the Attack on Labor

The Administration also used the enormous discretion of the executive branch to relieve business of many of the burdens of regulation. Building on the reforms of the Carter Administration, it effectively concentrated control of the regulatory process in the OMB, where David Stockman presided, and even without major legislative actions, it succeeded (through leadership changes, staff cuts, reduced budgets, changed agency rules, and other means) in gutting enforcement at major regulatory agencies of special concern to business. The

TABLE 4.1

Personnel: Authorized Permanent Positions for Selected
Executive and Independent Agencies

	FY 1980	FY 1984*	Percent Change FY 1980–84
Environmental Protection Agency	11,015	8,669	−21
Federal Grain Inspection Service	2,242	1,045	−53
Mine Safety and Health Administration	3,857	3,184	−17
National Highway Traffic Safety Commission	874	617	−29
Occupational Safety and Health Administration	3,015	2,355	−22
Office of Surface Mining	1,025	731	−29
Commission on Civil Rights	285	236	−17
Consumer Product Safety Commission	880	542	−38
Equal Employment Opportunity Commission	3,777	3,185	−16
Federal Trade Commission	1,665	1,131	−32
Interstate Commerce Commission	2,024	1,200	−41

*Estimated.

Source: Eads and Fix, Relief or Reform?, 152

notoriously complex and heterogeneous nature of the American administrative process prevents any adequate summary of the Reagan regulatory program here. But it is safe to say that it comprised another giant, if almost hidden, transfer program, shifting all sorts of costs away from business and onto the rest of the population.[38]

In the critical area of environmental regulation, the Administration simply refused to implement all sorts of key provisions of existing air- and water-pollution laws. Over Reagan's first term, EPA's overall budget was reduced by 35 percent (a cut of 50 percent was proposed), enforcement against strip-mine violations declined by 62 percent, prosecution of hazardous-waste violations declined 50 percent, and FDA regulation enforcement declined 88 percent. Exposure limits on hazardous chemicals were raised above previous EPA levels, sometimes on the order of 10 to 100 times. The number of "emergency exemptions" for business for restrictions on pesticide use more than tripled (in 1982, better than 97 percent of business requests for such exemptions were approved by EPA).[39]

The Administration's treatment of hazardous-waste problems may be taken as exemplary. At present, according to the Office of Technology Assessment, there are approximately 378,000 waste sites that may require corrective action. The vast majority (87 percent, on one estimate) pose threats of groundwater contamination. As of 1985, the Reagan EPA had put only 850 of these on its "priority" list for action. Of these, it cleaned up only six during its first term; whether they were cleaned properly and completely is sharply disputed. That year, with this record, the Administration proposed phasing out the "Superfund" for toxic-waste cleanup; for fiscal years 1984–85, it proposed no funding at all for the EPA's groundwater programs.[40]

In some areas, however, the Administration was prepared to spend money. When Reagan ran for office, he announced that "I am a Sagebrush Rebel," and soon went about the business of rewarding this business constituency. Early in its first term, the Administration announced plans to sell off as much as 35 million acres of federal land, at the low price of $17 billion. This proposal was eventually beaten back, but efforts at other "privatization" of natural resources continued. The Administration made massive sales of federal timber and embarked on an extensive leasing program of offshore oil and gas rights (originally proposed to cover one billion acres) and coal development rights to federal properties—all done in ways that turned resources over to private actors at below-market prices. It opened millions of acres of already degraded grazing land to private users, with usage fees set at less than a quarter of market prices. And it promoted enormous water projects, including the wasteful and environmentally disastrous Bonneville Unit of the Central Utah Project. This, too, was a major subsidy to business. On average, irrigators pay back only about 10 percent (without interest) of the massive investments made by the public.[41]

In other areas of "regulation" as well, the Administration led a broad attack on long-standing policies. It presided over a quiet revolution in antitrust policy (leading law professors to joke to their classes in the subject that they now were teaching "protrust") that helped spur one of the great merger manias in recent U.S. history. It gutted enforcement of voting rights, other civil rights, and affirmative-action programs. It launched a broad campaign of nondisclosure and secrecy in the executive branch, and while further institutionalizing business involvement in the promulgation of new regulatory standards, it declined to enforce provisions for public participation. Calculating accrued benefits over ten years, the Administration estimated the total "savings" from these and other programs of regulatory reform to be $150 billion; if the number is to be credited at all, virtually all of it should be credited to business.[42]

Finally, in what was a sharp break from prior policies—which had ranged from active promotion to malign neglect—the Administration mounted a wide-ranging offensive against organized labor, beginning with a string of anti-union appointments at the Department of Labor. As Secretary it brought in Ray Donovan, an obscure construction company executive from New Jersey who had been a leading fund-raiser for Reagan efforts there. Donovan's firm, Schiavone Construction, was a repeat violator of national health and safety laws. During the late 1970s, it was cited an average of ten times per year for "serious" violations (defined as involving "a substantial probability that death or serious physical harm could result") of the Occupational Health and Safety Act. (After a series of inconclusive federal investigations into charges that he engaged in kickbacks, bribery, and extortion schemes while at Schiavone, Donovan would later become the first sitting Department Secretary in U.S. history to resign under criminal indictment.) At OSHA itself, the Administration appointed Thorne Auchter, another construction company executive from a firm with a history of repeated OSHA violations. At the National Labor Relations Board, the Administration's first appointee was Robert P. Hunter, a former aide to anti-labor Utah Republican senator Orrin Hatch, a central figure in blocking Labor Law Reform. Among Hunter's other anti-labor bona fides was his authorship of the chapter on the Department of Labor in the Heritage Foundation's famous *Mandate for Leadership* policy blueprint for the Administration. There he urged many of the policies subsequently adopted in the Department, including the gutting of OSHA and the Mine Safety and Health Administration (moving both to a more "cooperative" relationship with industry) and closer review of the "pro-labor bias" at the Bureau of Labor Statistics (as well as sharp cutbacks in its funding). Hunter also found the NLRB to be too pro-labor and "ivory tower" in its approach. Among a host of procedural and policy recommendations, he urged greater use of injunctive powers against unions and the extension of coverage for Taft-Hartley's section 14(b).[43]

With Hunter on board, the Administration moved to replace outgoing NLRB chair John Fanning with John Van de Water, a Los Angeles-based management consultant who specialized in preventing or breaking unions. When this effort failed, it placed management lawyer Donald L. Dotson (formerly of Wheeling-Pittsburgh Steel and, earlier, labor counsel for Westinghouse and Western Electric) in that critical spot. Only months before his appointment, he had argued that "collective bargaining frequently means labor monopoly, the destruction of individual freedom, and the destruction of the marketplace as the mechanism for determining the value of labor," and held that the NLRB (under Carter and previous Administrations) had engaged in a "selective enforcement and perversion of the Labor statutes," exhibiting a "tendency to act as a legal aid society and organizing arm for unions."[44]

Later, Dotson and Hunter were joined by Patricia Diaz Dennis, another management lawyer (formerly of ABC and Pacific Lighting), whose appointment the Administration often described as a "triple," since she was a woman, a Hispanic, *and* a nominal Democrat who strongly supported the President. Finally, as Solicitor for the NLRB, to whom Dotson promptly gave enormous new powers, the Administration appointed Hugh Reilly, veteran staff attorney for the rabidly anti-union National Right to Work Legal Defense Foundation. Remarkably, he continued working for that organization even after accepting government employment.[45]

Such appointments heralded major changes in policy. At OSHA, for example, enforcement of existing law dropped precipitously, while the development of new workplace standards came to a virtual halt. Over the FY 1980–82 period, OSHA complaint inspections declined 58 percent, while follow-up inspections declined 87 percent. Citations for violations of the act also fell, dropping 50 percent for serious violations, 91 percent for willful violations, and 65 percent for repeat violations. At the bottom line, total penalties (including both state and federal programs) dropped 78 percent, while failure-to-abate penalties fell 91 percent. By the end of Reagan's first term, enforcement levels would have slid to a point where they provided virtually no deterrent to violations of the act. Manufacturers who violated the law could expect, on average, a penalty of only $6.50 for doing so. The agency also stalled repeatedly, and in some cases even suppressed its own studies of worker risk, in issuing standards for such known workplace carcinogens as asbestos, formaldehyde, and EDB. It would not be until June 1984 that the Reagan OSHA issued its first new final standard for a workplace carcinogen, which was immediately challenged in court as inadequate.[46]

Policy changes at the NLRB were even more dramatic. Especially after consolidating a solid majority of Reagan appointees in 1983, the Board began making major changes in basic labor-law doctrine—all in the direction of favoring management over unions. During the first five months of 1984 alone, it altered long-standing policy in a slew of lead cases: narrowing the scope of activities subject to traditional NLRB protections; broadening the permissible range of employer conduct in union representation campaigns; lowering the costs to employers of unlawful activity during such campaigns; freeing employers from the constraints traditionally imposed on work-relocation decisions by the collective-bargaining obligation; and otherwise narrowing or excusing the employer to make changes subject to bargaining without informing unions before the change is made, or by permitting employers wider latitude to end the bargaining process by declaring impasse. The Board also announced a broad new policy of deferring cases, whenever possible, to private arbitration, thereby shifting more and more of the costs of dispute resolution onto unions, and removing the government as an active player in the enforcement of many worker rights. More subtly, perhaps, the Reagan Board gutted much existing law through biased application of it, sometimes overturning the credibility findings of its own Administrative Law Judges and hearing officers in the process.[47]

In addition to being the most anti-union Board in history, the Reagan NLRB soon became the least efficient. The case backlog, or number of contested cases awaiting decision by the Board, grew dramatically, rising from about 400 cases when Reagan took office to a high of close to 1,700 cases by February 1984. By 1983, it would take the Reagan Board, on average, 627 days to move from the filing of an unfair-labor-practice charge to a final Board decision. Such inefficiency complemented the Board's anti-union animus. Because, as in any adjudicative system, the resolution of contested cases in one area (be that defined factually or in terms of the law) is typically related to the resolution of cases in cognate areas, the backlog had a huge and geometrically increasing bottleneck effect throughout the Board's regional system. And by slowing the processing of cases at the local level and stretching out the already nearly interminable proce-

TABLE 4.2
Reagan NLRB Bias

Contested Unfair Labor Practice Cases

	1975–76	1979–80	1983–84	1984–85
Complaint against employers sustained in whole or substantial part	470 (84%)	642 (84%)	189 (51%)	206 (52%)
Complaint against employers dismissed in whole or substantial part	92 (16%)	126 (16%)	181 (49%)	188 (48%)
Complaint against unions sustained in whole or substantial part	96 (73%)	84 (74%)	108 (86%)	110 (86%)
Complaint against unions dismissed in whole or substantial part	36 (27%)	29 (26%)	18 (14%)	18 (14%)

Representation Cases

Decisions in accord with employer's position	94 (35%)	73 (46%)	63 (72%)	65 (66%)
Decisions in accord with union's position	177 (65%)	86 (54%)	25 (28%)	34 (34%)

Source: AFL–CIO Lawyers Coordinating Committee, The Labor Law Exchange 4 (December 1985), 8.

dural delays at all different stages of the organizing and bargaining process, it made it that much more difficult for unions to organize new workers or effectively represent the members they already had.[48]

As it lay the foundations for these administrative changes in early 1981, the Administration was also moving forward on other parts of its programs. The budget and tax enactments of midyear, both of which (except for their military component) were strongly opposed by labor, promised to wreak untold havoc on union members' lives. A few weeks after they passed, in August, the President crushed a strike called by the Professional Air Traffic Controllers Organization, which had earlier been one of the handful of unions to endorse his 1980 candidacy. By then, of course, the vast Reagan recession that would mark the next two years had begun, throwing millions of workers off their jobs, driving the level and duration of unemployment to postwar record highs, prompting a host of "givebacks" and "concession bargaining" from unions, sharply reducing overall union membership, and, at least in the near term, fundamentally altering the bargaining climate between unions and employers. Cutbacks in unemployment benefits illustrated the synergy of the unemployment "cure" and the social-spending cutbacks. During the 1973–75 recession, unemployment insurance coverage reached as many as 80 percent of those who were officially without jobs; in January 1983, near the bottom of the Reagan recession, less than half the official jobless were covered; by the fall of 1984, only about a quarter were covered.[49]

By the end of Reagan's first term, the full extent and success of this attack would be evident. By 1984, for the third year in a row, average first-year settlements in major bargaining contracts would lag substantially behind inflation, major strike incidence set a postwar low, and unions organized fewer than 100,000 new workers through NLRB representation elections. Even in that year of economic recovery and boom, real average gross weekly earnings were 12.5 percent below their 1972 peak, while real adjusted hourly earnings were still in decline.[50]

Most striking were the figures on trends in membership over the 1980–84 period. During that time, total labor-organization membership dropped 2.7 million, and the private-sector unionization rate fell to a bare 15.6 percent of employed wage and salary workers. Union membership fell absolutely, and as a percentage of industry employment, in every major industrial classification, with no apparent relation to the underlying growth or decline in employment. In goods-producing industries, where total employment declined by 800,000, union membership declined by more than 1.8 million. In service-producing industries, where employment grew by more than 4.9 million, membership declined by more than 700,000. And in mining and construction, where employment remained stable during the period, unionization rates still plunged by 44.1 and 21.4 percent, respectively. Clearly, what began happening to labor in 1981 outlasted the Reagan recession.[51]

5/

The Democrats'

Response (1981–82)

Given their behavior during the late days of the Carter Administration, the first reaction of most leading Democrats to the Reagan onslaught was entirely predictable. Seeking to recapture business support, they acquiesced in, and in many cases helped promulgate, the right turn in public policy.

The Democrats were, for example, noisy supporters of the military buildup. Earlier, in considering the Carter Administration's FY 1980 and 1981 requests for sharp increases in military spending, a Congress controlled by the Democrats in both houses actually exceeded those requests in its final appropriations. During Reagan's first term, the Democratic House continued in this vein, granting him over 93 percent of the more than $1 trillion dollars in military obligational authority he requested over FY 1982–85.[1]

Democratic compliance in the area of social spending, as already noted, was less dramatic. Still, the House gave the Administration most of what it asked for in 1981, and, over the first term, ratified just under 50 percent of the Administration's impressive spending-reduction proposals. More generally, the Democrats did next to nothing to contest the Administration's basic strategy, which was to reduce benefits most drastically for those who could least afford it—low-paid workers and the poor—before moving on (perhaps in the second Administration) to cuts in the "middle class" social-insurance programs that comprised the bulk of the social budget.[2]

Last but by no means least, many Democrats supported the regressive Reagan tax plan, which everyone knew would eventually create almost unbearable pressures for further cuts in social spending. Even when, as in 1981, party leaders claimed to offer an "alternative" to the Administration's plans, their initiative was closely patterned on the Administration proposal. Costing the same, and equally regressive, it merely distributed the great corporate tax breaks to a slightly different range of firms.

Nor were these results merely a function of Republican alliances with the Southern "boll weevil" faction of the Democratic Party. Repeatedly, Northern Democrats, including prominent "liberal" Northern Democrats, facilitated or openly endorsed Administration initiatives. During the drafting of the tax bill, it was Democratic Illinois congressman Dan Rostenkowski (a perennial leader among congressional figures receiving PAC and other interest-group-related outside income) who, as chair of the House Ways and Means Committee, played a key role in the dizzying auction that eventually gave even leading business groups pause. During the debate over social-program budget cutting in 1981, it was House Speaker Tip O'Neill, the quintessential "Northern liberal," who declined to permit an "open rule" allowing amendments to individual spending-cut proposals. By forcing budget trimmers to take public stands on individual cuts, rather than just aggregate "reductions in the bloated federal government," the amendments such a rule would have permitted would probably have slowed the momentum of the Administration's attack. And in the Senate, John Glenn and twelve other Northern Democrats also voted "yes" on the final passage of the Administration's budget bill in 1981, while Delaware's Democrat Biden, New York's Moynihan, and several other Northern Democrats (including Howard Metzenbaum of Ohio, a favorite target of the right) voted in favor of the tax cuts. In short, it was clear from early on in the Administration that the Democrats were prepared to buy into major elements of the "Reagan" program.[3]

Potential Opposition

But while congressional Democrats and party elites did little to contest the new Republican order for many months, the Democrats' threatened mass base at length began to stir. As the full scale of the Reagan assault on social programs became apparent, unions, community organizations, church groups, social-welfare workers, and state and municipal employees sought to unite in opposition to the cutbacks. As the reality of the Administration's arms buildup sank in, resistance mounted to the Administration's aggressive policies in Central America, its insistence on a further militarization of the European theater, and its repeated destabilization of U.S.–U.S.S.R relations. As the economy sank into deep recession and unemployment reached a postwar high, millions of working Americans wondered about the wisdom of Reaganomics. Even the AFL–CIO showed signs of life. Pressured by the rank and file, Federation president Lane Kirkland called for vast "Solidarity Day" rallies in Washington, D.C., and other cities in the fall of 1981 to protest the Administration's cutbacks in social programs. And among the public at large, the President's approval rating plunged from a high of 68 percent in May 1981 to 35 percent by January 1983.

Clearly the audience for an alternative political message existed, and had this burgeoning opposition been able to seize control of the Democratic party, the consequences might have been interesting indeed. The problem was that the groups most strongly committed to presenting alternatives had almost no resources, while those that did were either halfhearted or actively hostile to any basically new message.

Nonunion popular organizations that were trying to mobilize against Reagan were living on shoestring budgets and were almost hopelessly divided among themselves. The Reagan cutbacks exacerbated their desperate condition, both by removing all sorts of subsidies and by grievously worsening the plight of their immediate constituencies. A 1982 survey by the Campaign for Human Development, the domestic anti-poverty agency of the Catholic Church, found that some 80 percent of the organizations it funded had been adversely affected by the budget cuts. Some 46 percent reported losing staff (primarily due to the cutbacks in VISTA and the replacement of the CETA program), with 23 percent reporting a loss of more than half their staff. More than 75 percent reported that the "new political and economic environment" affected the direction of their activities:

The greatest number of responses concerned increased effort on fundraising (in order): seeking funds from the private sector, new projects must pay for themselves, starting income generating projects, and seeking funds from state and neighborhood. The second largest area of new directions mentioned was increased involvement in the electoral process. Several mentioned they had to do more with less and that there was more pressure for them to change focus and provide services.[4]

Such experiences were hardly atypical. All across the service sector, deep cuts in funding, combined with the natural calamities of steep economic downturn, strained the resources of groups that might mobilize against the Administration. A survey of nonprofits early in the Reagan term found that more than 60 percent of the total income of legal service and housing and community development came from the federal government. But as noted in the previous chapter, the programs supporting such activities most directly—the community-service grant programs—were the object of sharpest Administration attack among all social-spending programs. Over FY 1982–85, non-profit social-service organizations lost 35 percent of the revenues they had been receiving from the federal government; housing, economic-development, and neighborhood-development organizations lost 30 percent; and education and research organizations lost 11 percent. In these three areas, the total loss in federal funds was just under $15 billion; as funds dried up, so did the capacities of countless community organizers and activists who worked in and around such programs. And where some money did get through, new limitations on the receipt of funds were commonly promulgated, as in the variety of restrictions on "advocacy" by recipients of Community Services Block Grant or Job Training Partnership Act (the successor to CETA) monies. Such restrictions were encouraged by the "new federalism" promoted by the Administration, which gave local and state officials more power in the distribution of funds. The net result of all these initiatives was that community organizations not only shrank but changed, giving substance to the Administration's slogan of "defunding the left."[5]

Within the labor movement, the situation was somewhat more complex. Unlike the community and church groups, the unions still commanded substantial resources. But save in a few unions suffering from truly catastrophic declines in membership, there was no real will to use them. The social ties, financial incentives, and organizational advantages that made accommodation with big business such an attractive option for top labor leaders in the 1960s were still operating. For all its bellicose rhetoric, what the AFL–CIO leadership really wanted was to find out if anyone in the business community was still interested in a separate deal.

In 1976, immediately after Ford's veto of common-situs picketing legislation, top labor leaders and business figures had formed the Labor-Management Group (LMG) to keep their lines of communication open. After business mobilized successfully against the Labor Law Reform Bill, however, the group disbanded, with Meany, Kirkland, and especially UAW president Douglas Fraser denouncing the proceedings. Only months before the much-ballyhooed Solidarity Day demonstrations, however, top labor leaders revived the LMG and recommenced a series of secret negotiations with the leaders of big business. In off-the-record meetings with select business leaders (including George Shultz, then still at Bechtel; Clifton Garvin of Exxon; Roger Smith of GM; Irving Shapiro of Du Pont; John Welch of GE; and Walter Wriston of Citibank) they attempted to find some common ground with the businessmen. The (limited) accords that emerged from these meetings appear to have encouraged the union leaders to continue searching for partners in a more general political arrangement.[6]

As usual, the AFL–CIO's moves in foreign arenas paralleled its actions at home. From the early days of Reagan's first term on, even as they denounced the Administration's domestic initiatives, top labor leaders actively supported the Administration in the promotion of "free trade unionism" abroad. Federation president Lane Kirkland and teachers union president Albert Shanker, for example, joined the rabidly anti-labor Orrin Hatch, who had led the fight against labor-law reform in 1978, on the board of the Administration's new and controversial National Endowment for Democracy (NED), which sought to pursue U.S. foreign-policy goals through a variety of informal, and largely uncontrolled, channels. By the end of Reagan's first term, the AFL–CIO's budget for foreign activities would be running in excess of $40 million annually, almost matching its total domestic budget. Of that foreign budget, roughly 90 percent would come from U.S. government sources—chiefly the Agency for International Development, the U.S. Information Agency, and the NED. The money was spent on many things: the further corruption of land reform in El Salvador, where labor worked to shore up the brutal regime of José Napoleón Duarte; the support of the anti-Sandinista CUS union in

Nicaragua, and the sponsorship of speaking tours by prominent Contras, including Alfonso Robelo and Arturo Cruz, in the United States; the promotion of Ardito Barletta's fraudulent election in Panama; and various attacks on the Philippine Labor Federation, the principal source of organized worker opposition to the regime of Ferdinand Marcos. Arguably, the AFL–CIO became the single most important actor in the Reagan Administration's more general policy of promoting controversial foreign-policy goals through private institutions—the official rationale of the NED, which by the end of Reagan's first term was giving the AFL–CIO 75 percent of all its grants. Clearly, labor was ready to deal.[7]

Business Democrats

And while labor leaders put out feelers, business Democrats regrouped. Aware that the times demanded something more then business as usual, the most venerated of all the New Deal Democratic business leaders, investment banker Averell Harriman, had already begun putting together a new Democratic pressure group. Organized principally by his wife Pamela, "Democrats for the 80's" first appeared in December 1980. On its board were Stuart Eizenstat, previously a top aide to Carter and currently a director of Hercules, a major defense contractor; former LBJ counsel (and Atlantic Institute director) Harry McPherson; and Robert Strauss, the former Carter trade adviser who is perhaps the best connected of all the leading Democrats to Wall Street and the multinationals. Another glittering bloc of multinational Democrats—including former Carter Secretary of State Cyrus Vance, McPherson, MCA's Lew Wasserman, Lazard Frères partner Felix Rohatyn, former Treasury Secretary and current Burroughs chief executive Michael Blumenthal, former Carter Under Secretary of State Warren Christopher, and Washington "superlawyer" (and Trilateral Commission member) Lloyd Cutler—bulwarked the new Center for Democratic Policy (later renamed the Center for National Policy). Max Palevsky, the major McGovern fund-raiser who had served as a member of Xerox's executive committee, and was now on the board of Intel, bankrolled a new journal, *democracy.*[8]

Older Democratically oriented think tanks also stirred. The Brookings Institution, whose carefully balanced and formally nonpartisan board has long been chaired by one of the best-known and most influential of all the multinational Democrats, Robert Roosa, added several new board members (including Bank of America chief executive Samuel Armacost, a liberal Republican). It also revamped its research programs and staff to compete more effectively with more right-wing, GOP-oriented think tanks like the American Enterprise Institute and the Heritage Foundation. Though everyone continued making all the usual disavowals about how the researchers operated with "complete independence," etc., these personnel shifts and other changes clearly had a major effect. In due course, *Industry Week* was gushing enthusiastically that Brookings "is sounding more like Ronald Reagan every day."[9]

With signs of discontent in the rank and file rising rapidly, the Democratic business groups and labor leaders opened negotiations over the shape of a Democratic "alternative" to Reaganism. Their most important step was the first—the Democratic National Committee elected a new chairman, Charles Manatt. A prominent lawyer and banker from California, whose law firm represented, or quickly acquired as clients, many firms with obvious interests in what happened in the Democratic Party (such as Northrup, a major defense contractor, and Nissan Motors, the Japanese auto giant), Manatt swiftly embarked on a sweeping reorganization of the party.[10]

His program was perfectly straightforward. Like most other business Democrats, Manatt wanted to strengthen the party's ties with the business community, rather than with blacks, community organizations, or the poor. To that end, he and his allies deliberately sought out millionaires and other wealthy business figures to run as candidates. They also tried to shore up the party's desperately straitened financial condition. Like many other institutions in trouble in the world economy, the Democratic Party was heavily in debt, and short-run relief required taking on more debt while struggling to pay off sums already run up. Under Manatt, who before he became DNC chair was mentioned as a possible future head of the American Bankers Association, the party's financial structure soon bore more than a faint resemblance to that of a debt-encumbered LCD being run under IMF surveillance. Major banks, including Bank of America and Chase, helped float the loans, which prominent business leaders of the party guaranteed.[11]

The party also attempted to strengthen its capacity for direct mail. Famously anemic when Manatt took over, the Democrats' use of these techniques did increase. But while the party raised some additional sums this way, and also began gradually to catch up to the Republicans in its use of computers and polls, some plain facts of American political sociology set severe limits on the party's use of the new technologies. The sheer facts of American social class, for example, virtually guaranteed that the party would always trail behind the GOP in appeals to the upper middle class—there were simply more affluent Republicans out there than Democrats. The role organized labor played in the party also helped limit the Democrats' use of direct mail. Since direct fund-raising appeals to union members would bypass the union leadership, many union leaders objected strongly to its use. Business Democrats, who were then at work trying to reincorporate the AFL–CIO within the party, did not press the issue.[12]

The most important step Manatt and his allies took to reform the party's finances, however, was their organization of the Democratic Business Council (DBC). Originally promoted by Byron Radaker (chief executive officer of Congoleum, the huge New Hampshire holding company whose Bath Iron Works subsidiary has been a major naval contractor since the days of Admiral Alfred Thayer Mahan), the DBC required annual contributions from each member of either $10,000 of the member's own money or $15,000 from the member's company. In return, the party invited members to participate in a regular series of task forces and study groups to develop party policies, as well as "quarterly meetings of a substantive nature held in Washington" and elsewhere, "where members can share their respective business, professional and political interests with the political leadership of America."[13]

With big business as a whole headed increasingly to the Republicans, the venture was a bit of a gamble for the heavily indebted party. But it proved a highly successful one. As they had done ever since the New Deal, labor-intensive manufacturers stayed away completely. While lower-ranking executives of Arco, Occidental, Chevron, and a few independents eventually signed on, most of the oil industry also declined to join. Vast numbers of executives from capital-intensive military contractors, however, snapped up the high-priced memberships, including officials of United Technologies, Signal, Tiger International, General Dynamics (which had several members), Boeing, and Grumman Aerospace. Leading financiers, including Bank of America board chairman Leland Prussia, and many investment bankers also joined, as did a huge bloc of real-estate magnates, some high-tech executives, a few mostly lower-ranking figures in various multinationals (such as General Electric), and many corporate lawyers. Executives from several natural-gas companies—a sector that has historically been interested not only in regulatory policy but in détente—also took out membership.[14]

Arms Control, Intervention, and the Nuclear "Freeze"

Organizing the DBC required considerable time. All during this period, however, the economy was collapsing, and a host of other issues—Central America, European relations, and trade policy among them—were generating new problems for the Reagan Administration. As a consequence, not only the mass public but important segments of big business began turning more clearly against the President.

For the Democrats, the gradual disintegration of Reagan's support in the business community presented both an opportunity and a danger—an opportunity because it brought many new recruits to their project of building a business-oriented alternative to Reaganomics; a danger because many of the firms newly interested in the party shared little beyond a disenchantment with Reagan's policies. Because virtually nothing else bound them together, in the longer term they could as easily destabilize the party as strengthen it. During much of 1981–82, however, the specific ways in which Reagan's coalition was disintegrating meshed almost perfectly with traditional Democratic themes.

As a glance down the roster of the top federal appointees of the Kennedy, Johnson, and Carter Administrations indicates, most top-level multinational Democrats came from companies that had strong orientations toward Europe. Though in the 1970s the attention of American business as a whole was shifting from Europe to the Pacific Basin, the Middle East, and other parts of the Third World, the old-line Democratic business executives that still dominated the party's elite structure disproportionately retained this orientation.

In early 1982, moreover, they, along with their handful of multinational allies that were still hoping to do business with the Soviet Union, made up precisely the parts of the business community with the biggest grievances with the Reagan Administration. For many reasons—including the Administration's huge military buildup (which included several systems denounced by critics as potential "first strike" weapons which promised to destabilize the European theater); Reagan's "Evil Empire" rhetoric; the disastrous effect high American interest rates initially had on European growth; the dispute with NATO allies over the construction of a pipeline to carry natural gas from the U.S.S.R.; American efforts to limit Europe's trade with the Eastern bloc; and the growing stalemate in arms control—a crisis was brewing in U.S.–European relations. Strong opposition from Europeans, criticism from friendly business elites in Latin America, and the certainty that a U.S. invasion of Central America would lead to massive protests (and damage to the property of American firms) all around the globe, were also fanning doubts among some leading multinationalists about the Administration's aggressive Central American policies.

Traditionally Democratic business elites thus had an opportunity to do good and do well at the same time. Many seized it with relish. Harriman, Thomas J. Watson, Jr. (whose family has long controlled IBM), and other prominent Democrats in whose global vision and corporate strategies Europe has long enjoyed a special place, sharply attacked the Reagan Administration for its neglect of arms control and allied relations. Several leading multinational Democrats joined the board of the elite Arms Control Association, including Robert McNamara (former Secretary of Defense and president of the World Bank, and now a director of Shell and many other multinationals, and a trustee of the Ford Foundation) and Admiral Bobby Inman (formerly Deputy Director of the CIA under Carter, and by then the head of MCC, the computer consortium whose moving spirit was William Norris, the longtime Democratic head of Control Data, close friend of Walter Mondale, and a champion of U.S.–U.S.S.R. trade). The Association, rather quiet for some time, soon reemerged as a strong and vocal critic of the Administration's arms-control policies.

The Rockefeller Foundation, whose president, Richard Lyman, was a Democrat, and whose board generously sampled multinational Democrats (including Roosa, McNamara, and Carter Defense Secretary Harold Brown) and the few remaining liberal Republicans, announced a major new program of grants for research on arms control. The Rockefeller Family Fund (organized by the Rockefeller grandchildren) set up another special arms-control program. So did the

Chicago-based MacArthur Foundation, whose board included several longtime Democrats such as Jerome Wiesner (White House science adviser to John Kennedy, past president of MIT, and now a director of such multinationals as Schlumberger, the giant French oil-drilling concern); the Ford Foundation; and the Carnegie Endowment for International Peace. Several major environmental groups also announced they were adding nuclear issues to their list of concerns.

This new interest was reflected in a spectacular rise in major foundation funding for work on arms control and nuclear issues. A recent study of foundation funding for "international security and the prevention of nuclear war" (ISPNW) issues over 1982–84 found that, among the seventy-four foundations studied, ISPNW grants more than tripled, rising from $16.5 million to $52 million. A little under 70 percent of this total was supplied by five big multinationally oriented foundations—MacArthur, Carnegie Corporation, Ford, Rockefeller, and Alton Jones. Of these five, three of the foundations, accounting for 57 percent of total ISPNW grants in 1984, had not made any such grants before 1980; the other two dramatically increased their existing programs after that date.[15]

Because they were tax-exempt, the foundations and environmental organizations had to take care to be officially nonpartisan. But multinational Democrats also set up a number of new organizations which were explicitly political. Paul Warnke, for example, head of the Arms Control and Disarmament Agency under Carter and the law partner of superlawyer Clark Clifford, joined high officials of the Council for a Livable World (whose board included Wiesner) to establish Peace PAC, a political action committee on nuclear-war issues. Other organizations with ties to the multinational Democrats, such as the Union of Concerned Scientists (headed for many years by Henry Kendall, an MIT physicist and Boston philanthropist whose father had chaired Roosevelt's Business Advisory Council at the height of the New Deal and helped found the CED), renewed their long-standing campaigns on arms-control and security issues.[16]

At almost the same time Sol Linowitz (a prominent international lawyer with Coudert Brothers, for many years chair of Xerox, and still a director of Time Inc. and many other concerns) began heading up an influential series of meetings between elites in the United States and Latin America. Financing for the project was provided by, among others, the Ford and Rockefeller foundations, the Rockefeller Brothers Fund, Chemical Bank, IBM–AFE, and Time Inc. Linowitz also drew a glittering array of U.S. multinational participants—including Time chair Ralph P. Davidson, Coca-Cola chair Roberto Goizueta, IBM–AFE chair Robert Pfeiffer, Chemical Bank chair Donald Platten, RKO General president Frank Shakespeare, and such familiar figures as McNamara, Muskie, Vance, and David Rockefeller—to the project. This "Inter-American Dialogue" was implicitly quite critical of Reagan Administration policies in Central America. Typical in tone and substance were its conclusions about "security and peace-keeping issues," offered at a time when the Reagan Administration was breaking off negotiations with the Soviets, accusing the Nicaraguans of being Soviet agents, and sabotaging the Contadora process:

> We all favor keeping Latin America and the Caribbean out of the East-West conflict to the greatest extent possible. It does not serve that purpose for the United States to oppose changes in the region simply because they diminish U.S. influence and hence are perceived as advantageous to Cuba and the Soviet Union, unless they are clearly related to basic security concerns. We believe that the United States can better achieve its long-term interest in regional stability, one shared by Latin Americans, by exercising measured restraint in the projection of its own power. . . .
>
> To deal with the hostilities in Central America, we favor dialogue: between the governments in El Salvador, Nicaragua, and Guatemala and the respective opposition movements in the those countries; between Nicaragua and each of its neighbors; between Cuba and all the countries of Central America; and between the United States and Cuba, and the United States and Nicaragua, respectively; as well as between the United States and the Soviet Union.[17]

Further evidence of business disenchantment with Reagan policies in the region came in the "Miami Report," another widely circulated statement, signed by another group of leading multinational business leaders, that echoed many of the criticisms of the Linowitz group. Even the Council on Foreign Relations distanced itself from the President: its annual report for 1982–83 pointedly avows that its views on Central America were "obviously at variance with" those of the Reagan Administration.[18]

By themselves, the multinational Democrats and their allies in the (predominantly Eastern, internationalist) press and the foundations were a force to be reckoned with. Their emphasis on arms control and the avoidance of armed intervention, moreover, laid the basis for a coalition with yet another powerful set of business interests the Reagan policies were then alienating—urban real-estate interests, particularly in the Northeast and Midwest.

Because the Reagan tax bills, passed earlier, made new investment so attractive, they could only accelerate the flight of business from central cities to the South and West. In addition, the Reagan budget presented in the fall of 1981 called for sweeping cuts in federal spending on a wide range of urban programs that primarily benefited older cities and declining regions—spending on housing, transportation, state and local fiscal assistance, trade-adjustment assistance, and urban infrastructure and development.[19]

Such cuts would not only devastate the poor, blacks, and blue-collar residents of these areas; together with the tax bill, they would also knock the props out from under many investments in real estate and other place-oriented business ventures. Real-estate interests building in the downtown areas of many large cities, for example, absolutely required mass transit for their projects' viability. Cars, in many cases, simply could not bring in enough people to make high-rise, intensive developments economical. Many projects, particularly for "urban development," were counting on other forms of subsidy as well. Nor were they the only major businesses with a special stake in the economic viability of these urban regions. The media had to worry about the decline of local audiences for its lucrative flagship stations in the East. As long as major regulatory hurdles remained in the way of interstate banking, local banks had to worry about protecting their deposit bases. And any number of other major business interests for whom a move out would be difficult and expensive—utilities, many small businesses, even some New York City financiers—could not afford to stand idly by and watch their communities decay or simply move to the Southwest.[20]

The result was, perhaps, inevitable. The elite concern with arms control and the military budget found a focus in the growing grass-roots campaign for a "nuclear freeze." The multinational Democrats and the real-estate interests coalesced behind efforts to reduce the Reagan arms budget by cutting—or, rather, restructuring—nuclear programs. From a decentralized campaign begun by a few committed activists, the movement for a freeze abruptly changed character. All of a sudden Eastern real-estate magnates with no known interests in any defense issue, such as the famous Donald Trump, began supporting a vaguely defined "freeze" movement. Foundations, investment bankers like Donald Petrie of Lazard Frères, and many members of the Forbes 400 contributed to groups like the Council for a Livable World, which, along with the Union of Concerned Scientists, became a bridge between the freeze movement and the more conservative, establishment-oriented arms-control movement. General Motors heir Stewart Mott funded a variety of peace groups, while other individual businessmen—such as American Minerals' Stanley Weiss—founded other groups. In Boston, a group of hotel and real-estate magnates underwrote the costs of informal discussions that helped start the New England anti-nuclear movement, probably the most successful in the nation.[21]

With the same media that was then criticizing Reagan's budget proposal providing extraordinarily favorable press coverage, the freeze movement took off. While professional groups unthreatened by the Reagan budget cuts (such as lawyers and accountants) generally held aloof, professionals in occupations threatened by budget cuts flocked to support activists who had previously worked on a shoestring. Physicians who never said a word about capping medicare fees now joined Helen Caldicott in Physicians for Social Responsibility. Church groups, which had temporized all through Vietnam, but which relied on federal grants that the defense buildup placed in question, joined the movement. So did many teachers' unions and educators that also faced big budget cuts if the Reagan military buildup continued.

By mid-1982, the anti-nuclear movement had become a powerful political force. But it had also moved far from the intentions of its original champions. Few of the business groups and foundations that now helped push it along wanted to explore the relations between multinational business, the use of force in American foreign policy, and social class. Accordingly, the critical content of the early freeze proposals largely evaporated. Allying with the "freeze" became little more than a way of disaffiliating with a military buildup of the size Reagan projected.

The height of the denaturing process was reached during the great anti-nuclear demonstrations of June 1982. Only days before 2.5 million people were scheduled to march in New York and Washington, events in Lebanon threatened to provoke a major superpower confrontation. After a private debate, sponsors of the anti-nuclear movement agreed to make no reference to the crisis in public.[22]

By then, however, Manatt and many multinational Democrats were moving to affect the character of the anti-nuclear debate in a way that would still further strengthen the Democrats' ties with the business community. Thanks to revolutionary developments in electronics, the technologies available for conventional war were in rapid flux. A whole new generation of weapons—precision-guided munitions, pilotless drones and robots, supersophisticated tanks, battlefield missiles and all sorts of aircraft-delivered weapons—held out the promise of a new kind of very expensive land war. The chance to combine capital-intensive infantry attacks with fabulously expensive tactical aircraft support was bringing the Army and the Air Force together around new strategies of "Air-Land battle" (whose name expresses its costly essence) and "Follow on Force attack." To varying degrees these were promoted in opposition to the Navy's own "forward strategy" of carrier-based offensive force projection against the Soviet Union. The sharpness of interservice rivalries grew under the Reagan Administration (whose huge buildup, as already noted, disproportionately benefited the Navy), as did the debate over these two different approaches to the projection of U.S. power. And it soon became clear that the dispute within the military had political potential for the Democrats.

Democratic military strategists such as Robert Komer (a Vietnam superhawk in the Kennedy and Johnson Administrations and an Under Secretary of Defense under Carter) had long been arguing for the virtues of "coalition defense." They wished to increase conventional capabilities through closer alliances and "burden sharing" with major allies, and grew agitated in contemplating the huge naval buildup. As Komer argued:

[T]he kind of carrier-heavy navy we are building, and the peripheral maritime strategy for which it is designed, cannot meet our basic strategic needs. Even if we simultaneously swept the Soviets from all the seven seas at the outbreak of a war, this could not alone prevent the U.S.S.R. from dominating the entire Eurasian landmass, including such vital areas as Europe, Japan/Korea, and the Persian Gulf oil fields. Only land and sea power as well could do that. . . . Moreover, the current costly emphasis on big carriers for offensive force projection is even eroding our ability to perform the essential naval mission of sea control.

Thus, he concluded, while carriers "are splendid for Third World conflict," the United States already had enough of them. More resources should go into land and air forces, while realizing the efficiencies that came from coalition defense. Other Democrats, including Samuel Huntington, took the Komer argument a step further. They argued that the new military technologies could afford the United States a chance to strike at Soviet forces in Eastern Europe with devastating force.[23]

In either version, the emphasis on building up conventional land and air forces, particularly in Europe, would permit large savings in the huge naval buildup and permit less reliance on nuclear weapons. Reciprocally, many prominent advocates of nuclear-arms control, including the famous "American Gang of Four"—Robert McNamara, McGeorge Bundy, Gerard Smith, and George Kennan—emphasized in their writings the importance of increased reliance on land and air conventional forces and a greater cooperation with the allies.[24]

These developments handed Manatt & Co. a providential way to square the circle. The Democrats could now endorse the "freeze," which implied the cancellation or scaling down of some big-ticket nuclear programs, such as the MX, the B-1 bomber (manufactured by Rockwell, which, unlike other contractors, had no personnel on the Democratic Business Council), and perhaps the D-5 missile for the Trident II submarine. Adding these savings to those gained by scaling back the naval buildup, both the multinationalists oriented toward Europe or a potential accord with the U.S.S.R. and the real-estate and other regional interests would gain. Because a whole new field of conventional weaponry would open up, however, even many military contractors would be satisfied. And this in turn kept such "middle of the road" (and distinctly unfrozen) Democrats as Sam Nunn of Georgia (home to Lockheed, the producer of the C-5A transport), a prominent advocate of conventional weaponry, happy too.[25]

As explicit commitments on the freeze faded, many Democrats even abandoned the rhetoric, and (following the Administration) shifted the earlier rallying slogans in favor of "build down" proposals on nuclear weapons. Sponsored by a group of mostly Democratic officials with very close ties to weapons producers, this notion proposed that the United States and U.S.S.R. destroy a certain number of nuclear warheads for each addition they made to their nuclear forces. Because they provided for the destruction of some nuclear weapons, such proposals could be plausibly passed off as "freeze"-inspired. In fact, they were really formulas for the further modernization of strategic forces. Depending on the ratio of what was to be destroyed to what was to be added and the nature of the weapons, they could legitimate the purchase of almost anything, in almost any amount. Added to the arguments for more conventional defense, they seemed at the time to be a perfect answer to many Democratic needs.

As the Reagan Administration's hopes to force down federal spending by inducing a budget crisis led to larger and larger budget deficits, the Democrats won more affluent friends. Faced with mounting deficits, virtually all segments of big business complained, but not with equal urgency. For weapons producers, for example, the deficits appeared as an entry in their profits column. Labor-intensive manufacturers, whose bargaining position against their workforces would almost certainly improve if the Administration succeeded (perhaps in a second term) in still deeper cuts in social spending, also had an incentive to stick with the President. But not everyone in the business community could afford to wait. In particular, investment bankers and insurance companies could hardly afford to stand quietly on the sidelines while new government debt exploded, since their prosperity depends on investor confidence in long-term bonds. Permanently growing deficits erode such confidence, since investors know that government and taxpayers will be almost irresistibly tempted—if not now, with Paul Volcker in charge of the Fed, then later, after he departs—to pay off the debt by merely printing money. Prominent members of both of these sectors thus became increasingly active in supporting the Democrats.[26]

The "Industrial Policy" Compromise

As the midterm elections of November 1982 approached, the Democrats looked considerably healthier. With money rolling in from all the sectors just discussed, the finances of the party and related groups like Democrats for the 80's were stronger. And with high interest rates weighing heavily on the quarterly earnings of RCA (owner of NBC) and other large concerns, the media had become far more interested in the costs of Reaganomics. By late 1982, it was easy to believe that the party might yet succeed in pulling itself back together. Just possibly it could even oust the incumbent in the next Presidential election.[27]

The party still lacked an important attraction, however—a distinctive economic alternative of its own. There was an excellent reason for this. Because imports were devastating thousands of union jobs in industries such as steel and autos, the AFL–CIO leadership absolutely had to have a commitment from the party to some degree of trade protection. Manatt and the party also hoped to recruit new allies among the burgeoning ranks of import-threatened manufacturers. But import restriction remained an explosive issue with many business Democrats, including most of the party's oldest, best-entrenched business supporters.

In recent years, a few investment bankers (and, probably, some real-estate interests anxious for both social peace and the survival of their regional bases in the Northeast and Midwest) had sometimes speculated whether carefully limited, temporary protections might not be advisable. For the long run, however, both they and the vast majority of Democratic businesses were still strongly committed to the party's traditional free-trade precepts. And while pressure from the Japanese and other foreign competitors was gradually stimulating many to rethink their stance, most remained skeptical about proposals that would channel government aid to certain industries, regardless of whether the money went to rebuild older, "sunset" industries or, as in proposals supported by some high-tech-oriented analysts, to new "sunrise" sectors.

As the 1984 primaries were eventually to suggest, these differences might well have been unbridgeable in ordinary times. But 1982 was no ordinary year. In what would eventually rank as the most economically disastrous period since the Great Depression, national income was plunging at a terrifying rate, while imports, interest rates, and unemployment were soaring.

For a while, this looming economic disaster had little effect on the hold the Republicans had over most of the business community. Enthusiastic about the huge tax cuts and looking forward to permanently dropping a substantial proportion of its work force, the bulk of the business community remained solidly behind the President. As the economy nosedived, however, the strain began building up. Manufacturers already in trouble from imports faced a giant new surge as rising interest rates forced the exchange rate of the dollar higher and higher. Firms needing an infusion of borrowed money faced rising capital costs, while firms that already owed money discovered that interest costs were taking most of their profits.

By the fall of 1982, many parts of the business community once loyal to Reagan were breaking ranks. In late September, a $1,000-a-plate fund-raising dinner sponsored by the Democratic National Committee was spectacularly successful in drawing prominent business donors; indeed, party leaders described it at the time as the most successful such event in the party's history. Some of these new business Democrats worried about Japan, others about domestic interest rates, the state of demand for their product, or the rapidly growing federal deficit. Whatever motivated them, however, all suddenly had reason to look kindly on positive government action and, as the suddenly swelling totals for many Democratic campaign committees vividly show, were prepared to pay for it.[28]

In the winter of 1982–83—after a relatively strong Democratic showing in the House elections, at close to the bottom of the depression, and with the ranks of the protectionists and interventionists growing within the party—Manatt and other party leaders convened a series of meetings with spokespersons for most major tendencies within the business community and labor unions.

Among those who participated in these discussions, the unions, spokesmen for threatened sunset industries (such as Chrysler's Lee Iacocca), and many investment bankers and multinational business executives (some of whom, such as Burroughs chairman Michael Blumenthal or Du Pont's Irving Shapiro, certainly had reason to fear long-run threats from foreign competition) eventually reached agreement on a compromise "industrial policy" plan. Strongly resembling earlier proposals by Shapiro, Anthony Salomon, and other internationalists developed during the Carter Administration's last year in office, the new plan called for a "development board" that combined a long-run commitment to free trade with authority to make temporary loans or grants either to troubled industries or to industries with extraordinary long-term growth potential. The plan also tacitly conceded a need to restrict imports temporarily in certain particularly hard-hit industries.

Formally issued by the Center for National Policy a year later, the "reindustrialization" plan contained some things displeasing to almost everyone. Labor and many newly protectionist firms would have liked a stronger stand on imports. High-tech spokesmen, such as the Foothill Group's Don Gevirtz, questioned both the emphasis on sun-set industries and the concessions on trade policy. And many free-traders naturally disliked any compromise with the principle of an open world economy. Nevertheless, at the time only commercial bankers and other strongly committed free-traders (such as University of Minnesota economist Walter Heller, a director of the Bank of Minneapolis and longtime member of the Trilateral Commission, who dissented formally from the development-board idea endorsed by Rohatyn and others on the committee), found the report unacceptable.[29]

Party Rules and "Reaching Down"
But the Democratic business leaders and labor chieftains were taking no chances. In June 1981, the DNC chartered a commission on party rules reform, headed by then North Carolina governor James B. Hunt, Jr., and in March 1982 it announced its adoption of the commission's proposals. Frankly intended to increase the control of party leaders over the rank and file, the rules changes rolled back most of the reforms of the early 1970s. They included a shortening of the primary and caucus season, the abandonment of mandatory proportional representation in state selection of delegates (in favor of various "winner take all" or "winner take more" alternatives), the reservation of 14 percent of convention delegate seats for "super-delegate" party leaders not committed to specific candidates, and the abolition of the "faithful delegate" rule compelling delegates to vote for the candidate they had pledged to support. Together, the changes were designed to advantage the early-front-running candidates and ensure that party insiders would be "heard" at the convention.[30]

Prodded by Cyrus Vance and some other business leaders, partic-ularly those sympathetic to the "anti-nuclear" movement, the party also warily eyed the possibility of increasing voter turnout. As noted earlier, American electoral participation is decisively class-skewed; the nonvoting population, as a group, is significantly poorer and less ed-ucated than the voting population. And because it is poorer, the non-voting population is also disproportionately—by conventional wis-dom, about 2–1—Democratic. Everything else being equal, it would seem then that increased voting participation would tend to help the

Democrats. Since most nonvoters (more than 70 percent) are unregistered, and registration is generally required for voting, a natural focus for any effort at increasing turnout would be an effort to increase voter registration.

The logic and general conclusions of this argument appeared to have been confirmed by the results of the 1982 elections, and reconfirmed throughout 1983 in a string of prominent local races. In the off-year congressional elections of 1982, before any significant increase in registration levels, voter turnout jumped 10 million over 1978. The greatest increases in turnout rates were among the unemployed (24.5 percent), blacks (15.6 percent), and blue-collar workers (13 percent)—groups that are overrepresented in the ranks of traditional nonvoters. True to form, the new vote split about 2–1 Democratic, with the party making its biggest gains in the South and Midwest, where turnout increased the most. In 1983, Democratic candidates would score victories in a series of mayoral races—including Chicago, Philadelphia, Denver, and Charlotte, North Carolina—which also featured large increases in turnout, preeminently among blacks and Hispanics (who are also overrepresented in the ranks of traditional nonvoters). In each of these races, large-scale registration drives were a prominent part of the successful Democratic campaigns.[31]

As Democrats looked to the Presidential election of 1984, a registration-based strategy for Democratic victory appeared to gain further credence. As already noted, despite his overwhelming electoral college victory Reagan's share of the popular vote in 1980 was unimpressive, and in several states his margins were razor thin. In fourteen states, accounting for 148 electoral votes, his margin was 5 percentage points or less; in ten of those, the election was decided by less than 20,000 votes; in four of those ten, it was decided by 5,000 votes or less. More immediately, in many states Reagan's victory margin was vastly exceeded by the number of unregistered voters. In sixteen states, it was less than 5 percent of the nonvoting population, and in several states it was only a small fraction of the unregistered population of groups that, if registered, could be expected to vote overwhelmingly Democratic. Black Americans, for example, vote about 9–1 Democratic, and in many states the Reagan margin was only a small percentage of the unregistered black voting-age population. The most dramatic examples were in the South, where the Reagan margin was only 3 percent of the unregistered black population in Tennessee, 4 percent in South Carolina, 6 percent in Alabama and Arkansas, 8 percent in North Carolina, and 9 percent in Mississippi. Even in the North, however, there were cases of the unregistered black population vastly exceeding the Reagan victory margin. In New York, Reagan's plurality was 165,000 votes; the number of unregistered blacks was 894,000.[32]

Assuming the Democratic nominee in 1984 did at least as well as Carter had in 1980 (and who could do worse?), such numbers suggested to many that even incremental increases in registration could make a big difference in the next Presidential election. Below the national level the case seemed even more compelling. In 1980, nine of thirty-four Senate races were decided by 2 percent of the vote or less. Republicans won seven of those, emerging with a 53–47 majority instead of (had they lost all nine) a 46–54 minority. In 1982, a shift of 1 percent of the vote in five states—Vermont, Rhode Island, Virginia, Missouri, and Nevada—would have meant a Democratic majority in the Senate. Even in the House, which presents the "case of the vanishing marginals" (the disappearance of districts where close party competition survives), there were still many close races. A total shift of only 44,000 votes would have changed the outcome in twenty House seats won by Republicans in 1982. Again, registration seemed to hold the key to possible Democratic victory.

A little over a year later, at the beginning of 1984, such thinking would be reflected in a memo to Manatt, written by DNC political director Ann Lewis, which argued that "the key to Democratic victory is *voter mobilization.*" Taking Carter's 1980 performance as a baseline for Democratic hopes, Lewis began with Reagan's 8.4 million margin of victory in that race. She thought that women, who had voted 47–45 for Reagan in 1980, would "not make that mistake" again, and the Democrats could pick up 2 million votes from the gender gap. Another 2 million would come as the Democratic share of those 5.7 million votes that had gone to Anderson in 1980, thus narrowing the gap to 4.4 million voters. The remainder could be made up through increased registration. Applying the conventional wisdom that new voters would split 2–1 Democratic, Lewis argued that increasing turnout 13.5 million over 1980 levels would give the

Democrats a net increase of 4.5 million votes (9 million Democratic voters, minus 4.5 million Republicans picked up along the way), thus ensuring victory.[33]

But while many within the party were advocating massive efforts at voter registration, party leaders were ambivalent. After all, the very characteristics that made nonvoters attractive candidates for mobilization into Democratic ranks—most importantly, the fact that they were poorer than the rest of the voting population—also spelled potential trouble for elite Democratic interests. Mobilizing the poor might threaten business Republicans, but it would also threaten business Democrats. Manatt and other party leaders had spent much of their time over the past two years extinguishing such threats—by acquiescing in the Administration's attacks on working people and the poor and reintegrating business interests into the party—and were not inclined to reignite them now. Nor was organized labor, the chief non-business actor in the party, anxious to rock the delicate arrangements it had entered into with business Democrats, or to disturb, as a full-scale mobilization surely would, its own intensely hierarchical organization. Thus, while party leaders began talking about voter registration as early as 1982, they did little about it at the time.

Others did, however. In 1981, the liberal New World Foundation, following up earlier efforts by the Rockefeller and Ford foundations, hosted a series of meetings of liberal funders interested in supporting nonpartisan voter registration efforts. In 1982, ABC and Harvard's Kennedy School sponsored a major symposium on voting participation, which brought liberal academics together to discuss the virtues of increasing participation. In 1983, the Ad Hoc Funders' Committee for Voter Registration and Education was formed to coordinate funding responses to a variety of independent groups interested in doing voter registration. Among those active in the Funders' group were representatives of the Arca, Field, Carnegie, Cummins Engine, New World, Norman, Playboy, Charles H. Revson, and Rockefeller foundations, as well as the Rockefeller Brothers Fund. Along with Coca-Cola, Philip Morris, the Rockefeller Family Fund, and, as a major giver, the Ford Foundation, these various foundations and corporations, led mostly by business figures with strong commitments to free trade and arms control, and in many cases already subsidizing the freeze movement, began subsidizing a variety of groups (some old, many new) doing voter registration work among likely Democratic constituencies. Almost all the new or revivified voter registration efforts they funded were as officially "nonpartisan" as the foundations and corporations that funded them. Informally, however, it was no secret that defeating Reagan in 1984 was the primary aim of the effort.[34]

In early 1983, as Reagan's popularity hit bottom, unemployment hit postwar highs, and many parts of big business seemed on the verge of shifting to the Democrats, that effort appeared far from vain.

6/

The Campaign

At the time the Democrats unveiled their industrial-policy statement almost everyone expected that either Walter Mondale or Edward Kennedy would represent the party in the next election. When Kennedy announced his withdrawal from the race, the torch fell effortlessly into Mondale's grasp. It was widely assumed—and the impression was assiduously cultivated by the Mondale camp—that the agenda worked out by the Democratic business groups and the DNC commanded support from the vast majority of the party and that, accordingly, the former Vice President would sweep easily to the nomination.[1]

The Mondale Camp

For a while during 1983, this scenario did indeed seem to be coming true. From its command post in the Washington office of Winston & Strawn, a leading international law firm headquartered in Chicago, the Mondale campaign appeared to embody perfectly the coalition Democratic business leaders were seeking to build. At its informal center was a group of veteran Democratic businessmen with glittering multinational credentials, including C. Peter McCullough of Xerox (prominent Democratic fund-raiser, member of both the Business Council and the Business Roundtable, and a director of many concerns); Irving Shapiro (just retired as CEO of Du Pont and co-chair of the Business Roundtable, but still active on the boards of such concerns as IBM, Du Pont, Bechtel, and Boeing); Michael Blumenthal (former Carter Treasury Secretary, head of Burroughs, and director of such companies as Equitable Life and Bankers Trust); and several members of the Dayton family (longtime friends of the candidate, whose huge Minneapolis-based retailing concern included on its board Bruce K. MacLaury, president of the Brookings Institution). Joining them were several prominent investment bankers who had long been associated with the Democratic Party, including Roger Altman of Lehman Brothers and Mondale's close friend Herbert Allen. San Francisco real-estate magnate (and Coalition for a Democratic Majority member) Walter Shorenstein, Mel Swig (the chair of Fairmont Hotels), and a number of other prominent real-estate members of the Forbes 400 "richest Americans" were also early members of the Mondale bandwagon.

For more than a year, Altman, Allen, and others in this group had been working to "educate" Mondale on their business-oriented views on taxes, social spending, and other issues. Under their guidance (and in some cases patronage, since Mondale was working for several of them), the candidate had begun a loudly proclaimed effort to fashion a "new," more centrist, business-oriented public image.[2]

While these businessmen prepped Mondale, a small army of policy analysts occupying the multinational middle of the Democratic Party advised the campaign, including Sol Linowitz, investment banker David Aaron (previously with Carter's National Security Council), Trilateralist Henry Owen (another former Democratic official), and Walter Slocombe (also formerly of the State Department and a member of the Atlantic Council of the U.S. and the Trilateral Commission). C. Fred Bergsten, a strong free-trade advocate and former Treasury official, whose new Institute for International Economics in Washington, D.C., had received a $4 million grant from the German Marshall Fund, advised the campaign on trade and monetary policies.

The Mondale campaign also raised funds, from all the natural opponents of Reagan policies identified earlier: real-estate magnates, including both Fred and Donald Trump; insurance executives, including Aetna Life's John Filer and Connecticut General head Robert D. Kilpatrick; liberal internationalists with strong ties to Europe, including Thomas J. Watson, Jr., and the head of the German Marshall Fund; and many investment bankers, including Goldman Sachs head

John L. Weinberg, Prudential-Bache chairman Harry Jacobs, William Hambrecht (whose Hambrecht & Quist dominated new issues in high tech), Irving Rothschild of Bear Stearns, and Peter Solomon of Lehman Brothers. Other business figures with a clear interest in arms control—such as Orion Picture's Arthur Krim (a veteran member of the advisory committee for the embattled Arms Control and Disarmament Agency) and grain dealer Dwayne O. Andreas (chair of the U.S.–U.S.S.R Trade Council)—also contributed. So did several members of the Rockefeller family; leading Democratic members of the Trilateral Commission (including Owen and international lawyer Richard Gardner); several top executives in communications, including Capital Cities chair Thomas S. Murphy (a business partner of Robert Strauss); executives of other capital-intensive internationally oriented businesses (including at least one from Control Data, from whose board Mondale was then prudently retiring); and Mondale's longtime friend John G. McMillian (on the board of whose Northwest Energy sat James Schlesinger, another Democrat with ties to both investment banking and the defense industry). Harold Brown, Carter's Secretary of Defense, and now a director of CBS, *The Washington Post*, and other multinationals, also advised Mondale informally. Over the course of 1983, many other liberal internationalist business figures who had previously backed Democrats (or, in 1980, Anderson) began to support the campaign, including Standard Shares' Irving Harris; Salomon Brothers' head John Gutfreund; Bear Stearns chair Maurice Greenberg; Morgan Stanley managing partner Richard Fisher; Lehman Brothers chair Lewis Glucksman; Goldman Sachs partner Robert Rubin (who eventually raised more than $1.8 million for the candidate); Brookings trustee James Wolfensohn; and, of course, Felix Rohatyn.[3]

In the latter half of 1983, however, the aura of Mondale's invincibility began to tarnish, for the coalition it was based upon was proving desperately unstable. The basic problem was twofold. First, after three years of Republican rule, the organized mass base of the campaign was literally disappearing. From the beginning, the *raison d'être* of Mondale's effort had been to find a compromise that both (parts of) big business and organized labor could support. That had been a guiding thought behind the party's industrial-policy proposals, and it was also the reason Mondale kept courting the support of the AFL–

CIO, whose precedent-shattering pre-primary endorsement he secured in October 1983. Reeling from imports, high unemployment, and the new assaults by Reagan appointees at the NLRB and Labor Department, however, labor was losing its organizational effectiveness, even among its own confused and frightened members. Many Democratically oriented community organizations, meanwhile, were demoralized and running out of money.

Second, the economic recovery changed the calculus of interests among Democratic business groups, particularly among the new arrivals that the DBC and the recession had pulled into the party. In particular, with labor so transparently in decline, many corporate figures were beginning to wonder why they should deal with labor and the poor at all, and not explicitly seek to rearrange the party's mass base. Free-traders who were willing to nod at limited protectionist initiatives at the bottom of a recession now began to question the need to compromise. Military contractors that had flocked into the DBC were tempted to gamble on getting a bigger share of the budget. As the military producers gained strength, the more ardent supporters of the freeze, cutbacks in military spending, and arms control sought to press their own concerns more vigorously. And with Mondale holding down most of organized labor, other candidates would be tempted to forge alternatives to the old Democratic coalition.

The Other Early Candidates

Splintering along these lines was evident across the spectrum of alternative candidates. On Mondale's left, for example, George McGovern, and California senator Alan Cranston stepped forward with programs calling for strong arms control, less bellicose Latin American policies, bigger cuts in military spending, and more social expenditures.

Far less interested in domestic economic policy and redistribution than McGovern, Cranston built his campaign mostly around the nuclear issue. Prominent freeze supporters, including Jerome Wiesner, McGeorge Bundy, George Kennan, and the Reverend Theodore Hesburgh (president of Notre Dame University and a longtime director of the Chase Manhattan Bank), served on his platform commit tee, while advocates of a freeze such as Victor Palmieri, Stewart Mott, and Council for a Livable World president Jerome Grossman contributed funds. Money also came in from other sectors and individuals already engaged in the struggle to cut military budgets and control the arms race, including leading real-estate magnates (the Dunfeys of New England, Lewis Rudin, Herbert Simon, Lawrence Tisch, among others) and investment bankers (including Donald Petrie of Lazard Frères, his partner Michel David-Weil, American Express's James D. Robinson III, Howard Stein of the Dreyfus Fund, Greenberg of Bear Sterns, and Gutfreund of Salomon Brothers). Cranston also raised considerable money from power centers in his home state, including Hollywood (20th Century–Fox chairman Allen J. Hirschfield and many actors); Silicon Valley (Intel's Robert Noyce, perhaps the industry's single best-known figure); wine producers (Ernesto Gallo, Robert DiGiorgio, the Wine Institute's PAC); growers (Sunkist); and area utilities (Pacific Lighting). In a sure sign that "anti-nuclear" no longer meant "anti-military," many weapons producers also contributed, including PACs associated with Signal, Rockwell, Aerojet General, and General Electric.

McGovern, by contrast, still scared most of American business, even its relatively "liberal" sectors. As a consequence, he received virtually no money, with such funds as he did get apparently coming mostly from a handful of investment bankers and other liberal internationalist business figures (including Andreas, Mott, Arthur Krim, and Pamela Harriman). A longtime supporter of Israel who had recently criticized the Israeli invasion of Lebanon, McGovern also received a few contributions from prominent critics of traditional American policy in the Middle East.[4]

But while Cranston and McGovern succeeded in causing some erosion in Mondale's coalition, neither had any real chance of cracking it open. The media and even many business supporters of military spending cuts were lining up behind "build down" proposals. Money was short, press coverage anemic, and to the extent that the candidates garnered any attention at all, coverage focused mostly on the improbability of their winning.

In McGovern's case, the press was openly hostile. When he announced his candidacy in 1983, much of the media focused on what they thought had been a laughable campaign for the Presidency eleven

FIGURE 6.1
Percent of Candidate Airtime (NBC)

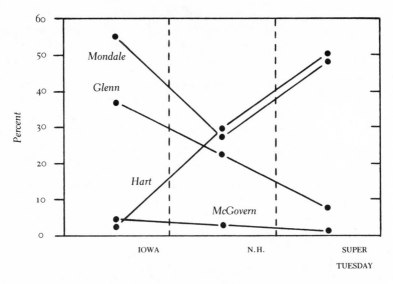

Source: Adams, "Media Coverage," 11

years before. At CBS the fact that McGovern had sometimes been called "Mr. McGoo" by junior staffers in that effort was the most most prominent bit of information offered on the new candidate. Many other commentators kept referring to him as "McStassen," drawing a pointed comparison between McGovern (who had run for the Presidency only once before and won his party's nomination) and perennial candidate Harold Stassen. His candidacy, as *Newsweek* explained, was one more "unmistakable" sign that "McGovern craves another chance to cavort in the limelight." In this vein, throughout 1983, McGovern received a disproportionately small share of media coverage. While he ranked third with voters as a preferred candidate (fourth after Jackson announced), and as late as December 1983 was still almost three times as popular as Hart and eight times as popular as Reuben Askew (the least favored in the Democratic group), he ranked last in media coverage. Later, when the primary season got under way, the press bias became even more evident. In Iowa, McGovern unexpectedly finished third, with 13 percent of the vote, barely 2 points behind Hart, whose own showing was 30 points behind Mondale's winning 45 percent. Hart benefited mightily from his Iowa performance. The week after, he received ten times more coverage on NBC than he had the week before and five times more coverage on CBS. McGovern's airtime, by contrast, actually *declined* as a proportion of network campaign coverage, falling to a tiny fraction of that accorded Hart. The media, clearly, were prepared to hear some "messages" from the electorate and not others. Given their thin backing and negligible coverage, the two left-liberal candidates were destined to generate some excitement among voters and then be overwhelmed.[5]

On the right the story was entirely different, as money was gushing in in torrents and a major media buildup was in progress. Ironically, the most potent theme of this burgeoning opposition to Mondale appears to have inadvertently originated with some of his own business supporters. Though it is difficult to pin down, because no one will speak for the record, it appears that a substantial bloc of business-oriented Democrats were nervous about the concessions the party's industrial policy had made to labor on the trade issue. Subsequently, one of the dissenters from the statement of that policy, high-tech venture capitalist Don Gevirtz, declared that he hoped Mondale, whom he said he could support, would simply change his mind. A few months later, Robert Strauss assured a Western European audience that Mondale's endorsement of domestic-content legislation for the devastated auto industry should not be taken too seriously, since it was only offered "for the purpose of getting the nomination of our party."[6]

Despite such signaling, in the summer of 1983 leading Democrats at the Brookings Institution and other organizations, including the New York Federal Reserve Bank, began a behind-the-scenes press campaign against the industrial policy. One later averred that their purpose was to warn Mondale away from supporting labor too strongly, not to defeat him. Regardless of their actual intentions, one of the main themes of this campaign—that the Democratic industrial policy represented an unconscionable surrender to "special interests"—quickly was seized upon by many interests hostile to the whole Mondale effort. Thus was born the deadly charge that—amplified again and again by the media, the business community, and eventually the Republicans—would do so much to destroy the Mondale campaign.

Glenn

With the "special interest" theme sounding everywhere, it was probably inevitable that the chosen instrument of right-thinking Democrats would put himself forward as the candidate of the "general interest." And because he was a member of the Trilateral Commission—whose members received the most favorable press coverage of all candidates in 1976 and 1980—it also was probably fated that much of the press would credit this claim during the vast buildup of his candidacy.[7]

No one else, however, should have. Initially launched on a conservative, internationalist platform that was as implicitly hostile to labor, social welfare, and the protection of the environment as it was openly in favor of vast military expenditures, Ohio senator John Glenn could at any moment have been linked to a host of very special interests by any reporter who bothered to check with the Federal Elections Commission. The campaign's PAC list alone was stunning. Included were contributions from a broad range of military contractors (Hughes Aircraft, Grumman, the Explosives Manufacturers Political Action Committee, Fairchild, American Shipbuilding, Lockheed, LTV, Rockwell, Signal, Colt Industries, Atlas, TRW, Ticor, United Technologies, and something called Spacepac); utilities (American Electric Power, Ohio Edison, El Paso Electric, Dayton Power and Light, Ohio Power, Utah Power & Light, and Georgia Power); and any number of other companies willing to invest in a Democrat more conservative than Mondale (including American Motors, Lehman Brothers, AT&T, L. F. Rothschild, Donaldson Lufkin Jenrette, Federal Express, MCI, Mead, Merrill Lynch, Mellon National, GTE, the National Association of Realtors, and Nike). Executives and inside directors from health-care industries (including Humana's Wendell Cherry), some media concerns (including Ann Cox Chambers, owner of the Cox chain of newspapers and broadcasting stations), and other multinationals (including Philip Morris and Textron) also unrolled their bankrolls. Glenn's fund-raising efforts in Texas were particularly impressive. The "Good Government Fund" of the famous Houston law firm of Vinson, Elkins, Connally & Searls made a substantial contribution; so did many famous individual Texans, including Ben Barnes (a former lieutenant governor and now a business partner of John Connally), James A. Elkins, Jr. (of the same family as the law firm), three of the four fast-rising Bass brothers, William

Hobby (the lieutenant governor and a member of a family in the Forbes 400), and many ranchers and oilmen, including Clint Murchison, Jr., George P. Mitchell, C. H. Murphy of Murphy Oil, and Houston's James Calaway, Sr.

Puffed by many of the same interests that are now urging the Democrats to move right to attract voters, the Glenn campaign took off. Indeed, had no primaries ever taken place, Glenn might have won the nomination by acclamation. But despite the blizzard of press notices (which his flattering portrayal in *The Right Stuff* can hardly have hurt), when the primaries did come Glenn did not do well, even among the conservative white Southerners he was said to have enthralled. How could this have happened?

Part of the explanation is obvious, though now that the revisionist movement is sweeping the party it is unlikely to be deemed widely fit to print: Only a comparative handful of Democratic voters in any region—North, South, East, or West—in fact want a conservative candidate. Though because of its low information levels and the high costs it faces when trying to act politically, the Democratic electorate can be almost endlessly confused, divided, and misled by party elites, the Glenn campaign's speedy demise strongly suggests that Democratic voters can still recognize a registered Republican when they see one, and do not like them.

But there were other factors as well. One great handicap to the Glenn candidacy came from a serious split that soon developed within his core support among conservative, defense-oriented Democrats. Some prominent interests backing Glenn's campaign had fairly close ties to Arab businessmen. Glenn, in addition, had been a strong advocate of the controversial sale of F-15 aircraft to Saudi Arabia in 1978. Many otherwise hard-line activists in groups like the Coalition for a Democratic Majority, accordingly, distrusted him, and stayed with Mondale, even though they were also wary of Aaron, Cyrus Vance, and other Mondale advisers they considered insufficiently hawkish. As the Glenn camp noticed the slippage from this quarter, it made clumsy efforts to backpedal. These, however, only led to resignations and defections in Glenn's own organization.[8]

The Glenn candidacy's orientation toward military power also hurt in a second, more subtle way. In addition to turning off some members of the electorate, Glenn's strong commitment to increasing military spending assuredly alarmed the urban real-estate interests now gathering in support of Mondale's campaign for "fairness" to their regions. Virtually none of the real-estate developers on the *Forbes* 400 list outside the state of Ohio made any contribution to the Glenn campaign. Most investment bankers and other business interests alarmed by regional disparities also held aloof. This had real consequences that went beyond the vast financial implications. In many parts of the Northeast, real-estate interests are almost indistinguishable from the local political machines.

Finally, there is some evidence that disputes over trade and industrial policy tarred the Glenn campaign. Glenn's initial backers appear in the main to have been strong free-traders who believed his lukewarm support of domestic-content legislation simply reflected the political necessities of his Ohio base. But the Glenn campaign also took in substantial contributions from a number of manufacturing interests hurt badly by foreign competition, including some agribusiness interests in Florida concerned about Mexican imports; executives or major owners from import-damaged firms, such as International Harvester's Louis W. Menk or Ford's own Henry Ford II; and the PACs of such firms as Cleveland Cliffs Iron and the near-bankrupt Wheeling-Pittsburgh Steel. In a "not for attribution" conversation, a top-ranking member of a firm that supported Glenn confirmed to us that part of the motivation for that support was a belief that Glenn would implement a conservative industrial policy. To the extent that an attempt to straddle the trade issue contributed to his defeat, Glenn, like John Connally four years before, discovered the pitfalls of a business coalition that was very wide, but very shallow.

Hart

With McGovern and Cranston a safe bet to be unable to raise much money or attract favorable media attention, by mid-1983 the contest for the Democratic nomination was shaping up as a two-horse race between Mondale and Glenn. Yet Mondale's compromise on trade and Glenn's strong links with defense contractors and heavy industry and utilities (indicating that he would severely curtail social spending and scale back environmental protection) did open space for a dark-horse candidate who was brave enough to try to find a new way to combine the classic Democratic formula of the past—free trade and an affirmative role for government in society—with the practical necessity of being considerably more conservative than a figure like

McGovern. Because such a candidate would be totally committed to free trade, his industrial-policy proposals would not be portrayed by the media as protectionist. Because he did have an industrial policy, he could hope to rally at least some of the multinationals and high-tech concerns then looking nervously over their shoulders at the Japanese. Since many of those multinationals were deeply interested in Europe, and the high-tech companies helped make weapons systems, this new dark horse could move to occupy the ground where the establishment anti-nuclear movement was heading, and come out in favor of both arms control and bold new weapons programs, while opposing U.S. military intervention in Central America. Because the ceiling on nuclear weapons and implied limitations on naval spending would set limits on the overall rise in the military budget, at least some new money would be available for social spending—or, as a shrewd candidate would probably put it, "social investment." Because virtually no heavy industry would support a liberal free-trader, such a candidate could also be a strong environmentalist.

More than the logical possibility for such a candidacy existed. As in 1976, when another committed free-trader with virtually no name recognition, but vast elite support, had come from nowhere to capture the nomination, the peculiar structure of the Democratic primaries advantaged a campaign with this kind of focus. The opening caucuses took place in Iowa, a state whose major industry was agribusiness. Committed to free trade and increased wheat sales to the U.S.S.R., the state's alert and organized farm groups could help offset Mondale's strength with the unions. Even more promisingly, the second primary took place in New Hampshire. Just emerging as a high-tech center, New Hampshire was still what it had been at the time when its economy was dominated by labor-intensive textiles and shoes—one of the most anti-union states in the country, but one where liberal Boston media carrying programs and syndicated new columns from New York and Washington papers could easily reach the small, environmentally sensitive Democratic electorate.

With Mondale locking up most of the mainstream liberal money in the business community, however, and Cranston and McGovern ever-present threats on the (voting, but not contributing) left, this was a tall order. What interests could have the overwhelming cultural force to attempt a coup of this scale?

At the time Colorado senator Gary Hart began running as the darkest of dark horses, the implicit answer of most commentators to this question was "movie stars." Such publicity as Hart gained focused largely on the early funds Hollywood supporters such as Robert Redford, Goldie Hawn, and Neil Diamond brought him. But while the media focused attention on Hollywood, Hart's Kennedyesque good looks and stabbing gestures, and the excitement he was said to rouse among nearly invisible crowds, a far less publicized coalition of supporters began to gather around and contribute.

Theodore Sorensen, once special assistant to President Kennedy and now a top international lawyer who had played a pivotal role in several major deals (including the one that let South African industrialist Sir Harry Oppenheimer's diamond cartel into Zaire), became the head of the campaign. Under attack by the right for years, Sorensen was a strong champion of arms control. Richard Gardner, who as Carter's ambassador to Italy and former member of the Trilateral Commission had built a strong reputation as an advocate of free trade and a strong U.S. presence in Europe, emerged as an early adviser. Another early Hart supporter, Mike Medovoy of Orion Pictures, came from the same firm as Arthur Krim, which had recently produced the controversial *Under Fire*, a movie that sympathetically portrayed the fall of the Somoza regime in Nicaragua at the hands of the Sandinista guerrillas.[9]

The true extent of Hart's early elite support, however, is best revealed by his fund-raising. Headed by Paine Webber Capital Markets Group president Michael Johnston, and aided by Regis McKenna, who handled public relations for many leading electronics firms in Silicon Valley, and Atlanta attorney (and Delta Air Lines director) David Garrett, this was a far cry from the ramshackle, shoestring operation its press image suggested.

Johnston himself reportedly raised more than $600,000. Several figures associated with IBM, probably the most profitable of all multinationals and the one with perhaps the biggest stake in Europe (as well as the firm that has long supported the work of Richard Garwin, science adviser to the Committee on East-West Accord), also made very early contributions. Among these were T. J. Watson, Jr., whose ideas on industrial policy and the need for assisting "sunrise" industries strongly resembled some of those Hart was promoting, and Nicholas deB. Katzenbach, IBM's general counsel and a director of both that firm and *The Washington Post*. Other early contributors included Sydney Gruson, previously in charge of European operations for *The New York Times* and now that concern's vice-chairman (Hart himself was a partner in a real-estate investment with a member of the *Times's* Washington bureau); Denver oil billionaire Marvin Davis (on the board of whose 20th Century–Fox Films Henry Kissinger sat); Seagram's chairman Edgar Bronfman; and Boston real-estate developer and *Atlantic* publisher Mortimer Zuckerman.[10]

Local Colorado businesses also contributed extensively. Just then emerging as a regional oil and high-tech center, Denver was crowded with entrepreneurs who knew Hart, and liked him: Among those were Denver developer Gary Antonoff, attorney Ben Stapleton, Lee White, the regional director of public finance for Smith Barney in Denver, attorney Norman Browstein, and a great many independent oilmen whose holdings in the United States would have jumped in value if Hart's proposal to put some limits on the commitment of American ground troops to the Persian Gulf area had ever actually been implemented.[11]

As impressive as all this support was, it proved insufficient. If only reporters working with concerns whose directors and top management were contributing to his campaign could straight-facedly describe Hart as an "outsider," the candidate's financial base did remain thin, and funds did not flow to Hart as abundantly as they did to Mondale and Glenn. Though, in marked contrast to its treatment of the other minor candidates, *The New York Times Magazine* had given Hart a boost by providing space for a major essay describing his neoliberal views on military reform, during much of 1983 the campaign was in straitened circumstances.[12]

One response to the money shortage was a refocusing of campaign strategy. In a move that would later come back to haunt the campaign, Hart and his advisers decided to concentrate all their resources on the early primaries. This had one costly consequence—that in the later primaries many states would not even have full slates of Hart delegates on the ballot. But it also had a big advantage. Because requirements for federal matching funds included ceilings on spending in individual states, Mondale and Glenn could not outspend Hart in the early primaries. If he concentrated all his resources on Iowa and New Hampshire, he had the potential to match them, almost dollar for dollar. Here, however, was a rub. "Potential" did not imply "actual." Though Hart could spend the money in a concentrated burst, he first had to get it, and the level of contributions in early summer 1983 was well below what was required for even a fully funded campaign in Iowa and New Hampshire. Hart needed more money, and he needed it quickly.[13]

In July the dark clouds hanging over Hart's future suddenly broke, as a series of transactions of almost mythical dimensions began. The First American Bank of Washington, D.C., loaned Hart $150,000. In the next weeks, it loaned him $300,000 more. Over the next few months, as contributions continued to nosedive, further huge loans from this bank kept his candidacy going. By the time of the New Hampshire primary, his debt to First American amounted to just under a million dollars.[14]

By itself, the size and strategic timing of the loan to a "dark horse" candidate should have stimulated some comments in the media. The identity of the bank's chief owners, however, should have made the story front-page news: Kamal Adham, former head of Saudi Arabian intelligence; Faisal al Fulaig, past chairman of Kuwait's National Airline; and Crown Prince Mohammed, son of the president of the United Arab Emirates. The American directors were no less sensational: Armand Hammer, Stuart Symington, and, the concern's chairman, Clark Clifford.

But the American media rose to the challenge. Though stories about First American's attempts to purchase banks in New York State and its dealings with various regulatory agencies had been appearing regularly in *The New York Times, The Washington Post,* and other papers for over three years, in the heat of the election campaign scarcely a word appeared anywhere on Hart's arrangement. The handful of tiny notices that did appear fleetingly mentioned that the bank was Arab-owned, but did not pursue details.[15]

Because no one is ever likely to speak for the record, any nuanced assessment of this extraordinary situation is very difficult to make. Previously a strong supporter of Israel, Hart had already won support from many Americans interested in that country, including *Atlantic* publisher Zuckerman and Martin Peretz, owner of *The New Republic.* But when a proposed congressional resolution calling upon the United States to relocate its embassy to Jerusalem came up for discussion, Hart declined to back it—a stance that led to a major controversy during the New York primary a few months later (when stories about the Saudi loan briefly surfaced, and Hart had to backtrack in public).

A close look at the American directors of the bank, however, suggests strongly that factors other than those bearing on the Middle East might have played a role in their perception of Hart as a candidate. Clifford, Hammer, and Symington, after all, virtually incarnated the political coalition Hart aspired to build—liberal on trade and domestic policy, strong on conventional defense, but willing to negotiate on arms control. Along with all his other credentials, Clifford happened to be the law partner of Paul Warnke, who was even then organizing the resistance to the Reagan Administration's nuclear program and arms-control proposals. Symington's ties to weapons producers stretch back many years; some had been among the core supporters of his abortive Presidential drive in the late 1950s. And Hammer, perhaps the best-known American businessman in favor of dealing with the Soviet Union, was a director of an organization that claimed both Symington and Clifford as members—the Committee on East-West Accord.

Whatever motivated the bank to make the loan, and Hart to accept it, the fact is plain that it kept him in the race. While other wealthy contributors (including oilman Arthur Belfer) aided his campaign in the final weeks before Iowa, by itself their assistance would not have been enough. And it is equally plain that while the mass media could with equal justification have hyped either McGovern or Hart for their "astonishing" showing in Iowa, the media pushed Hart far more strongly and consistently.

Jackson

In the meantime yet another candidate had entered the race—a candidate who happened to be black. In American politics, the mere fact of such a candidacy is worthy of extended notice; that it continued as long and successfully as it did only underscores the need for attention; and because the effort now figures in so many discussions of Democratic alternatives, we would ideally like to examine its many twists and turns in detail. But that would require a book in itself. We confine ourselves to a few points. [16]

What was most fascinating about the Jackson campaign, in our view, was that it exposed the fundamental tensions that now define the Democratic Party. That the campaign ever got airborne at all is surely attributable to the vacuum that was forming within the party on domestic economic issues. Aside from his anemic industrial-policy proposals, Mondale was largely avoiding these questions. Backing away from even nominal commitments to the goal of full employment, he and most of the rest of the party had accepted a business-oriented definition of America's problems. But millions of people still out of work, facing rising imports and downward mobility, could hardly be expected to get excited about the corresponding initiatives. At campaign rallies, in discussion groups, in private conversations, one could almost feel the tension: was any candidate going to speak to this great, suffering mass?

Neither was any candidate (aside from McGovern) prepared directly to address the growing tension between U.S. domestic needs and foreign-policy objectives. Though many Democratic candidates professed support for the freeze and "peace," they used the term evasively and did not link these issues directly to the average citizen's economic and social well-being. Instead, moralism and sentimentality filled most of their rhetoric. Virtually no one declared that the U.S. interventions in Central America came at the expense of the cities and the poor. Nor did anyone note that a massive American military presence abroad lowered the rate of return a multinational had to have before it could decide safely to invest overseas. All spoke in circumlocution, and the electorate saw only through a TV glass darkly.

In these circumstances, Jesse Jackson's "rainbow" was no mirage. An audience really existed out there, and it had not yet heard any candidate address its interests. Moreover, Jackson, an eloquent speaker who had long been involved in the grass-roots politics of the civil-rights movement, could plausibly come before community groups and dissident union locals to make the case. But if the initial promise of the Jackson campaign was great, so too were the obstacles it faced. The chief drawback, as usual, was money.

As McGovern had already discovered, in the America of the 1980s virtually no white business groups were interested in subsidizing another poor people's movement on the model of the 1960s. Neither, increasingly, were many black business leaders. Though some frankly conceded the inability of "black capitalism" ever to dent inner-city rates of black unemployment, more and more of these groups (with establishments disproportionately concentrated in trade and a few service industries) concentrated on campaigns to win franchises and dealerships from larger Fortune 500 companies and expand their share of government contracts and small business loans. While these efforts could be justified as attempts to rectify the results of past practices of racial exclusion, the logic of the situation was very ambiguous. Hostile critics did not fail to note that Jackson's millionaire half brother was himself operating two franchises, while others observed that a number of top Jackson campaign operatives, including Cleveland businessman Arnold Pinckney, were under investigation by various state and federal authorities.[17]

For a while, the Jackson campaign marched on, sustained by its own enthusiasm, grass-roots fund-raising efforts in black churches, and some aid from a few liberal international groups and foundations (including David Rockefeller, Jr.). Some multinationals (including Coca-Cola) that have long cultivated relations with both American and Third World blacks also contributed. Well known for his views on the Middle East, Jackson was also puffed by some portions of the U.S. media that have long been interested in tilting American foreign policy toward the Gulf states.[18]

But the campaign ran on a shoestring, and white-dominated unions largely declined to respond. As the pressure mounted, Jackson perceptibly changed direction. Though he continued to talk rainbow on many occasions, in practice his rhetoric and attention focused increasingly on the black community.

It is in this context that the frequent charges of anti-Semitism leveled at Jackson should be assessed. Relations between blacks and Jews have been famously troubled now for more than a decade. Many factors are involved—the neoconservative movement in the Jewish community, central-city economics, and foreign policy, among others. Whatever the sources of tension, however, what is clear is that the pattern of cooperation between many black and Jewish groups that marked the heyday of the civil-rights movement in the 1960s has broken down. With suspicion and mistrust rife, one strand of black nationalist leadership has emerged in recent years that appears assuredly anti-Semitic, if that term is to have any meaning at all. And because that leadership's emphasis on autonomous black economic development parallels the broader movement in favor of "black capitalism," some of its policy pronouncements resonate beyond its immediate circle.

As the Jackson campaign turned its attention to getting black votes, it tended on several occasions—not merely in the famous "let's talk black" discussions brought to light by *The Washington Post*'s Milton Coleman—to employ some of that inflammatory rhetoric. It also loudly refused to repudiate a grotesque assortment of threats and disparaging remarks about Jews by Louis Farrakhan, the Black Muslim leader in Chicago who had joined the board of Operation PUSH, Jackson's old community organization, early in 1983. It would not be until June, after the primary season had ended, that Jackson would forcefully condemn Farrakhan's statements. [19]

As the campaign concentrated increasingly on the black community and foreign-policy questions, Jackson's fund-raising efforts also focused more exclusively on some black business groups and those with a longtime interest in policy toward the Middle East. In the end, Arab-Americans (some of whose contributions were refused by Mondale) raised considerable sums for Jackson. Several Americans long noted for their stands on the Middle East—notably James Akins, formerly the U.S. ambassador to Saudi Arabia—also contributed to the campaign. Operation PUSH, which Jackson campaign aides claimed operated independently of the campaign, received $200,000 from the League of Arab States and $10,000 from the government of Libya. [20]

Mondale Triumphant

For some weeks after he won the New Hampshire primary, Gary Hart was the cynosure of the nation. Moving from victory to victory, he briefly seemed on the verge of knocking Mondale out of the races. Then Mondale surged back as the campaign moved to New York, Pennsylvania, and Illinois, and held on when it drifted West for the final primaries. Though he lost California and Ohio, in the end he defeated Hart. How does one explain this remarkable turnabout?

One part of the answer is so obvious that even the mass media got it right—organized labor's declining political clout carried most weight in the heavily unionized states, and their primaries came later in the season. Another reason is but a bit less subtle—the rules written by

TABLE 6.1

The Democratic Primaries

Time Period		Total Vote	Percentages			
			Mondale	Hart	Jackson	Other
Hart upsurge	2/28–3/13	3,124,220	30.4	35.1	13.4	21.2
Mondale comeback	3/20–4/10	5,560,279	43.6	34.4	19.0	4.0
Homestretch	5/1–5/22	4,954,615	36.8	37.2	21.2	4.9
Super Tuesday	6/5–6/11*	4,036,293	39.8	39.6	18.4	2.2
TOTALS†		17,675,407	38.2	36.5	18.5	6.9

*6/11: North Dakota only.
†Excludes Puerto Rico.

Source: Walter Dean Burnham, "The 1984 Election," 211

the Kennedy and Mondale people before the campaign even began helped Mondale. While Mondale's share of the actual vote in the Democratic primaries was only 1.7 percentage points greater than Hart's, within a few days of the close of the primary season he was able to claim a commanding 52–32 percent lead in his share of actual delegates. This was more than enough to lock up the nomination before the party convention.[21]

But a good deal more can be said about the Mondale victory than these obvious points.

First of all, Glenn's withdrawal strengthened Mondale immensely. As an analysis of Glenn's campaign contributions makes plain, much of his conservative, military-oriented constituency would not transfer to any other Democrat. Accordingly, one sees many business figures in the FEC data who list a primary contribution to Glenn and also contributions to Reagan and the Republicans. On the other hand, those Glenn backers that stayed (in whole or in part) with the Democrats figured to go mostly to Mondale. As a consequence, when Glenn pulled out, Mondale, whose campaign seemed to be reeling, suddenly had the best of both worlds. He now enjoyed an even more affluent audience that would reward a move toward the right, especially on national-security issues. At the same time, he still had his carefully tailored "fairness" theme to tug at Hart's free-market-exalting neoliberalism from the left.

Mondale played both themes superbly. In late January he had opened negotiations with various groups favoring the freeze, and apparently some freeze supporters expressed their willingness to support him (others, however, including Helen Caldicott, declined). As Glenn folded, however, Mondale moved further to the right. Though he preserved links with the freeze and arms-control movements, he conveniently forgot his earlier misgivings over the Grenada invasion. Coming out in favor of a tough stand on Latin America, he called for a "quarantine" of Nicaragua and talked up the "Communist threat." While he did so, the hardest of the hard-line Democrats—including at length even James Schlesinger—gathered round him. So did many of Glenn's financial backers, including the Stephens brothers of Arkansas and publishing executive Robert Farmer.[22]

Hart, by contrast, encountered increasingly heavy weather among Democratic business elites. In the first flush of his primary triumphs, many comparatively liberal, pro-arms control, multinationally oriented business figures moved toward him, including Lewis Branscombe of IBM and investment bankers Glucksman, Gutfreund, Arthur Altshul, and Donald Petrie. Trilateralists Lloyd Cutler and Victor Palmieri contributed, as did McGeorge Bundy and William Colby. Apple Computer founder Steven Wozniac (a Hart delegate from California) and others from Silicon Valley also pitched in.

Most business Democrats, however, recoiled. Particularly as Hart moved more firmly toward the anti-interventionist position on Central America that Linowitz had promoted, and Mondale was now abandoning, they raised sharp questions about his "character'" that were echoed widely in the media. One right-wing political action committee actually singled him out as a target for "independent" expenditures on negative publicity. No less damaging to Hart was his inability to crack Mondale's hold on the real-estate interests. Quite striking in the FEC data, this phenomenon vividly illustrates the potency of the "fairness" issues with elites who simply could not afford pure neoliberalism.

As Mondale reconsolidated his elite support, their money began to weigh heavily in the outcome. Though hamstrung by FEC rules on its own expenditures, the campaign benefited extensively from more than a hundred "delegate committees" it had previously encouraged to form—both to evade the limits on total expenditures and to avoid any financial loss from Mondale's public pledge not to accept funds from PACs (the committees were happy to take the money). Though Hart eventually complained about this scam and garnered some useful publicity, by that time the damage was already done. Even after Mondale promised to repay the money to the businesses and unions that had donated it, he did not do so immediately, but instead took out a bank loan in May (when he was a far surer bet for the nomination) for an additional $400,000, which he declared to be an escrow account for the contributions. Then he simply waited until November for the FEC to act on Hart's complaint, after which the delegate committee monies were paid back—not to their original donors, but to the U.S. Treasury as part of a settlement the Mondale camp agreed to with the FEC.[23]

Back in the late spring, meanwhile, in Texas and other late primaries Hart's campaign again began to run short of funds. Though he had proved he had voter appeal at least equal to Mondale's, the latter's elite-directed machine was proving too much. Texas provided a striking illustration of the candidates' contrasting fortunes after Glenn's withdrawal. Aware that "the Glenn people" "held the key to the rest of the money" and that "if they all moved together, it meant another $800,000–$1 million," Mondale personally flew to the state. From his hotel suite he "began dialing the phone numbers of bankers, businessmen, and Democratic Party contributors." Texas business leaders who had previously backed Glenn responded: the efforts of Mondale and his staff there in just two days in late May brought in more than $425,000. And only days before the decisive round of primaries in New Jersey, California, and other states, David M. Roderick, the president of a major likely beneficiary of Mondale's industrial policy, the United States Steel Co., also endorsed him for the nomination, if not necessarily for the White House.[24]

Though Mondale lost California and other states on June 2, he managed to win New Jersey. Now the advantages he received from the new Democratic rules became palpable. Within days, enough unelected or previously uncontrolled delegates had committed themselves to allow him to announce that he had gone over the top. And as it became increasingly clear that this was true, more and more of the party moved to coalesce around the former Vice President. Though the bad blood flowing between Hart and Mondale was evident, both sides had considerable incentive to settle. Mondale wanted to avoid a bitter convention fight, and Hart would need help retiring his large campaign debt. Eventually, after efforts by Edward Kennedy and several Democratic businessmen to mediate, the two sides did reach an accommodation. Hart was permitted to keep up the appearance of a campaign and to address the convention in prime time.

Once it was clear that Mondale had the nomination wrapped up, attention shifted to the question of his running mate. Because the point is so important to an assessment of who was running whom, we note the obvious—that the famous round of public pilgrimages to Mondale headquarters by prospective Vice Presidential nominees started at the invitation of the Mondale headquarters. Rather clearly intended to unify the party by persuading all factions that they were being heard, the proceedings may have been used by his political enemies to hurt Mondale's public image by underscoring his debts to various "special interests." But his campaign surely did not have to do it.

In retrospect, it is apparent that the Mondale campaign was trying to take a new leaf from a very old book. Quite like many New Deal Democratic candidates, Mondale was hoping to reach out to a fairly well-organized mass interest group that could add something to what was clearly becoming a fairly conservative business-led campaign. Accordingly, after taking a perfunctory look at several conservative Southerners, Mondale's campaign began inventorying various "minority" candidates.

Two black mayors, Wilson Goode of Philadelphia and Tom Bradley of Los Angeles, were among those considered. The invitation to Goode was generally interpreted merely as a way of thinking him for his support in the critical Pennsylvania primary. Bradley, on the other hand, who had worked closely with top executives from Arco and other leading firms in his city's business establishment, clearly attracted Mondale campaign operatives. San Francisco mayor Dianne Feinstein, who was a close political ally of real-estate magnate Walter Shorenstein, and whose husband was also a major Bay Area real-estate power broker, campaigned vigorously for the job. A strong drive also developed for San Antonio mayor Henry Cisneros. A prominent Hispanic political leader in Texas, Cisneros was originally a protégé of Boston Brahmin Elliot Richardson (who was alleged to say he did not even know Cisneros was a Democrat until the word leaked that he was being considered for the VP slot). He owed his political career, however, primarily to two famous Texas Democrats: Belton

Johnson, who at the time of Cisneros' rise co-owned the fabled King Ranch, and "Asphalt King" H. B. Zachary.[25]

And of course, as all the world now knows, Geraldine Ferraro, a liberal Queens Democrat married to yet another New York City real-estate figure, was also under consideration. Backed strongly by many Eastern women's groups and praised by some labor leaders and other congressmen, Ferraro eventually got the nod. The historic designation of a woman candidate for Vice President by one of the major parties succeeded in bringing some excitement to the Democrats. For a few days, Mondale looked like a bold innovator, and after Ferraro's first press conference, the new ticket began rising in the polls.

But Ferraro's selection was virtually the last happy decision by the Mondale campaign, which now made a series of fatal moves. Only days after the Ferraro announcement, Mondale named Bert Lance chairman of his campaign committee. The news that Jimmy Carter's former OMB chief would direct Mondale's efforts shocked many in the party, who remembered how Lance had departed under a cloud in the Carter Administration. Lance was also a close ally of several prominent Arab investors and had maintained friendly relations with Jesse Jackson's campaign. As protests piled in, and the American-Israel Public Affairs Committee organized an emergency breakfast to complain, the Mondale campaign backed down and announced that Lance's role would be scaled back. No less damagingly, on the eve of the convention Mondale surprised almost everyone by proposing to replace Charles Manatt as DNC chairman. But Manatt, a pivotal figure in the whole series of compromises that had brought Mondale the nomination, simply had too many allies to be dislodged. Besieged by an army of major contributors, Mondale backed down again. Manatt, he announced, would stay on.

The convention itself proceeded smoothly. With Jackson, New York governor Mario Cuomo, and others making memorable speeches, it was considerably more radical in its tone than the actual ticket, and brought Mondale a final lift in the polls to a virtual dead heat with Reagan. The tone of the convention and a few incidents in the Mondale campaign itself briefly alarmed some of Mondale's business backers, who complained to the candidate that "there has been some unfortunate choosing of words" in describing the Democratic Party's residual obligations to working people and the poor. But they need not have worried. As calls to revive the spirit of the New Deal still echoed in the convention center, he made the final blundering concession to business that turned an uphill struggle into a political charge of the light brigade.[26]

Mondale and the Deficit

Desperate for money and a few favorable press notices, he had made a fatal bargain. By the early summer of 1984, virtually all sectors of the business community were up in arms over the size of the deficits projected by the Reagan Administration for the next several years. But the protests came most intensely from those parts of business that were already close to Mondale and the Democrats—investment bankers and insurance company executives.

To the Mondale campaign—whose economic advisers consisted almost wholly of investment bankers, such as Robert Hormats of Goldman Sachs, or economists with close ties to finance (including at least one who had actually worked for the Committee for a Responsible Budget, funded in part by the American Council of Life Insurance and closely associated with the CED)—the agitation about the deficit appeared to be a golden opportunity. Here was a chance for Mondale, at one stroke, to shed the charges of "special interest" domination. By presenting a tough fiscal program and calling dramatically for a tax rise, he could throw Reagan on the defensive and demonstrate his ability to make tough decisions. He could secure support from major parts of the business community and obtain more favorable press notices.

In June, agitation within the business community over deficits crested. Led by a bipartisan group of former Treasury Secretaries, more than a hundred business organizations descended on Washington to lobby for budget cuts. As the business groups lobbied, Mondale discussed the problem with influential Democrats and made a tentative decision to make a major public statement. Investment banker Harry Jacobs, Jr., chair of Prudential-Bache, told the press that "Democrats, as a matter of business policy, need to take a strong and aggressive position on curbing deficits," and that "as a businessman, that's a contribution I can make to the Democratic platform." In July, two investment bankers who were later publicly identified as sources of Mondale's new "thinking on the need to reduce budget deficits"—Robert Rubin of Goldman Sachs and Roger Altman of Lehman Brothers—traveled to his Minnesota home to discuss the tax plan. At the convention, Mondale announced he would raise taxes, if elected.[27]

To the immense relief of Reagan strategists (who later confessed their anxiety that Mondale would steal the tax-reform issue from them), Mondale also turned aside pleas from many leading Democrats for a sweeping endorsement of tax reform. In this, Mondale was at least practicing the virtue of consistency. Because the "fair tax" and other reform proposals in the air threatened the special treatment of capital gains that was so important to investment bankers and the unique advantages enjoyed by real estate, neither of these key Democratic business constituencies had any enthusiasm for the reform issue. In abandoning it, Mondale merely confirmed the alliance with Democratic business elites that his promise to raise taxes had already signaled.[28]

But the costs were high. Though Mondale appears to have thought he might gain the whole world, all in fact he had done was to sell his own soul, and that of his party.

The investment bankers and insurance company executives in the campaign were, of course, gratified. Even if Mondale lost, their preeminent issue would be massively publicized and the party would be committed in advance to major efforts at deficit reduction after the election. No one else, however, saw much reason to cheer. Less directly concerned than the financiers (and, for those on the outside, sometimes skeptical that Mondale really meant what he said), most industrialists preferred to wait for a second Reagan Administration to chop social spending to the bone. Nor were industries hurt by the high exchange rate of the dollar moved by Mondale's claims that lower deficits would lead to lower interest rates. Aware, as one multinational Democrat admitted, that if Mondale won, "labor would have a stronger voice," these firms were hardly enthusiastic at the prospect of conceding in wages what they might gain on lower interest and exchange rates. And for all his talk, even Mondale's commitment to lowering interest rates was doubted by many; after all, he never made a major issue of the Fed's tight-money policies.[29]

Poor and middle-class Americans also were unimpressed. Could even Jesse Jackson rouse a crowd of the unemployed to march, sing, and demonstrate in favor of higher taxes? Without any jobs program at all? Many dispirited organizers of the foundation-sponsored "get out the vote" drives soon realized that the answer was probably no.

The General Campaign

Shortly after the convention, the mess of Ferraro's personal finances surfaced. The public learned that in her financial disclosures to Congress beginning in 1978, the Vice Presidential candidate had claimed an exemption from disclosure of her husband John Zaccaro's income, holdings, and liabilities, although the exemption (which applies only in those cases where the member of Congress does not know about, contribute to, or benefit from such finances) did not apply. At the time she claimed not to know about Zaccaro's activities, Ferraro was an officer and half owner of a company with her husband; she had also failed to note the source of her husband's income, a disclosure requirement not subject to any exemption. The public also learned of Ferraro's illegal financing of her 1978 campaign, during which she had borrowed $130,000 from her husband and children, who were permitted to loan her only $1,000 apiece. Having been ordered to return these funds by the FEC (which also assessed Zaccaro and the Ferraro campaign committee civil fines), Ferraro raised the money in part by selling a property and mortgage interest, which she had purchased for $25,000, for $100,000. To Congress, she reported her $75,000 capital gain on that transaction as worth only $15,001 to $50,000. To the IRS, Ferraro and Zaccaro made all sorts of other false disclosures. Close scrutiny of the tax returns they finally made public in August led to their paying the IRS $53,000 in back taxes and interest. Finally, the public learned of the shady business dealings of Zaccaro himself. These were extensive and would eventually lead him to plead guilty to attempted fraud in a Queens real-estate deal in exchange for a pledge from New York prosecutors to drop two other charges against him and not sentence him to jail. Back in August, however, the most colorful revelation was the news that Zaccaro had made insider loans to himself from a trust he "conserved" for an elderly, imcompetent widow.[30]

Thereafter only divine intervention could have saved Mondale, and signs were abundant that the greatest of vested interests was also registering Republican. The Archbishop of New York, John O'Connor, was wondering in public how Catholics could in good conscience vote for someone with Ferraro's views, while instructing the candidate in public that she had "said some things about abortion relative to Catholic teaching which are not true." Harassed by media attacks on Ferraro's tangled finances, Mondale's campaign sank lower and lower in the polls. With most of the business community behind him, more than two-thirds of the press formally endorsing him (to a historic low of 9 percent for Mondale), and campaign contributions breaking all records, Reagan had an easy time.[31]

Certain to capture a heavy majority of upper-income groups, all the President had to do was to split off a minority of the working-class vote. Unless the poor voted in unprecedentedly large numbers, he would win by a landslide.

The Reagan campaign, accordingly, dusted off the old tried-and-true formulas for consternating blue-collar voters. Aware, thanks to its highly sophisticated polling operation, that most affluent American men and women would not vote against their economic interests merely because the President endorsed some eccentric views on social issues, the White House stepped up its appeals to conservative religious groups. The President praised Jerry Falwell, campaigned at Catholic shrines, appeared on stage with Catholic bishops, and denounced abortion. He also associated himself with the Olympics, wrapped his campaign in the flag, and scored it with country music.

The White House also sat by while conservative groups operating "independently" of the campaign raised and spent some $10 million for the President's reelection on their own.

Last but hardly least, all the powers of incumbency were working for Reagan at the end of the campaign. The huge political business cycle was hitting its peak, with spectacular increases in personal income in the second quarter of 1984. Still suffering from criticism of parts of his weapons program, the President pushed ahead with his huge Strategic Defense Initiative ("Star Wars"), announced at the very end of the recession. With at least $26 billion in appropriations over its first five years, and almost infinite amounts promised down the road, the Star Wars program (even more than the rest of the Reagan military buildup) represented a lucrative alternative to the Democrats' industrial-policy proposals. It subsidized sunrise sectors and high-tech concerns feeling pressure from the Japanese, without forcing them either to compete directly or to make a general compromise on trade. Continuing its peacemeal approach to the trade issue, in September the White House issued its long-awaited plan for the American steel industry. Here it broke with its professed free-trade "principles" and pledged to roll back steel imports, and gave its negotiators until December to work out market-sharing agreements with the Europeans and Japanese. In contrast to plans put forward by some Democrats and earlier adjustment schemes implemented under Carter, however, it did not ask the industry for commitments on reinvestment or employee retraining. In short, Reagan was offering something to almost everyone except workers and the poor.[32]

In the final weeks of the campaign, Mondale accused Reagan of having a secret plan to raise taxes after the election. Until Reagan's announcement of an upcoming summit with the Soviets, he flogged away at the arms-control and nuclear-terror issues. In a memorable speech at George Washington University, he stepped up his rhetoric and briefly seemed to come alive:

This election is not about jelly beans and pen pals. It is about toxic dumps that give cancer to our children. This election is not about country music and birthday cakes. It is about old people who can't pay for medicine. This election is not about the Olympic torch. It is about the civil-rights laws that opened athletics to women and minorities who won those gold medals. . . . This election is not about slogans, like "standing tall." It is about specifics, like the nuclear freeze—because if those weapons go off, no one will be left standing at all.[33]

But Mondale still did not have a jobs program to offer, and when the campaign even made noises about redistribution from the rich, his business supporters sharply complained—at one point drawing from Mondale the reply: "Oh my goodness, I'm so sorry. There's nothing wrong with wanting to be rich. I want to be rich.") Returning again and again to the deficit issue, the Mondale campaign turned aside proposals from veteran media men Tony Schwartz and others for a series of hard-hitting attacks on the Republicans. Once again, the business figures in his campaign need not have worried. The Democratic candidate had almost nothing concrete to offer voters, other than higher taxes.[34]

The Democrats also declined to push hard on efforts to register new voters. Many nonpartisan groups, to be sure, ran registration efforts aimed at likely Democratic voters. There were more than a hundred of them, supported by about $5 million in foundation and other funding in 1983–84. In addition to canvassing and other traditional registration techniques, several groups attempted strategies of "wholesale" registration, signing people up at social-service waiting rooms, welfare centers, surplus-food distribution lines, and the like. One organization, Human SERVE (Service Employees Registration and Voter Education), attempted to persuade social-service agencies, both private and public, to offer registration as a regular service.

But these groups had many problems. As a general matter, their acute decentralization and lack of partisan focus blurred the effectiveness of the effort. Each organization had its own individual strategy, focus, and geographic range, and with rare exceptions (commonly in particular cities), the many different efforts overlapped their activities haphazardly or worked at cross-purposes. In addition to wasting scarce resources, the lack of coordination provoked sharp disputes over tactics and turf. White-led organizations attempting to use wholesale-registration techniques in black communities were sometimes assailed by black organizations using more traditional techniques. Those that were particularly aggressive in their tactics (sometimes resorting to civil disobedience) were often attacked as "disruptive" by less radical organizations. And so on. The lack of partisan focus, which was a precondition for foundation funding, also meant that the groups had to limit their direct attacks on the Administration and engage only in the most general sorts of voter "education." This effectively required that the very reason many of the groups engaged in the effort at all— to throw Reagan out of office or, more adventurously, to disrupt the Democratic Party from below—had to be kept obscure from those they attempted to register. It also meant that they spent at least some of their resources registering Republicans.

Nor did the Democratically oriented nonpartisan efforts have the field to themselves. Recognizing that at least some effort would be made to organize likely Democratic voters, the GOP resolved in 1983 to mount a major registration project of its own. The official GOP war chest for this effort was $11 million, more than twice what was eventually raised by Democratically oriented groups. It was supplemented by the "independent" registration efforts of more than 170 trade associations (including major drives by the U.S. Chamber of Commerce and the Realtors Association), close to ninety different corporations, a variety of right-wing lobbying organizations (including the American Defense Foundation), and the huge American Coalition for Traditional Values, a group of 40,000 conservative preachers. While precise figures are almost impossible to come by, this added an estimated $12–$15 million to the GOP-oriented side.

In addition to being much better funded, these efforts were far more coordinated and sophisticated. Clear lines of authority ran from the national GOP operation down through state and local organizations. Resources were allocated on the basis of a national registration plan that mounted drives in all fifty states, but targeted twenty-eight (disproportionately from the South and West) for special attention, with additional targeting of particular congressional districts. Having picked its geographic targets, the GOP used census, motor vehicle, credit bureau, and board of registrars data, shuffled and reshuffled ("merged and purged") in computer runs, to locate likely Republican subjects within them. Working off lists of such likely Republicans, paid phone-bank staffers would call prospects to assess their political sympathies firsthand. Once located, unregistered Republican "identifiers" were systematically canvassed or offered registration forms through the mail. Such operations were a far cry from part-time volunteer activists working a surplus-cheese line.

In addition to being outstaffed and outorganized, the Democratically oriented nonpartisans repeatedly encountered resistance to their efforts. Where state rules mandated that registration take place at official registrar offices, they found that those offices kept only business hours and were often closed at midday, making it difficult for working people to get to them without losing pay. In some cases, unsympathetic local officials advertised (or allowed their local allies to advertise) that registrants' names would be checked against welfare rolls. Where states permitted "deputy" registrars, they found that local officials reserved this privilege for "respectable" groups, or members of the local machine, or limited the sites at which deputies could work (frequently excluding such sites as housing projects or welfare and unemployment offices). Where mail registration was available, they found that they could only get a limited number of cards at a time, or that the cards were not available in Spanish, or were available but illegible. Where, through deputization or postcards, they attempted to register people in social-service waiting rooms, they found local officials who barred the way or threw them out. And where, as happened in a handful of states and localities, sympathetic governors or mayors or county executives ordered that registration be made available to social-service recipients, they found Republicans waiting with restraining orders, or the White House threatening, should the practice continue, to cut off funding for the social services themselves.

Throughout all this, the national Democratic establishment sat on the sidelines. There was still talk of voter mobilization, but it was mostly just talk. After months of Democratic stalling on the issue, Mondale's own field director, Mike Ford, urged him desperately to spend the money needed (on Ford's estimate, $12 million) to register 5–6 million black, Hispanic, and union voters. But this was not to be. Despite various pledges to spend $5, $10, or $13 million on a national effort, the Democrats wound up spending only about $2 million, most of which was expended late in the campaign on "get out the vote" drives. Of that, about half went to state officials, many of whom had been hostile to the original registration efforts; the other half apparently went to a variety of groups, mostly black-led, with former Jackson staffer Ernest Green (who had been taken on by the Mondale campaign to appease Jackson) dispensing the monies. By the time the money was distributed, Ford had left the campaign.[35]

Nor did the DNC supply much nonmaterial support. When organizers encountered resistance from local and state Democratic officials, and asked the DNC to use its clout to stop it, they were turned aside. And it was only late in September, less than a month before most registration rolls closed for the season, that Manatt was even moved to write to major Democratic executives at the state and local level to urge their cooperation in voter-registration efforts.[36]

Despite the vastly different levels of support for the two efforts, the end result was a rough draw between the nonpartisan Democratically oriented groups and the GOP and its "independents." Both could take credit for about 3.5 million of the approximately 7 million new people registered through group activity. Turnout went up absolutely, but stagnated as a percentage of the eligible electorate. So much for the "reaching down" effort that Samuel Huntington and other revisionist Democrats labeled a "proven failure" immediately after the election.[37]

Meanwhile, as the Democrats temporized on this and other issues, top aides to the President (as well as a special team of reporters working for *The Washington Post* and *Newsweek* who had been in on the secret) kept silent about a potentially explosive campaign story—that there really was a secret tax plan. Officially laid plans to further cut the budget of the EPA (leading soon after the election to the resignation of William Ruckelshaus, the Weyerhaeuser VP to whom Reagan had recently given the post after a major scandal) were also not discussed. While Reagan reassured audiences that the United States would simply grow out of $200 billion annual budget deficits, J. Peter Grace and other top business supporters prepared a massive anti-deficit ad campaign to begin on election night. Asked later about the cynicism of this move, especially given that the company paid only a 0.2 percent tax rate on profits over 1981–84, Grace would later explain that "we are not concerned about the deficit," rather, "we are concerned about the level of spending."[38]

On election day, an electorate that knew nothing of this voted. There were no surprises. Faced with a choice between someone who at least talked about growth, and delivered one of the greatest political business cycles, and someone whose only firm promise was to raise taxes, the half of the electorate that made it to the polls opted decisively for growth. Blacks, Jews, and the very poorest Americans voted for Mondale. Everyone else, in percentages that rose directly with income, voted overwhelmingly for Ronald Reagan.

7 /

Aftermath:

The Legacy of 1984

With Mondale's catastrophic loss to Ronald Reagan, we return to our starting point. Was it pressure from voters that inspired the Democrats to make their right turn in the 1970s? Were the "special interests" of organized labor, blacks, women, and the poor responsible for the party's failure to define electorally successful alternatives to Reaganism? Are voters the chief force pushing the party further to the right in the wake of the 1984 disaster? Have Reagan and the Republicans succeeded in forging a new political coalition that will dominate the next thirty years of American politics in the way the Democrats dominated the old New Deal party system?

By now, the answers to at least some of these questions should be obvious. Organized labor, black and women's organizations, and community groups representing the poor and other ordinary Americans may have disappointed their mass constituencies in important respects. They may frequently have failed to recognize the dangers of their own lack of coordination, or not come to grips with the deterioration of the American economy and the radical differences between the present context of their organizing efforts and the Great Society environment in which many of them emerged. They may have become dependent on business patronage, and contented themselves with advancing the interests of the best-organized, most affluent parts of their constituencies. They may even be insensitive to the merits of some reform proposals—including proposals for restructuring the delivery systems for health care and other social services—that could significantly cut costs while improving the position of those they claim to represent. But they cannot possibly be charged with running the Democratic Party into the ground.

They have never run the party. They have always occupied the lower rungs of a hierarchy that had other, more powerful interests on top—principally capital-intensive and multinationally oriented big business and its allies among urban real-estate magnates, military contractors, and portions of the media. As we have sought to show, all the crucial decisions that have brought the Democrats to where they are today were made by actors who either had close ties to this bloc or were—as in all Democratic Cabinets from Kennedy through Carter, or the principal economic and foreign-policy advisers to Mondale in 1983–84—themselves prominent members of it.

These business interests—and not workers, blacks, or the poor—were responsible for designing the fragmented, bureaucratized, litigation-prone regulatory programs and social-service delivery system whose costs ballooned in the 1970s. They promoted the vast urban-aid programs that were frequently little more than subsidies to developers, downtown merchants, and real-estate companies. Along with many Republican business groups, they pushed for the combination of regressive tax relief and a major military buildup that provoked the budget squeeze of the late 1970s and produced the even more disastrous one of the 1980s.

These business groups, and some of their GOP allies, were also the primary forces behind the Carter Administration's politically disastrous decisions to tighten the money supply, and cut social spending, immediately before the 1980 election—steps which handed the White House to the Republicans on a platter. They were also the force that inspired the government to make essentially no response to the flood of imports that devastated the U.S. industrial base in the 1970s. They were the power that openly boasted of their intent to make Mondale focus on the deficit during the 1984 Democratic convention, and encouraged his suicidal pledge to raise taxes without offering tax reform. They were the ones who complained during the campaign at the slightest mention of redistribution to workers and the poor. And they are the ones who now say that the "public" has spoken and that the Democrats should move even further to the right.

But what public is being invoked here? As we argued at length at the outset, the basic structure of American public opinion remained unchanged over the last decade. On particular issues of social welfare, "New Deal" concerns, civil rights, relations with the Soviet Union, and U.S. military intervention abroad, mass opinion has actually moved slightly leftward since Reagan assumed office. The only major exception to stable or increasing "liberalism" was the sharp rise in support for military spending at the very end of the 1970s, and that was notably brief. There is no way to sustain the claim that there has been a broad, stable right turn in mass sentiment in America, no matter how many times revisionist Democrats tell us that is the case. Nor is there convincing evidence that the public has "realigned" in electoral terms; the data on party identification and voting do not support the charge. It is simply not true now, and has never been true, that the majority of ordinary Americans want ever-deepening cuts in social security and social-spending budgets, or insist that unemployment stay indefinitely at about 7 percent (what the American Enterprise Institute's Herbert Stein now trumpets as "close to the lowest unemployment rate consistent with avoiding a speeding up of inflation," that is, what most neoclassical economists define as "full employment"), or believe that the poor should be punished for not having jobs, or endorse a Federal Reserve policy that the Fed's own board and all top Washington policymakers recognize is certain to increase the unemployment rate. It is not true that most Americans favor playing "nuclear chicken" with the Soviet Union, or believe government has no special responsibilities to help minorities and women in labor markets, or think consumers should not be protected, or cheer on the pollution of the environment, or rejoice at regressive tax reform. Now that even majority support for increased weapons spending has melted away, it is high time to admit the obvious. American public opinion has not caused the right turn in public policy. What caused it was the disintegration of the New Deal system itself.[1]

That system is now dead, killed off not by voters but by a dramatic realignment of major investors in the political system. This realignment was occasioned by structural transformations of the world political economy and the position of the United States within it—a set of changes that first shocked American elites, then led them to form new coalitions, and advance new programs, to turn away from the New Deal.

Reversing the Right Turn

But if one concedes that America is now experiencing what amounts to party realignment without any corresponding voter realignment, one is led automatically to ask whether this state of affairs can continue, and under what circumstances it might be reversed. Answering this last set of questions, we should emphasize, does not depend at all on one's personal views about desirable public policies. In principle, an inquiry into the stability of America's new party system can be conducted as clinically as one might examine, say, the extent of Walter Mondale's support among leading American investment bankers, or the number of real-estate magnates on the Forbes 400 list who contributed money to his campaign. All that is necessary is to focus sharply on the key question—who is going to make the gigantic investments in time and money that a reversal of the politics of the last decade would require?—while bearing in mind the usual qualifications that should always attend social-science inquiries into complex and imperfectly understood phenomena.[2]

From this clinical standpoint, one conclusion seems plain. While resistance is unpredictable, and the current quiescence of American politics could always be interrupted by a dramatic upsurge of action from below, in the absence of a major depression the rightward drift of both political parties is unlikely to be reversed in the near future. While it may slow somewhat, and certain of its more exotic manifestations may moderate significantly, America's new right-center political order seems here to stay. The social forces that have a structural interest in opposing it are simply too weak.

Consider what the task would require. To reverse the right turn of America and the Democrats, some set of investors would essentially have to replicate the work of the center, and particularly the right, over the last fifteen years or so, pouring millions of dollars and person-hours into political organizing at all levels. While there is a sense in which the population, which still cleaves to the ideals of the New Deal, is already persuaded, vast amounts of time and effort would be required to mobilize this generalized sentiment in favor of specific programs and particular candidates.

One would have to find a way to conduct detailed studies rebutting the innumerable reports on innovation, productivity, the future of social security, tax incentives, and all sorts of other policy matters that have gushed from the American Enterprise Institute, the Heritage Foundation, the American Council for Capital Formation, and (lately) the Brookings Institution and others centers of subsidized research. Once one did the research, one would somehow have to disseminate it, by gaining access to the media and persuading newspapers, magazines, and broadcasters to do an honest job of reporting on activities that are against the interests of their owners and publishers. One would also have to find a way to prevent the dismissal of the younger, untenured academics who did such work.[3]

As one roughed out proposals and began to catch the attention of the public, a new set of political organizations would have to be created. Mechanisms to reach the vast number of nonvoters would be required, including expensive, time-consuming voter-registration and education campaigns. Widespread and escalating government surveillance, intimidation, and sabotage of dissident groups—manifest recently in the Reagan Administration's growing use of the FBI and other government agencies against peaceful dissenters from its Latin American policies—suggest that a small army of lawyers would also have to be recruited, to make sure that alternative candidates gained access to the ballot, and that dissident voters gained access to the polls. Even assuming all this apparatus was in place, the process of campaigning itself would be enormously expensive, requiring whatever alternative candidates that did emerge to contend with the efforts of a rich and powerful opposition.

The center and the right satisfied these different requirements of holding political power in America by spending fabulous amounts of money. In 1983 alone, just three of the literally hundreds of conservative foundations—Olin, Pew, and Scaife—spent $26 million promoting various right-wing causes. Over the past decade, Scaife has spent more than $100 million. The *annual* research budgets for Brookings, AEI, Heritage, and ICS total more than $40 million alone. We have already noted the approximately $1 billion corporations spend each year on "advocacy advertising" and "grass-roots" lobbying. Where could opponents of America's right turn possibly obtain resources on this scale?[4]

Surely not, we think, from the most obvious quarter that springs to mind—organized labor. Though conservative organizations like the National Right to Work Committee continue to picture the AFL–

CIO as a financial Tyrannosaurus Rex, stalking the political land-scape and devouring everything in its path, the rapidly shrinking la-bor movement in fact could not come near to matching the resources commanded by the firms in the Business Roundtable alone, even if its constituent labor unions sold everything they owned, right down to the autographed pictures of past Democratic Presidents that adorn the walls of their headquarters. In 1982, the last year for which we have reliable data, the combined net income of national and inter-national unions and associations (including the AFL–CIO) was $324 million. Corporate profits that year totaled $156 billion, almost 500 times as much.[5]

And as the resources of the union movement shrink, the gap be-tween those resources and its needs grows. Consider the question of union membership. As noted at several points already, the unionized percentage of the work force has been dropping for three decades, with the rate of that decline increasing substantially over Reagan's first term. By September 1984 unions claimed only 15.6 percent of employed wage and salary workers in the private sector, the lowest level since the New Deal. What would it take just to *halt*, not even reverse, this membership decline? Given "natural" attrition through retirements and changes in firms' location and organization, if unions engage in no representation elections before the NLRB they can be expected to lose about 3 percent of their share of the total work force over the course of any given year. One way to answer the question, then, is to calculate what level of NLRB activity would be necessary to make up the difference. In 1984, this would have required orga-nizing 390,000 workers. But unions netted only 68,000 new mem-bers that year through NLRB elections, about a sixth of what was required.[6]

But even if unions had the organizational and monetary resources to maintain the needed level of activity, there is very little evidence that the leadership of the labor movement (if not all leaders of indi-vidual unions, let alone all union members) would use their re-sources to this end. The past twenty years of stagnating commitments to organizing, and the suicidal pursuit of aggressive foreign-policy goals, do not give much reason to hope. There have been some re-cent signs that top labor leaders are not quite as smug about dwin-dling membership as Meany was. And it is true that, thanks to pres-sure from below, the AFL–CIO's hawkish foreign-policy establishment, while still immensely powerful, is no longer quite the omnipotent and insensate monolith it was under him. Still, the top levels of the Federation, and of most unions, remain dominated by a conservative white male gerontocracy that deeply opposes any mobilization that threatens their own power (as any successful mobilization of workers surely would); that considered the decision to endorse Walter Mondale before the primaries a move of almost Napoleonic boldness; and that remains on foreign policy well to the *right* of dominant views within such business-dominated organizations as the Council on Foreign Relations.[7]

Even where they have the inclination, community organizations are even less likely to have the resources for such a campaign. Though a few years ago some analysts detected a "renaissance" of neighborhood organizations, the truth is quite different. Outside of a few large cities where tenants-rights organizations or broad-based neighborhood associations do exist, and parts of the Southwest, where powerful Hispanic organizations are waging strong campaigns, most neighborhood organizations are special, limited-purpose organizations, established to achieve definite, particular goals (such as blocking condominium development, lobbying for better housing, or organizing safety patrols for their neighborhoods). If they broadened those goals, they would almost certainly break into quarreling blocs based on income and other social characteristics. Moreover, the few tenant-rights and "public interest" groups that have survived find the going tough indeed. Often they have merely stimulated local opponents to organize and then been overwhelmed, or been coopted into local political machines dominated by developers and other business interests. Their desperate search for resources has also led many to become dependent on, and thus dominated by, grants from local, generally quite conservative, foundations. More than a few have become totally corrupt. And those that have not, such as ACORN (Association of Community Organizations for Reform Now), are in bad financial shape.

These material constraints at the local level are even more pointed for the handful of national organizations run by opponents of America's right turn. Consider the case of the movement in opposition to U.S. policies toward Latin America. The most important research center for this movement, the North American Congress on Latin America, has a total yearly budget of $475,000 with which it publishes a monthly journal, runs conferences and other consultations for activists, and supports a staff of twelve full-time people (most with advanced degrees and most in their thirties or forties), who are paid $16,500 a year. The full-time activists in the major "solidarity" organizations—the Nicaragua Network, the Committee in Solidarity with the People of El Salvador, and the Network in Solidarity with Guatemala—are paid $750 a month. The executive director of PACCA (Policy Alternatives for the Caribbean and Central America), an important sponsor of alternatives to present U.S. policies in Central America, is not paid at all for his full-time job. And as of November 1984—while Reagan was relishing his campaign victory, and the United States was spending about $10 billion a year pursuing his Administration's goals in Central America—the most prominent coalition of groups opposed to current U.S. policies in the region, the Central America Peace Campaign, was down to one paid staffer.[8]

It is sometimes said that these material constraints can be mooted by favorable press coverage. This we doubt. The only way to relieve deficiencies of time and money is through time and money. No opposition can proceed without organization, and favorable press attention, while it can contribute to organization, is certainly not a substitute for it. More immediately, the press is itself a major investor in American politics, and there is no reason to anticipate a halt in its own rightward drift. As already noted, virtually the entire press endorsed Ronald Reagan for reelection in 1984. Many of the important elements of it that did not—*The New York Times*, *The Washington Post*, the Cox-Chambers chain of newspapers—are concerns whose owners, directors, or top management were active early players in the 1984 campaign. While we would like to credit the constant refrain from journalists that their own private interests do not intrude on their news reporting, the comprehensive neglect of the real political economy of the 1984 election by the media makes this difficult.[9]

At any time during the primaries, for example, any reporter could have exposed the Glenn campaign's pretensions to being above "special interests" by simply walking over to the Federal Election Commission and inventorying his contributors. Given the immense curiosity about Gary Hart in the wake of the early primaries, the huge First American Bank loan to his campaign would have made a sensational story, but it was never told. And of course only Balzac could do justice to those many members of the media who kept referring to Mondale supporters among women, blacks, and unions as "special interests," while the Republican campaign piled up the stacks and stacks of cash it received from corporate PACs and affluent Americans.

Nor does the media reporting of the vast post-election campaign to move the Democratic Party to the right inspire much confidence in its disinterested impartiality. Almost every "independent" political analyst quoted in the media these days has strong ties to one or more interested groups, at least some of whose corporate sponsors are involved in the effort to move the Democrats to the right—the American Enterprise Institute, for example, or the Trilateral Commission, or the Coalition for a Democratic Majority, or any number of lobbyists for higher military spending. Their common sponsors, however, are rarely identified, as the general press neglect of the Four Seasons gathering attests.

One has to reckon also with the vast campaign other sectors of the business and legal communities have waged against the liberal establishment media's alleged bias or even "libel" of business and conservative figures or causes. With most of the liberal press looking over its shoulder at groups like Accuracy in Media, Fairness in Media, the American Legal Foundation, and the Capital Legal Foundation, it is an even less likely ally for any serious attempt to reverse present policies.

If labor, community groups, and the press are currently improbable vehicles for a new mass political movement, it is hard to think of anyone else who might stand in for them. As the Mondale campaign made clear, virtually no Democratic business group has a stake in expanding the party's mass base. To gain the support of the millions and millions of poor nonvoters and marginally identifying blue- and white-collar workers, the Democrats would actually have to offer them something—perhaps a progressive tax code, or full employment, or unionization with real power for the rank and file, or enhanced social programs. In the fitful, anxious world political economy of the 1980s, the party's dominant business elites are not prepared to do this. And so instead they recommend that the party chase a voting bloc with preferences apparently rather close to their own—Southern whites. The idea is that this is one bloc of voters whom the Democrats can gain by literally doing nothing. For all their peculiar cultural institutions, however, white Southerners are no dumber than the average American voter. They too want jobs, education, and economic well-being. If the Democrats offer only bread and circuses and a few more missiles, these voters will have every reason to stay with the Republicans, or more likely in the case of low-income voters, drop out of the system altogether.

Sources of Instability

While an economic catastrophe, or an unanticipated upsurge in popular protest, might drastically alter all calculations, an early reversal of the American political system's right turn thus seems most unlikely. But while both political parties are now dominated by conservative business groups and their allies, the American political universe is still a long way from being a stable, closed system. Both parties are vehicles for strongly contradictory interests which are almost certain eventually to collide.

If any theme emerges from our review of the disintegration of the Democrats since the mid 1960s, it is the party's inability to assemble any stable political coalition at all. It is true that narrowing the party's mass constituency has now been embraced by virtually every elite group in the party as a solution to this problem, and one can hardly doubt such instability will diminish if the party is able to move right and ignore the needs of its old mass base. But the heterogeneity of the American business system and the conflicting imperatives of a turbulent world economy are almost certainly enough to guarantee continuing conflict even among Democratic elites.

No matter how hard they try to shrink their mass base, for example, Democratic elites are unlikely to reach agreement on the role a steadily weakening labor movement should have in the party. Nor, though many may eventually sell out, take their losses, and adjust their investments—and their policy views—the Northeast and Midwest real-estate interests are likely to abandon efforts to cut the military budget or protest their existing tax concessions. Much the same can be said for the investment bankers, free-trading multinational interests, emergent protectionists (whose strength in the party appears recently to have risen a bit), and other interests in the party's elite. Such elite divisions, of course, can interact with more popular impulses. Jesse Jackson and the contradictory political movement he fanned is as likely to divide the party after the election as before it.

Many of these contradictory forces could be glimpsed in the post-election contest to replace Charles Manatt as head of the Democratic National Committee, a process that produced not one, but several candidates. The early favorite, Paul Kirk, Jr., had served for eighteen months as the party's national treasurer, where he had helped develop the controversial "soft money" fund-raising techniques that allowed Democrats like T. J. Watson, Jr., and venture capitalist Stuart Moldow to make legal contributions far in excess of the FEC national campaign limits. A Massachusetts lawyer with close ties to Edward Kennedy, Kirk also won backing from most of organized labor. Supported by New York governor Mario Cuomo and others in the party, former California Democratic chair Nancy Pelosi also made a bid. So did political consultant Robert J. Keefe, known for his close ties to Robert Strauss and other influential Democratic leaders.[10]

Because so much maneuvering took place offstage, and virtually no one will speak on the record now, it is impossible to say for certain how the bargaining went. Hints in otherwise uninformative press reports suggest that Kirk allied with many members of the Coalition for a Democratic Majority to oust Gary, Indiana, mayor Richard Hatcher (a Jesse Jackson supporter) from his slot as DNC vice-chair. In response, Jackson threatened to lead a third-party movement. Kirk also sought to defuse impressions that he was a Kennedy puppet by sponsoring a resolution requiring him to remain neutral in the 1988 Presidential race. In the end, Pelosi and Keefe withdrew, and a new candidate entered the race—former North Carolina governor Terry Sanford. A former public governor of the American Stock Exchange, Sanford is one of the best connected of all Democrats to big business. But as someone who served as governor of North Carolina at a time when textiles were far more important in that state's economy than now, he has had rather cooler relations with the AFL–CIO. His involvement in efforts to stimulate the interests of Arab investors in the South have also been criticized by some in the party. Nevertheless, he was a strong candidate, and barely lost.[11]

But Kirk's election did not stop the turmoil. He sought to nominate a black woman backed by labor for DNC treasurer, which was widely interpreted as an effort to squeeze one of the millionaires at the Four Seasons meeting, Florida real-estate developer E. William Crotty, out of a key role. Kirk urged Crotty instead to run for the post of finance chairman against his friend San Francisco attorney

Duane Garrett, but Crotty refused, and major party financiers threatened to stop contributing. Many prominent Democrats joined Sam Nunn and other party leaders in forming the new Democratic Leadership Council, independent of Kirk and the DNC, a move that Kirk strategists feared would take away the "cream of the party's leadership" and leave them with the "special interests" and Jesse Jackson. This prompted Kirk to make his own right turn, including his open feud with Kirkland and an appointment of Crotty to head the party's National Financial Board of Directors. More maneuverings followed.[12]

What is most important in this chronology, of course, is the overall dynamic, which is unmistakably to the right. But the many negotiations and difficulties underscore the existence of continued tensions within that rightward course.

More immediately, to return to a question raised at the outset of our discussion, America's transit to a new, center-right party system does not imply that the Republicans will dominate that system in the way the Democrats dominated the New Deal party system that has ended. In the long run, the most powerful force tending to destabilize American politics will probably be the continuing economic crisis. Even in the short run, this seems increasingly likely to lead to major policy collisions within both parties. But it may have a particularly destabilizing effect within the GOP.

Republican Troubles

The basic problem is stark indeed. Despite all the officially sponsored optimism that gushed in the later stages of Reagan's 1984 political business cycle, Reaganomics has failed to solve America's economic crisis. For the fourth business cycle in a row, the level of unemployment reached at the peak of the cycle has been higher than that of the cycle before. By historic standards, real interest rates remain high. The trade deficit is now running at the unprecedented rate of $150 billion annually. The full-employment budget deficit—a measure of budget imbalance that would be registered in the unlikely event that the U.S. economy succeeded in getting back to full employment—has already reached the Brobdingnagian amount of $200 billion dollars. Even more ominously, the high dollar is now devastating not only all the old manufacturing sectors but also the high-technology industries touted as the industrial base of the future. In 1985, for the first time, the United States ran a negative balance of trade in semiconductors, one of the driving forces of the "fourth industrial revolution." Even large, previously highly profitable firms like Wang Industries, Control Data, Apple, and Texas Instruments are retrenching. In many cases, they are moving more production abroad and cutting back on reinvestment in the United States. And for all the hoopla surrounding the Reagan tax cuts' miraculous "supply side" effects, the best recent econometric estimates of American productivity growth suggest that the "Reagan revolution" had no salutary effect on the American economy's anemic long-term rate of productivity growth.[13]

Perhaps most menacing of all, the post-election slowdown of the Reagan political business cycle is creating an explosive situation in much of the rest of the world. Crushed by high U.S. interest rates, growth in the Third World collapsed in 1981–82, completely reversing the trend in the world economy since the 1960s. As growth fell, so did foreign investment, while the outflow of loans from commercial banks plummeted. Though the huge U.S. election boom briefly revived world demand, the election is now over, and the American economy is flattening. Unless it is offset, this could easily bring on a world recession.

This is a development the rest of the world cannot afford. Urged on not only by Fidel Castro but also by many indigenous business interests, Latin American elites are increasingly balking at the harsh terms the IMF requires from countries trying to stretch out the debt their countries increased in the late 1970s. Fearing social revolution (and often low domestic profits for local business), the Latin Americans are threatening to default on their loans. In Africa and even previously booming East Asia, the prospect of a declining demand for exports is raising fears of an economic slowdown, accompanied by increased political instability and debt repudiation. In Western Europe, elite anxiety is rising about the social consequences of more years of slow growth. And lagging world demand, combined with aggressive oil-exploration efforts in some non-OPEC countries and the growth of the spot oil market, has sent world oil prices plunging. Though salutary for the world as a whole, the drop in oil prices is generating a giant wave of anxiety that runs from Riyadh to Houston.

The Reagan Administration is not blind to these disasters, and has a strategy with which it is trying to meet the situation. Finance ministers of the United States and the other major countries in the so-called Group of 5 (the United States, Great Britain, France, West Germany, and Japan) have recently announced a program of central bank intervention to push the dollar down against foreign currencies. The Administration and several other allied governments are also pressing Germany and Japan to reflate their low-inflation economies by expanding government spending and cutting taxes, in an effort to prevent the catastrophic decline in world demand that might lead to a wave of debt repudiation and guerrilla insurgence on the periphery of the world economy. In the case of Japan, these steps would open up a way for the Japanese to grow without expanding their exports as rapidly. Because the expansion would result from fiscal rather than monetary stimulation, it would help take upward pressure off the dollar.

The Administration is also pushing the Japanese to open up their heavily regulated financial system and reduce their many nontariff barriers to U.S. exports. There has also been some discussion of temporary Japanese controls on capital exports. These moves, favored by many multinationals anxious to stave off rising demands in the United States for tariff protection from foreign competition, are intended to lower the value of the dollar against the yen, and redress the hugely unfavorable U.S. balance of trade with Japan. To further bolster opposition to protection, supporters of free trade within the Administration are seeking Administration support for a new, far-ranging series of multilateral trade talks that would help moderate existing trade disputes and reconfirm a U.S. commitment to free trade.

The Administration has also introduced a sweeping new tax bill, which not only has the usual Reagan goal of securing more income for the wealthy (reflected in both its essentially proportional rate structure and its proposed abolition of the deduction for state income taxes) but also the objective of promoting the international economic competitiveness of U.S. business.

Prodded by Treasury Secretary Baker and Fed chair Volcker (plus, of course, any number of anxious banks), the Administration is also gearing up to deal with the debt crisis. At the recent IMF meetings in Seoul, Baker outlined a program under which the IMF and World Bank would expand their surveillance of Third World economies to spur their acceptance of more liberal economic policies. Major private banks would be encouraged to continue lending to the Third World, and official lending by the World Bank and other agencies would substantially rise. With support from the Administration, the World Bank's executive directors are also putting finishing touches on a proposed Multilateral Investment Guarantee Agency (MIGA). Conceived as a Bank subsidy, with authorized capital of $1 billion, MIGA is designed to entice multinationals back into the Third World by insuring them against a variety of political risks.[14]

These ambitious plans, however, face many obstacles, leading one to doubt whether they can possibly be realized without pulling the Republican Party apart.

By itself, for example, the widely heralded attempt to push down the dollar can do little but buy time for the Administration. Given the explosion of private currency markets and exchanges in the 1970s, central bank currency reserves and borrowing arrangements now add up to a fraction of total world financial flows. As a consequence, central bank intervention in the foreign-exchange markets cannot hope to reverse fundamental trends in the world economy. Only coordinated macroeconomic management by the five governments can do that. Specifically, if the dollar is to fall in the medium term, and world demand is to be sustained, the currency-intervention agreement must be followed by fiscal expansions in Germany and Japan. (Monetary expansion would lower the value of these currencies against the dollar and defeat the purpose of the whole exercise.) And since the Fed will not keep lowering U.S. interest rates while the deficit remains so large—both because of its own desire to force the budget down and because financial markets might well interpret such a move as a prelude to another dollar crisis, stemming either from an impending monetization of the deficit or (more likely) from a strengthening of inflation due to expansionary pressures—the U.S. deficit must also be cut severely.[15]

All of these outcomes, however, are certain to be heavily contested. Germany seems likely to mount at least a modest effort to reflate, but this move will be resisted by many German industrialists and bankers, who blame the Bonn summit agreements of the late 1970s for the subsequent rise in the German inflation rate. Neither are the Japanese likely to expand as much as the Administration hopes, though some Japanese officials have cooperated in currency intervention and made some noises about restricting their capital flows to the

United States. The latter would take pressure off the dollar, but because it would cut severely into foreign investment in U.S. financial instruments and penalize precisely those sectors that are most interested in closer U.S.-Japan relations, it will certainly generate powerful opposition in both countries. And whatever the outcome of the struggle, in the long run the Japanese are almost certainly not going to dismantle the regulated financial system and carefully orchestrated schemes for industrial targeting that have helped lift their country from a pile of rubble in 1945 to what now seems likely to be the world's dominant economic power in the next generation. In all probability, despite some cooperation on the currency front, the Japanese will listen carefully to the Administration and talk politely of the importance of mutual understanding. Then, after making a few concessions, they will try to run their export surplus as high as possible.[16]

And if the response of such "allies" is disappointing, then the Administration will have very few cards left to play. In the last months of 1985, after massive organizing efforts and a vast publicity campaign, it finally succeeded in getting Congress to pass legislation mandating a balanced budget by 1991. But while the bill led (briefly) to much rejoicing in financial markets, the White House and its allies in the business community did not succeed in breaking the stalemate that has existed ever since real-estate and other regional interests mobilized in response to the original tax bill in late 1981. Instead of giving the President the sweeping authority he had sought to determine where spending cuts would come from, the Democratic-controlled House forced a compromise that vested administrative responsibility for the cuts in the hands of the Comptroller General. The measure also laid down relatively strict rules for the Comptroller to follow as he apportioned the cuts, which have the effect of distributing them about equally between military and social spending. In a separate action, the House flatly rejected a budget proposed by the White House that would have cut social spending enough to raise military outlays without substantial new taxes.

The Gramm-Rudman-Hollings Act's passage probably tends, on balance, to make a real "Reagan revolution" in domestic policy slightly more likely. But it also creates many new problems for the White House. Because the Pentagon is subject to the cuts, many weapons producers and military planners are strongly critical. Defense Secretary Weinberger and other officials are issuing new warnings about the intentions of the U.S.S.R., and are openly campaigning to disavow the unratified (but informally adhered to) SALT II treaty. Opponents of Gramm-Rudman have also challenged it in court, seeking to have it declared unconstitutional. The D.C. Circuit Court of Appeals has found part of it so, in a decision now pending before the Supreme Court. In the meantime, of course, the first round of cuts mandated by the bill is drawing protests from those affected—both rich and poor.[17]

If the Supreme Court finally declares the bill unconstitutional, or the legislative coalition in favor of the bill cracks under pressure to raise spending ceilings in the next session of Congress, the Administration (and the financial markets) will find themselves back where they were in 1984 in regard to the deficit. While it now appears that the most extreme deficit projections are unlikely to be realized, the deficit will still be enormous. As a result, a truly grave threat to the heart of the Reaganite program—vast increases in military spending with no major new taxes—will still exist.

As we write, it appears that the Administration has not yet abandoned its hope of gaining authority to make the cuts fall almost entirely on domestic spending. In reply to the suit on the bill's constitutionality, the Administration is arguing that the bill is constitutional, but that the delegation of power to the Comptroller is not. If the Supreme Court concurs, the President might acquire the right to make the cuts.

Whatever is decided on the constitutionality question, however, it is unlikely that this or later Administrations can forever put off the question of taxes. Even a constitutional budget-balancing bill may well be revised slightly in later Congresses, especially if the Democrats do well in 1986 or 1988. A severe economic downturn might also compel a temporary suspension of its provisions. Either eventuality would again create pressures to close at least some of the deficit through increased taxes, forcing whatever Administration is then in power to choose between the competing demands of various sectors of big business. Such choices could easily split the GOP apart, which is why the White House has done everything it can to avoid making them since Reagan took office.

At the moment, the overwhelming need to secure revenues at least equal to those raised by current tax laws is snarling the Administration's own tax proposals. Oil and gas interests, working through Vice President Bush and other sympathetic Administration figures, have already forced major revisions in the treatment originally accorded their industries in the proposal. Just as they did before the election, investment bankers, insurance companies, developers, and many other business interests are fiercely resisting proposals to simplify the tax code by eliminating provisions favoring them. Many business interests and citizens groups in areas like the Northeast and Midwest have opposed the President's attempts to abolish the last vestiges of the New Deal in the states by eliminating provisions allowing the deductibility of state and local taxes. And many heavy-manufacturing firms fear that the new proposals would provide the coup de grace in their long fight with foreign competition.

As the President and Congress, especially the Democratic-controlled House, debate the bill, the need to make concessions is causing the bill's original partisans to rethink their support. Congressman Jack Kemp and many supply-siders, for example, have strongly criticized compromise elements of the President's proposals. More tellingly, many multinational and other big businesses that originally backed the bill are reconsidering. At the October 1985 meeting of the Business Council, for example, executives from Exxon, GM, AT&T, Prudential, and other large firms—many of whom had initially welcomed the plan—criticized it.[18]

Backers of many substitute proposals are also quietly mobilizing. A few business leaders are talking up a sales tax, presumably with more of an eye to the future than the present. Support for an oil-import surcharge is also growing. Originally proposed by a coalition of Southwestern oil producers and pro-Israeli groups centered mostly, though not exclusively, in the Democratic Party, this measure has attracted more attention as the full dimensions of recent Saudi oil-pricing policies are appreciated in the West. After trying for some time to persuade other OPEC countries not to undersell, the Saudis moved aggressively to compete by lowering their own prices. This not only immediately raises their own sagging revenues; it also raises the prospect of further steep drops in prices. Because a drop in world oil prices to below $13 a barrel makes at least some of Britain and Norway's huge investments in expensive North Sea oil uncompetitive, and might well topple the Nigerian government, these producers—who have thus far declined to cooperate with the Saudi efforts to maintain the cartel—may begin to fall into line. If they do, then it is possible (if, because of all the other imponderables, such as the Iran–Iraq war and the growth of the spot oil market, scarcely certain) that OPEC would regain some of its market power.[19]

In the very long run, the world might once again face another rise in prices, though the discovery that oil demand was elastic after all, and all the new supplies discovered since OPEC, would tend to restrain future rises. Partisans of an oil tariff argue that by holding the U.S. prices up as the world market declines, U.S. producers will continue to have an incentive to search for domestic oil, substitution away from oil will continue to be encouraged, and the United States will therefore be more secure in the long run.

The oil tariff, however, has powerful opponents. It would block out oil from the Middle East, where some of America's largest oil companies are still lifting, and Mexico, which expects to pay its bank debt by exporting oil to the United States. It would also tend to raise energy prices for domestic manufacturers already in trouble from world economic competition. In addition to these affected interests, some domestic oil interests, fearful that new oil taxes would lead to further government regulation of their industry, are also opposing the proposal.[20]

Yet even if, as we suspect, the Reagan Administration succeeds in cutting domestic spending enough over the next year or so to avoid a large tax rise, while managing to pass a heavily watered-down version of its tax bill, other policy choices confronting it are likely to open deep fissures within the party.

For example, no matter how successful the Administration is at chopping the domestic budget, it cannot possibly hope to fund the Pentagon at the levels needed to completely satisfy many in the defense industry and the Republican Party. By moving toward serious arms-control negotiations with the Soviets, it can open space for significant reductions in military spending and ease pressures for a tax rise. But it will also outrage innumerable businesses, consultants, and even universities tied in with the Pentagon, and will particularly mobilize the affluent, well-organized contractors for the most obviously vulnerable weapons systems—the B-1 bomber, the MX and other missile systems, the grossly distended 600-ship Navy, and, increasingly, the Strategic Defense Initiative.

And every day that the dollar stays high, the tide of imports that is now submerging American industry swells, while exports continue to decline. The continuing trade crisis adds to the protectionist pressures now rising in both parties and contributes to the economic decline of American farmers, who rely heavily on exports. Should protectionist legislation—either in the complex form now being advocated by some neoliberal Democrats, or the across-the-board import surcharge sponsored by Motorola and other concerns, or the "mutual trade" scheme now promoted by Republican Newt Gingrich—pass, all chances that Third World countries can ever succeed in repaying their debt go up in smoke. So, in due course, would the entire multinational trading system built up since the end of World War II.[21]

But, as suggested above, the Administration's attempts to coordinate macroeconomic policy with its allies are already in trouble, and its hopes to stem the rise in protectionism through a new round of GATT negotiations may well be unfounded. Third World countries oppose the U.S. demands to include services (such as banking services) and telecommunications in the negotiations. The French want talks on a new international financial system to come first. Though the Japanese—who badly want a new round themselves, since they will sell most of the goods in it—have worked to narrow differences between the United States and the rest of the world, these differences may be unbridgeable. Assuming the talks are actually held, they are certain to require years, making it difficult to believe they will solve the Reagan Administration's domestic problems. In the event that they do succeed, the protectionist parts of the party are almost certain to rebel, breaking up the fragile compromise that originally helped the Republicans come to power.[22]

And as the trade issue remains unresolved, more and more American industries are likely to press for some response to Japanese "targeting" policies: not only export subsidies and exchange rate changes, but more positive industrial policies reminiscent of those the Democrats experimented with in 1983–84. Because they raise burning questions of competitive rivalry and government subsidies, however, all these initiatives are certain to generate major controversies. Disputes over industrial policy, in addition, will fuel further controversies over interest rates and savings. These will probably revive the campaign, originally triggered by the pressures of high interest rates on industrialists (and particularly many Southwestern oil producers) and agribusiness, for action to restructure the Federal Reserve Board and to place one or more aggressive reflationists (that is, almost certainly, inflationists) on the Fed.

While it struggles with these pressures, the Administration will be wrestling with another dilemma: how to come up with a persuasive rationale for bailing out the international banks, while slowly allowing American farmers to go broke. At the moment, most of American agriculture is in a severe depression. Mortgage foreclosures, rural bank failures, and other signs of oncoming disaster are abundant. The Farm Credit System (FCS) is on the verge of bankruptcy. While the Administration will probably rescue the FCS, grain exporters and most other urban interests are dead set against spending any more money to raise prices of farm products that are already well above world market levels. The Administration and its business supporters also fear that farm relief would bust the budget.

The international debt crisis is a different story. Here the Administration is willing to act, and as observed above, has already made a series of far-ranging new proposals. It is unlikely, however, that Secretary Baker's Seoul initiatives will suffice. Though leading American banks have indicated their willingness to make modest new loans to the Third World, smaller U.S. bankers and some foreign banks (which are less heavily exposed in Latin America, the place where Baker's proposals would have their greatest impact) appear to be dragging their feet. In addition, some powerful U.S. figures—including a handful of corporate executives who run big family-controlled industrial corporations and representatives of some parts of domestic industry that want credit markets to look inward—steadfastly oppose bailing out the banks through the World Bank or other means. And even some analysts with close ties to banks have suggested making Third World countries, rather than U.S. taxpayers, put up the money for the World Bank's multinational insurance fund.[23]

In the face of this resistance, the Administration has moved very cautiously. In the absence of a crisis that would give it leverage, it has not yet indicated just how it plans to relieve the banks of their debts. Hints in speeches by Baker and other Administration figures suggest that the World Bank may end up with many of the bad loans, but this is far from a sure thing. Because the value of the World Bank's outstanding bonds would plunge if it loaded up with uncollectable Third World debts, the Administration and the banks cannot simply use it the way some large banks used specially created subsidiaries to hive off their doubtful real-estate investment trust loans in the early 1970s.

In addition, no matter how the Administration finally rescues the banks, its plans for restarting growth in the Third World will still have to surmount many other obstacles. Though both the banks and the Administration are well aware that Third World regimes are not lemons that can be squeezed indefinitely, they simply cannot afford to throw good money after bad. In addition, the Administration and the multinationals realize that the debt crisis has handed them a historic opportunity to roll back the tide of state-owned enterprise in the Third World and open more of those areas to the multinationals. On both grounds, accordingly, the Administration and the IMF will condition debt relief for the Third World on structural economic changes designed to create a more "liberal" economic climate in those countries.

Inevitably, at least two groups in the Third World will be squeezed severely—the masses of poor and ordinary working people and the indigenous entrepreneurs who in the 1970s sought to challenge the multinationals in their own countries. Inevitably, too, those who are squeezed will try to strike back by commencing revolutionary agitation. And, inevitably, some of these aggrieved groups will welcome aid from whoever will offer it, including the Soviet Union or Cuba. In all probability, the upshot of this will be deeper U.S. involvement in the Third World as the collection agency of last resort. At "best," the United States will provide aid and arms to assist repressive regimes in disciplining their increasingly restive populations. At worst, the 600-ship Navy will pay off as a social investment after all.

While it strives to avoid direct U.S. military intervention, the Administration and the Fed will be attempting something at home which, in its way, is almost as delicate and potentially grave. Given the difficulties facing the Administration's efforts to coordinate macroeconomic policy with the allies, there is no real alternative to Paul Volcker's transforming the United States into the buyer of last resort. That is, to guarantee that the global economy grows (and as much of the debts as possible are paid), the United States will have to buy from the Third World whatever goods the allies will not. This, however, will require higher growth at home, with concomitant risks of inflation. The Administration (along with banks and multinationals worried about the international economy and weak domestic concerns) might bring themselves to accept this, provided that their dollar deposits are protected by simultaneous reductions in European interest rates. But this is certain to meet powerful opposition from bondholders and companies concerned about domestic U.S. wage growth. If it occured too rapidly and for too long, moreover, it might lead to another huge dollar outflow and another "corrective" rise in interest rates.[24]

With so many pitfalls facing them, there is little reason to believe the Republicans will succeed in consolidating themselves, as the Democrats did in the days of the New Deal, as the overwhelmingly dominant party in America. Though as long as America's right turn defines the new political system the Republicans are likely at the national level to enjoy a sort of "elective affinity" with the dominant trends of American culture, the party itself is likely to splinter. At a minimum, one might anticipate the distance between "moderates" and the "right" to grow more distinct. Increasingly dissatisfied with the moderates' desire to compromise on the budget, taxation, and U.S.–Soviet relations, as well as their desire to maintain free trade, protectionists like Helms and the most hawkish internationalists are likely to emphasize the incomplete character of the "Reagan revolution." In using the President's name as a banner for their cause, these new Jacobins will not be deterred by the fact that many of them were sharply critical of Reagan even during his first term or by the fact that some of their number even talked of denying him renomination. They will, however, be handicapped in their advance by the slide in commodity prices, especially the decline in oil prices. As the wealth of many of their major donors declines as abruptly as it rose in the 1970s, conservative publicists and evangelists may face a balanced-budget crisis of their own.[25]

Some, no doubt, will react in innovative ways—perhaps by attaching themselves more closely to South Africa or finding a new niche in the moderate evangelical center. (Pat Robertson, the noted TV evangelist and son of a former U.S. senator, who is considering seeking the GOP Presidential nomination in 1988, is currently being advised by a committed supporter of George Bush.) Others may seek to differentiate their messages by moving further to the right.[26]

Meanwhile, what might be termed the "multinational middle" of the GOP is likely to consolidate its grip on foreign and economic policy in the Administration. Even within this group, however, the money-supply and interest-rate questions, as well as regulation and trade issues, are likely to divide its members. As we write, only Congressman Jack Kemp has put forward any new proposals that seem to have any hope of bridging some of the differences among the warring business sectors. In a striking move away from his earlier espousal of a quick return to the gold standard, Kemp has recently joined neo-liberal Democratic congressman Richard Gephardt (who is also thinking of running for President) in a proposal for a new monetary conference. Because it promises to control swings in interest and exchange rates, the idea of such a conference is potentially attractive to many industrialists, and because it might provide additional support for a soft landing for the dollar, it has at least some support from international financiers as well. With Kemp continuing to advocate free trade (in contrast to many of his followers, such as Gingrich), his identification with the money question might perhaps bring about an otherwise improbable alliance between supply-siders and the multinational financiers who would otherwise be expected to prefer Bush or Baker.

But not even a whole wave of innovative proposals would suffice to paper over the real differences of interest within the GOP. Instead, as Bush, Baker, Kemp, Dole, Pierre Du Pont, and other Republican Presidential hopefuls cut each other up in the primaries, some parts of the business community—particularly the capital-intensive sectors that can afford to live with labor—are likely to roll over to the Democrats, and the new American party system's center of gravity may shift very slightly.

On the Democratic side, interested parties will assiduously fan impressions that a wholesale reversal of policy trends during the Reagan years is in prospect. Absent a major renewal of mass politics, however, this is most unlikely. The Democrats could, after all, put forward a broad popular program of manifest appeal and general benefit. They could mobilize those vast reaches of the electorate (poorer, younger, blacker than the rest) who now abstain from voting altogether. The reason they do not do this is not because they do not know how, but because they do not want to. And they do not want to because such a mobilization would require that the people mobilized actually be offered something, and elite Democrats have very little that they want to give. While they would like to defeat the Republicans, they are not about to subsidize a broad popular coalition inimical to their own economic interests.

As a consequence, the "exciting new Democratic ideas" that the mass media will be heralding over the next few years are unlikely to include full employment, protection of employee rights through the spread (and revitalization) of unions, reestablishment of unemployment insurance coverage, or any of the well-argued proposals for more ambitious economic reform put forward by Democratic analysts in recent years. Instead, the Democrats will put forward plans which may suggest or connote those proposals but in fact attend quite traditional concerns of the party's elite constituencies. Put simply, if the burning issue is growth—to restart the world economy, to pay off debts, to fight protectionism, or whatever—the Democrats do have some natural advantage over the Republicans. Even quite modest rates of economic growth, if sustained for very long, are highly likely to bring a rise in wages. Accordingly, if the Fed and the multinationals seriously intend to run the economy closer to full employment, they are almost certain to come face to face with the problem that bedeviled Carter in 1977–78, before Volcker took over—how to restrain wages. Like Carter, various Democratic policy analysts will probably experiment with a variety of proposals to achieve this, including various tax-incentive-based programs of wage-price control, schemes to improve labor mobility, and any number of plans for compensating "social investment." The Democrats have a natural advantage over the Republicans in the implementation of such a program, because its success requires the cooperation of labor and organized labor still remains overwhelmingly with the Democrats.

While debate over this narrow range of political alternatives continues, and the Democrats, like the GOP, fight over protection and military spending, they will generally move down the path trod by Mondale in the last stage of his campaign and attempt to put together a coalition of business interests (including, perhaps, some of the high-tech industries that must respond to the Japanese challenge and that are hurt by the high dollar), professionals, and other upper-income Americans who cannot accept Republican policies. In the late 1980s, as parts of the South are devastated by imports, and the slide in agriculture, oil, and other commodity prices threatens to ruin large parts of the West, the Democrats may discover that the constituency for state intervention is considerably larger than it was in 1984. Coupled with the readiness of Southern Democrats—contrary to common revisionist claims—to elect blacks and women to major public offices (as happened in the fall of 1985 in Charles Robb's own Virginia), and even mayors who support gay rights (as happened in Houston), this appeal could help the party. Because it will still probably offer somewhat more to average people than what the Republicans are likely to offer, and because so many powerful business constituencies are likely to get behind it, the party could easily succeed in electing a Democratic President in 1988 or 1992.[27]

Merely changing the party that occupies the White House, however, will not reverse the current drift of U.S. public policy. By itself it will not put millions back to work, or produce a more intelligent and humane response to foreign competition, or revive the progressive income tax. By itself, surely, it will not secure a fuller democratization of American life—the basic popular promise of the New Deal. And it will hardly ensure the promotion of independent organizations, or subsidies to participation, or public funding of the electoral process, or a serious effort to reach and involve the nonvoting electorate, or any of the essential moves that such a democratic renewal would require.

Absent a sudden upsurge from below, or until economic catastrophe forces a new alignment of American business elites, the new, more conservative party system will be maintained. Democrats and Republicans will squabble and maneuver. The costs to the population will rise. But the basic structure of the party system will remain unchanged. America will continue its right turn.

Appendix /
A Note on Campaign Finance
and Its Statistical Analysis

This study relies at many points on evidence derived from the analysis of campaign contributions. Because the contribution data are so important to our argument, we use this Appendix to explain how we analyzed them.

Like everyone else who writes about American elections, we have some familiarity with, and certain definite views about, the identity of the major actors in U.S. business and politics. Accordingly, we track the campaign activities of as many of these people as we can through newspapers and magazines, campaign finance data, and any other means that promises useful information. Such information has been used at many points in this study.

From a social-scientific viewpoint, however, such procedures—though common in law, historical studies, and even most contemporary political science—inevitably raise suspicion. Put directly: Why are we confident that the patterns of coalition formation among large investors that we identify as pivotal to election outcomes reflect real movements among investor blocs, and not simply our impressionistic judgment of newspaper coverage, or a selective sampling of those names we happen to recognize in the FEC's mountains of data on campaign contributions?

Responding to this question requires reference to two sorts of methodological considerations. The first is general and theoretical, and goes to the heart of the "investment theory" of political parties that informs this essay: Why concentrate on large investors? How do we recognize them? In what sense do they define party systems? And so on. The issues involved here are complicated, and this is not the place to attempt a full and systematic consideration of them. Still, the essential points of the investment approach can be summarized simply and nontechnically. The issues of a political campaign are conceived as defining a multidimensional space. Different investors occupy various positions in that space, and they back candidates whose issue positions are close to their own.[1]

In the data analysis for this book, our aim was to follow as closely as possible (so that our results could be directly compared) the operationalization of the original "New Deal" coalition of the 1930s presented in earlier work by Ferguson. But we also sought to take advantage of the much better data on investors and campaign contributions that are available of the 1980s. This brings us to the second, and more mundane, methodological consideration: What data did we obtain from the FEC and other sources, and how did we work them over?[2]

For the present study we obtained a microfilm copy of the FEC's vast alphabetical list of individual contributions to races for the Presidency, Congress, and the Senate. This list covers certain other contributions as well, such as contributions to groups like the National Congressional Club. Advertised as being complete from January 1983 through December 1984, it also included the handful of 1982 contributions to the campaign organizations of some Democratic candidates who started early. We supplemented (and checked) this "master file" with separate computer printouts from the FEC which recorded individual contributions to the (national) Committee for the Future of America, the PAC that preceded Mondale's formally organized campaign committee; the PAC (rather than individual) contributions to all major party candidates that took them; and individual contributions to all the major Democratic candidates discussed in the text, Askew and Hollings, and the many Republican campaign committees.

We then prepared a list of "major investors" whose contributions we wished to examine systematically.

First, all members of the Forbes 400 for 1984 were placed on it. In a few cases, this called for some delicate judgments. The Forbes list includes a number of families as well as individuals. For the former, we tried to identify the senior member(s) of the family that appeared to control investments; in cases where children were actively involved with a parent on the list, we took note of the young member's campaign contribution as well. In a very few cases, we could not identify anyone; in those cases we made no assignment. [3]

Next, we added to this list the top officers (identified in standard business directories) of the top 150 industrials on the Fortune 500 list for 1984 (ranked according to assets). Because the *Fortune* industrials would be a quite inadequate index to the rest of the economy, we added into our sample the top officers of leading firms in the "service" sector. These included the top officer(s) of the thirteen largest banks, ten largest utilities, and eight largest life insurance companies (all ranked by assets), and the seven largest transportation companies (ranked by operating revenues). [4]

The number of "top officers" sampled varied with firm size. Because the investment approach to analyzing parties lays great emphasis on the pressures that bear on the very largest investors, for the ten largest industrials, the three largest banks, and the two largest insurance companies we analyzed contributions by at least three high officials in each firm. In most cases, we analyzed the contributions of the two top officials of the firm and (because of the pivotal role played in negotiations with government) the general counsel, if he or she served also as a director. If the general counsel was not a director, we went to the third-highest-ranking official. In the few cases of ties in rank between two officials, we took both; if the firm is known to have an active controlling owner, we checked on him or her as well. For the other firms noted above, we sampled only the top officer. [5]

Finally, because none of these methods yields much insight into "Wall Street," we inventoried the top twenty investment banks, as ranked by *Institutional Investor* for 1984. Because some of these firms are partnerships, and many are highly secretive (some flatly refused to identify their leadership for us), delicate judgment again had to be made. Where firms published a list of "managing partners" or a chair with a hierarchically structured bureaucracy and board, we took the managing partners, or the four highest-ranking partners. In a few cases where we could with confidence identify the leading partners (e.g., Michel David-Weil and Felix Rohatyn at Lazard) we put them into the sample; otherwise we took the first four names off an alphabetical list of partners. [6]

One can always quibble with sampling procedures, the coverage of particular sectors, and other details. The really important question, however, is whether adoption of reasonable alternative procedures would make any difference to the results. In 1983–84, the answer to that question is clear. Outside of a handful of sectors—notably investment banking, real estate, insurance, and some multinationals—comparatively few major investors contributed anything to the Democratic Party. Often the numbers of those who did are too small even to permit statistical tests.

For industries that did have an appreciable number of Democratic contributors, however, we ran statistical tests of the industry's difference from all other investors in our sample. Because we do not believe that the legally restricted contributions reported by the FEC yield very much useful information on the actual quantity of resources expended, we treated the data as though it simply signaled a preference for holding at least some Democrats within a portfolio of politicians that might also include some Republicans, and used x^2 tests on 2 × 2 contingency tables, with the group to be analyzed separated from the rest of the sample. We compared industries to all other investors first with regard to their general support for Democrats, then for their support for liberal Democrats (Cranston, Hart, McGovern, Mondale); conservative Democrats (Askew, Glenn, Hollings); and willingness to support *both* liberal and conservative Democrats.[7]

Needless to say, aggregating firms at the level of sectors risks concealing important intra-sectoral differences (just as aggregating in terms of size may distract attention from important differences between sectors) vis-à-vis the major parties. In the case of the insurance industry, which instanced several prominent Democrats (with a straightforward interpretation discussed in our text), the small number of cases, and some special problems of data interpretation, made statistical testing meaningless. For the industries that had significant results, however, the significance levels are indicated in the Appendix Table.

This statistical analysis provides strong support for several parts of our argument. The .01's in the table tell us that there is less than one chance in a hundred that the differences between the industry and our sample are due to chance. In other words, as the text claims, real-estate developers and investment banks are disproportionately Democratic compared to all investors, and disproportionately willing to support liberal Democrats. They do not, however, differ substan-

APPENDIX TABLE
Industry Support for the Democrats

Compared to All Investors

Group (Number of Cases)	Support for Democrats	Liberal Democrats	Conservative Democrats	Both Liberal and Conservative Democrats
Realtors/developers	52%*	45%*	13%	6%
(71)	(37)	(32)	(9)	(4)
Investment bankers	36*	32*	18	14*
(111)	(40)	(35)	(20)	(15)
Top 30 multination-als	27	·15	17	6
(52)	(14)	(8)	(9)	(3)
Rest of top 150	18†	10*	18	10
(121)	(22)	(12)	(22)	(12)
All top 150	21	12	18	9
(173)	(36)	(20)	(31)	(15)
Total investors	26%	18%	13%	6%
(781)	(199)	(143)	(103)	(47)

Compared to All 199 Democratic Investors

	Support for Liberal Democrats	Support for Conservative Democrats
Realtors/developers	86%‡	24%*
Investment bankers	88†	50
All Democratic investors	72	52

*Statistically significant at at least the .01 level.
†Significant at at least the .05 level.
‡Significant at at least the .06 level.

tially from all investors in their willingness to support conservative Democrats alone. That is, as we have also argued, conservative Democrats attract not only these sectors but others.

The figures for the top 150 firms have a potentially interesting interpretation. As discussed in our text, a considerable number of these firms contributed important support to the Democrats during the New Deal era. More recently, however, most have abandoned the Democratic Party. Hoping to pick up possible sectoral (and other) differences within this bloc, we ran separate tests for differences (in the percentage offering support to various Democratic candidates in the 1984 election) between the top 150 firms (which are mostly multinationals) and all other investors, between the top 30 firms and all other investors, and between the next 120 firms and all others. (We also separately analyzed the oil companies among the top 150 firms. Their ranks include a considerable number of national or independent petroleum producers that are huge by comparison with the rest of U.S. industry, but small by comparison with the multinational giants—comparing them to all other investors.) As our table indicates, significant differences emerged only for the 120 firms below the top 30 multinationals; these 120 were noticeably less likely than all other investors to back Democrats. (Since the results for the oil companies were not significant, they have been deleted from the table.) In our view, this supports the claims in our text regarding the general position of the multinationals and the oil industry vis-à-vis the Democratic Party today. Given that the top 30 firms tend to be the most capital intensive and multinationally oriented of all these firms, however, it seems likely that within the multinational bloc itself there remain vestiges of the old tie to the Democrats, at least in the sense that the probability of supporting a Democrat still appears to increase with capital intensity and orientation to an open world economy.[8]

Our argument also suggests that this pattern of differentiated support by different industries contributed importantly to the final outcome of the primaries. Between primary candidates, at least in most cases, the comparatively small number of observations makes statistical tests for industry differences impossible. One must rely on economic theory and information about specific candidates or investors to carry the argument. We were, however, able to test the most important hypothesis explored in the text for the eventual Mondale victory over Glenn and the more conservative Democrats—that the powerful real-estate bloc in the party, with its strong interest in regional economic aid, could not afford to embrace a candidate so solidly committed to increasing military expenditures. That hypothesis was born out. Compared not to *all* investors, but to all *Democratic* investors, real-estate developer unwillingness to support conservative Democrats was indeed significant at the .01 level. That is, the "liberalism" of the real-estate bloc is no mirage. Also compared to all Democratic investors, investment bankers were also significantly more willing to back liberal Democrats. To conclude our data analysis, then, investment bankers and real-estate developers were disproportionately Democratic, as our text insists. And the real-estate element of the party cannot afford conservative Democrats, which is a major reason Glenn lost, and turmoil over the deficit and the arms race continues.

Notes

Revisionist Democrats

1. *Washington Post*, 28 November 1984. Our discussion of the meeting is based on the *Post* article and an interview with one of the participants.

[To prevent the text from becoming hopelessly cluttered, subsequent references will be grouped together in longer footnotes at the end of paragraphs.]

2. Ibid.

3. Ibid.

4. On the CDM forum and the Babbitt and Robb speeches, see *New York Times*, 29 November 1984; *Washington Post*, 29 November 1984; and *Washington Times*, 3 December 1984. On the Phoenix 40, see David Altheide, *Creating Reality* (Beverly Hills: SAGE, 1976), 188–89; and Peter Wiley and Robert Gottlieb, *Empires in the Sun* (New York: G. P. Putnam, 1982), 174. Information on Babbitt's ties to the Phoenix 40 came from a telephone interview with Donald Devereux, a veteran journalist in the Phoenix metropolitan area, 5 October 1985. Devereux notes that Babbitt's relations with the 40 have a complicated history and have recently shown signs of strain.

5. Typical of press reaction to the CDM forum were the comments of Morton Kondracke, an executive editor of *The New Republic* (whose owner, Martin Peretz, has long been associated with the Coalition for a Democratic Majority), who hailed the instructive qualities of Babbitt's speech: "School should begin right away, with all the prospective 1988 presidential nominees as the class." See *Washington Times*, 3 December 1984.

For Huntington's analysis of the Democrats, see Samuel P. Huntington, "The Visions of the Democratic Party," *The Public Interest* 79 (Spring 1985): 63–78. For one important statement of his views on the Vietnam War, which includes an argument for strategies of "forced urbanization" of peasants there, see Huntington, "The Bases of Accommodation," *Foreign Affairs* 46 (July 1968): 642–56. For his contribution to the Trilateral Commission's "Report on the Governability of Democracies," see Michel Crozier, Samuel P. Huntington, and Joji Watanuki. *The Crisis of Democracy* (New York: New York University Press, 1975), 59–118.

6. Huntington, "Visions," 65.

7. Ibid., 65.

8. Ibid., 67.

9. Ibid., 71.

10. For the quoted remarks, see "Visions," 77. The recommendation on the 1988 Democratic ticket is at 78.

11. *Christian Science Monitor*, 26 December 1984. For Scaife's subsidy to *The Public Interest*, see John S. Saloma III, *Ominous Politics* (New York: Hill and Wang, 1984), 34; and Thomas Byrne Edsall, *The New Politics of Inequality* (New York: W. W. Norton, 1984), 120.

12. *New York Times*, 30 January 1985.

13. For the quotes from Nunn and the Kirk supporter, see *New York Times*, 1 March 1985. For the goals of the Democratic Policy Commission, see *New York Times*, 16 May 1985.

14. Quoted in *Time*, 19 November 1984, 65. Strauss's assertion is the only direct evidence for this claim offered, for example, by Huntington. See his "Visions," 75.

15. For the Kirk and Biden quotations see *Wall Street Journal*, 15 August 1985.

16. For the seminal characterization of this basic opinion structure, see Lloyd A. Free and Hadley Cantril, *The Political Beliefs of Americans* (New Brunswick, NJ: Rutgers University Press, 1967). The suggestion that the view reflects adaptation to a nonsocialist interventionist state is made in Walter Dean Burnham, "American Politics in the 1980s," *Dissent*, 27 (Spring 1980): 151.

17. For a useful survey of tendencies in public opinion during the postwar era, which notes the leveling off in increasing liberalism after 1973, see Tom W. Smith, "Atop a Liberal Plateau? A Summary of Trends Since World War II," *Research in Urban Policy* 1 (1985): 245–57.

18. Versions of this argument have been around a long time. See, for example, Norman H. Nie, Sidney Verba, and John R. Petrocik, *The Changing American Voter* (Cambridge: Harvard University Press, 1976), 192: "In the New Deal era, citizens cast issue votes in relation to those domestic economic issues for which the New Deal stood. By the fifties those issues faded." For a more recent invocation of the argument, see William A. Galston, "The Future of the Democratic Party," *The Brookings Review* 3 (Winter 1985): 16–24. Galston was Walter Mondale's issues adviser in the 1984 campaign.

19. Throughout this paragraph we have drawn on Stanley Kelley, Jr., "The New Deal Party System, 1952–1985" (Paper presented to the Seminar on Democracy and the Welfare State, Princeton University, 10 October 1985).

20. For a compilation of major polls on regulation, on which we draw in constructing Table 1.1, see Robert Y. Shapiro and John M. Gilroy, "The Polls: Regulation—Part I," *Public Opinion Quarterly* 48 (1984): 531–42; idem, "The Polls: Regulation—Part II," *Public Opinion Quarterly* 48 (1984): 666–77.

21. The NORC survey results are reported in Seymour Martin Lipset, "The Economy, Elections, and Public Opinion," *The Tocqueville Review* 5 (Fall–Winter 1983): 446.

22. All data in this and the preceding paragraph are from Lipset, "The Economy, Elections," 444–49.

23. For the lack of support for domestic spending cuts in early 1985, see *Washington Post*, 20 January 1985. The quote is from CBS News/*New York Times* poll, "Post-Election Poll, November 8–14, 1984," 4; cited in Seymour Martin Lipset, "The Elections, the Economy and Public Opinion: 1984," *PS* 18 (Winter 1985): 29–30.

24. *New York Times*, 27 January 1986.

25. All data from Lipset, "The Elections, the Economy," 30, with the exception of the "abortion on demand" result. That comes from a 18–20 January 1985 ABC News poll, reported in ABC News/*Washington Post* poll, "Reagan's Ratings High: GOP and Dems at Parity on Party Identification."

26. For the Harris report of increasing support for affirmative-action programs, see *Boston Globe*, 14 October 1985. Note again, as the text indicates, that this support does not extend to rigid quota systems.

27. See the discussion in Smith, "Atop a Liberal Plateau?"

28. The Harris results in this and the preceding paragraph are reported in Everett Carll Ladd, Jr. (with Marilyn Potter, Linda Basilick, Sally Daniels, and Dana Suszkiw), "The Polls: Taxing and Spending," *Public Opinion Quarterly* 43 (Spring 1979): 127–28. The H. & R. Block survey is reported in John F. Witte, *The Politics and Development of the Federal Income Tax* (Madison: University of Wisconsin Press, 1985), 342. For the trade-off data, see *Changing Public Attitudes on Government and Taxes* (Washington DC: Advisory Commission on Intergovernmental Relations, 1981), 12, cited in Witte, 363. For the low salience of the issue, despite increasing burdens for the average family, see Everett Carll Ladd, "Tax Attitudes," *Public*

Opinion 8 (February–March 1985): 8. For the declining progressivity of the tax system, see Joseph A. Pechman, *Who Paid the Taxes, 1966–85?* (Washington DC: The Brookings Institution, 1985).

29. The January 1985 reading is from an ABC News/*Washington Post* poll, cited in "Opinion Roundup: Tax Americana," *Public Opinion* 8 (February–March 1985): 23.

30. The Gallup figures are reported in Lipset, "The Economy, Elections," 450. Other polls show increased support for military spending peaking earlier, in 1980.

31. See polls reported in *Public Opinion*, 7 (April–May 1984): 36.

32. On press views and their relation to public assessments of military spending, see David P. Fan, "Defense Spending 1977–84: Influence of the Media on Public Opinion" (Unpublished manuscript, University of Minnesota). Fan's data come from a computer-assisted analysis of Associated Press dispatches, which on this issue are probably a good indicator of the general climate. He shows that changes in public opinion closely follow ("correlate" well with) prior changes in mass-media coverage.

33. All data in this paragraph reported in Lipset, "The Economy, Elections," 451; Lipset also draws the analogy between 1983 attitudes and early 1970s attitudes.

34. Data from Lipset, "The Economy, Elections," 454–55.

35. Quoted in *New York Times*, 24 January 1985; cited in Lipset, "The Elections, the Economy," 30.

36. Data from Lipset, "The Economy, Elections," 453; *Gallup Report* 220–221 (January–February 1984): 14.

37. All data in this paragraph are from Caribbean Basin Information Project, *On a Short Fuse: Militarization in Central America* (Washington, DC: Caribbean Basin Information Project, 1985), Section 5.

38. Daniel Yankelovich and John Doble, "The Public Mood: Nuclear Weapons and the U.S.S.R.," *Foreign Affairs* 63 (Fall 1984): 44–45; the "live and let live" summary of American attitudes is at 44.

39. All data in this and the preceding two paragraphs come from Yankelovich and Doble, "The Public Mood," 33–46.

40. All data in this paragraph from the Gallup Poll, various issues, and were confirmed by the authors in an interview with the Gallup Organization, 11 October 1985.

41. All figures from the Gallup Poll, various issues.

42. See the careful treatment in D. Roderick Kiewiet and Douglas Rivers, "The Economic Basis of Reagan's Appeal," in *The New Direction in American Politics*, ed. John E. Chubb and Paul E. Peterson (Washington, DC: The Brookings Institution, 1985), 69–90.

43. ABC News poll, "49-State Landslide More Than Personal Victory for Reagan," 3.

44. The ABC News/*Washington Post* poll which is the source for Table 1.3 is reported in Thomas E. Cronin, "The Presidential Election of 1984," in *Election 84: Landslide Without a Mandate?*, ed. Ellis Sandoz and Cecil V. Crabb, Jr. (New York: New American Library, 1985), 58. Readers will note that one row in the table sums to slightly more than 100%; those figures are in the original source. The figure on the percentage of voters identifying Reagan's conservatism as something that mattered to them comes from a CBS News/*New York Times* poll, reported in the *New York Times*, 11 November 1984; the figure on only 5 percent agreement comes from a Yankelovich poll reported in Walter Dean Burnham, "The 1984 Election and the Future of American Politics," in *Election 84*, 237.

45. The literature on the 1980 election is now too large to permit discussion of individual books and papers. For the conclusion of "dealignment," however, see Walter Dean Burnham, "The 1980 Earthquake: Realignment, Reaction, or What?," in *The Hidden Election*, ed. Thomas Ferguson and Joel Rogers (New York: Pantheon, 1981), 98–140. On the lack of a "mandate" for Reagan, see, in particular, Arthur H. Miller and Martin P. Wattenberg, "Throwing the Rascals Out: Policy and Performance Evaluations of Presidential Candidates, 1952–80," *American Political Science Review* 79 (June 1985): 359–72; and James M. Enelow and Melvin J. Hinich, "Estimating the Importance of Issues: An Empirical Analysis of the 1980 American Presidential Election Based on the Spatial Theory of Voting" (Unpublished manuscript, October 1984).

For other studies of the 1980 election, see W. E. Miller and J. M. Shanks, "Policy Directions and Presidential Leadership: Alternative Interpretations of the 1980 Presidential Election," *British Journal of Political Science* 12 (1982): 266–356; Douglas A. Hibbs, "President Reagan's Mandate from the 1980 Elections," *American Politics Quarterly* 10 (1982): 387–420; Paul R. Abramson, John H. Aldrich, and David W. Rhode, *Change and Continuity in the 1980 Elections* (Washington, DC: Congressional Quarterly Press, 1982); Austin Ranney, ed., *The American Elections of 1980* (Washington, DC: American Enterprise Institute, 1981); Ellis Sandoz and Cecil V. Crabb, Jr., eds., *A Tide of Discontent: The 1980 Elections and Their Meaning* (Washington, DC: Congressional Quarterly Press, 1981); Gerald M. Pomper, ed., *The Election of 1980: Reports and Interpretations*; and Ferguson and Rogers, *The Hidden Election*.

On dealignment in 1984, see Burnham, "The 1984 Election," 204–60; and David W. Brady and Patricia A. Hurley, "The Prospects for Contemporary Partisan Realignment," *PS* 18 (Winter 1985): 63–68, as well as the discussion below.

46. For notice of the increasingly Republican Electoral College, see Everett Carll Ladd, "As the Realignment Turns: A Drama in Many Acts," *Public Opinion* 7 (December–January 1985): 2–7. We are less impressed with the string of Republican victories since 1968 than many observers. The 1968 victory, of course, was a squeaker, and three of the others (1972, 1980, 1984) were special cases. On 1972, it is enough to note that the party's nominee, McGovern, was sharply opposed within the party, as well as massively attacked outside it. On the peculiarities of 1980 and 1984, see the discussion below.

47. Democratic losses in the House will rise to fifteen seats if Republicans are successful in their fight over Indiana's 8th District, now the subject of lengthy recount proceedings.

Ferejohn and Fiorina note that Republican gains in the Senate in 1980 were potentially misleading, at least if taken as evidence of sweeping realignment. Many of the Democratic senators who lost office then had already shown themselves to be weak candidates, winning with very slim margins in 1974—a bad year to be a Republican. See John A. Ferejohn and Morris P. Fiorina, "Incumbency and Realignment in Congressional Elections," in Chubb and Peterson, *The New Direction*, 103–4.

48. All data in this paragraph from Burnham, "The 1984 Election," and idem, *Democracy in the Making: American Government and Politics*, 2nd ed. (Englewood Cliffs, N.J.: Prentice-Hall, 1986), 306.

49. For the GOP swing in House elections over 1982–84, see Ladd, "As the Realignment Turns," 7. Harkin ran 10 points ahead of the Democratic national ticket, and Simon ran 8 points ahead; see *New York Times*, 8 November 1984. For all other data in this and the preceding paragraph, see Burnham, "The 1984 Election." Note that the denominator on voter participation used here is the potential electorate, and not the more commonly used voting-age population (VAP). The VAP includes aliens and convicted felons, who cannot vote, while excluding Americans living abroad, who can.

A useful review of congressional elections in the 1980s, which also concludes that any "realigning" forces, if they exist, have not yet had an impact on congressional elections, is provided in Ferejohn and Fiorina, "Incumbency and Realignment," 91–115.

50. Among the other surveys reporting a rough parity between Republican and Democratic identifiers in late 1984 were the ABC News/*Washington Post* exit poll, the CBS News/*New York Times* exit poll, and the University of Michigan's 1984 National Election Study.

51. All data except the August 1985 reading from *Gallup Report* 220–221 (January–February 1984): 31; August 1985 results reported in *New York Times*, 30 August 1985.

52. All data but the fourth quarter 1984 reading on party identification from *Gallup Report* 228–229 (August–September 1984): 33; fourth quarter 1984 data, also from Gallup, reported in Kelley, "The New Deal Party System."

53. This paragraph draws heavily on Kelley, "The New Deal Party System."

54. The results on split-ticket voting are from Gallup, and are reported in Ladd, "As the Realignment Turns," 6–7. The congressional-district splits are noted in Ferejohn and Fiorina, "Incumbency and Realignment," 100. The literature on the declining significance of parties as intermediaries in voting decisions is huge. For a useful recent study, see Martin P. Wattenberg, *The Decline of American Political Parties, 1952–1980* (Cambridge, MA: Harvard University Press, 1984).

55. On the trends in party identification among young voters in the 1920s, see Thomas Ferguson, "Elites and Elections, or What Have They Done to You Lately? Toward an Investment Theory of Political Parties and Critical Realignments," in *Do Elections Matter?*, ed. Benjamin Ginsberg and Alan Stone (Armonk, NY: M. E. Sharpe, 1986).

56. For the Republican fiasco in converting Democrats, see *Time*, 2 September 1985, 23.

57. The literature on the close relation between economic performance and voter approval is vast. See, among other sources, the contributions in *Contemporary Political Economy*, ed. Douglas A. Hibbs, Jr., Heino Fassbender, and R. Douglas Rivers (Amsterdam: North Holland, 1981), and *Economic Conditions and Electoral Outcomes: The United States and Western Europe*, ed. Heinz Eulau and Michael S. Lewis-Beck (New York: Agathon, 1985), and references cited therein. The "prediction" of a 59.4 percent Reagan share of the two-party vote is derived from Edward Tufte's familiar two independent variable regression equation; see the calculations in Burnham, "The 1984 Election," 255–56. See as well Steven J. Rosenstone, *Forecasting Presidential Elections* (New Haven: Yale University Press, 1983); idem, "Explaining the 1984 Presidential Election," *The Brookings Review* 3 (Winter 1985): 25–32. For a review of the accuracy of different forecasts in 1984, including several forecasting models relying heavily on economic performance, see Michael S. Lewis-Beck, "Election Forecasts in 1984: How Accurate Were They?," *PS* 18 (Winter 1985): 53–62. Note that the relevant voter evaluations of economic performance need not only be retrospective; they can also include an evaluation of future performance. See, for example, Michael S. Lewis-Beck, "Economics and the American Voter: Past, Present, Future" (Paper prepared for delivery at the 1985 Annual Meeting of the American Political Science Association, New Orleans, 29 August–1 September 1985). Some analysts have questioned the magnitude (not the existence) of economic-performance effects on voting. See D. Roderick Kiewiet, *Macroeconomics and Micropolitics* (Chicago: University of Chicago Press, 1983). Of course, judgments of magnitude can vary, depending on the election. See Kiewiet and Rivers, "Economic Basis."

58. Data in this and the preceding two paragraphs from Kelley, "The New Deal Party System."

59. For claims about the centrality of the mass media as a causal factor in recent U.S. political revels, see, among others, Sidney Blumenthal, *The Permanent Campaign* (New York: Simon & Schuster, 1982), and Burnham, "The 1984 Election." For the religious right, see, among others, J. K. Hadden and Charles E. Swann, *Prime Time Preachers* (Reading, MA: Addison-Wesley, 1981), as well as the discussion of the comparative significance of religion in American political life in Burnham, "The 1980 Earthquake," 132–40. For the growing importance of business organizations, see Edsall, *New Politics*. Among the many recent studies of U.S. economic decline, see Frank Ackerman, *Hazardous to Our Wealth: Economic Policies in the 1980s* (Boston: South End Press, 1984); Gar Alperovitz and Jeff Faux, *Rebuilding America* (New York: Pantheon, 1983); Samuel Bowles, David M. Gordon, and Thomas E. Weisskopf, *Beyond the Wasteland: A Democratic Alternative to Economic Decline* (Garden City, NY: Anchor, 1984); Barry Bluestone and Bennett Harrison, *The Deindustrialization of America: Plant Closings, Community Abandonment, and the Dismantling of Basic Industry* (New York: Basic Books, 1982); Joshua Cohen and Joel Rogers, *On Democracy* (New York: Penguin Books, 1983); Mike Davis, "The Political Economy of Late-Imperial America," *New Left Review* 143 (January–February 1984), 6–38; idem, "Reaganomics' Magical Mystery Tour," *New Left Review* 149 (January–February 1985), 45–65; Kenneth M. Dolbeare, *Democracy at Risk: The Politics of Economic Renewal* (Chatham, NJ: Chatham House, 1984); Otto Eckstein, Christopher Caton, Roger Brinner, and Peter Duprey, *The DRI Report on U.S. Manufacturing Industries* (New York: McGraw-Hill, 1984); Martin Feldstein, ed., *The American Economy in Transition* (Chicago: University of Chicago Press, 1980); Robert H. Hayes and Steven C. Wheelwright, *Restoring Our Competitive Edge: Competing Through Manufacturing* (New York: John Wiley, 1984); Robert Z. Lawrence, *Can America Compete?* (Washington, DC: The Brookings Institution, 1984); Robert Lekachman, *Greed Is Not Enough: Reaganomics* (New York: Pantheon, 1982); Ira C. Magaziner and Robert B. Reich, *Minding America's Business: The Decline and Rise of the American Economy* (New York: Harcourt Brace Jovanovich, 1982); S. M. Miller and Donald Tomaskovic-Devey, *Recapitalizing America: Alternatives to the Corporate Distortion of National Policy* (Boston: Routledge & Kegan Paul, 1983); Kevin P. Phillips, *Staying on Top: The Business Case for a National Industrial Policy* (New York: Random House, 1984); Michael J. Piore and Charles F. Sabel, *The Second Industrial Divide: Possibilities for Prosperity* (New York: Basic Books, 1984); Bruce R. Scott and George C. Lodge, eds., *U.S. Competitiveness in the World Economy* (Boston: Harvard Business School Press, 1985); Robert B. Reich, *The Next American Frontier* (New York: Times Books, 1983); Stephen Rousseas, *The Political Economy of Reaganomics: A Critique* (Armonk, NY: M. E. Sharpe, 1982); Lester C. Thurow, *The Zero-Sum Society:*

Distribution and the Possibilities for Economic Change (New York: Basic Books, 1980); idem, *The Zero-Sum Solution: Building a World-Class American Economy* (New York: Simon & Schuster, 1985); and Alan Wolfe, *America's Impasse: The Rise and Fall of the Politics of Growth* (New York: Pantheon, 1981). Last but hardly least, see Paul Sweezy and Harry Magdoff's regular "Review of the Month" editorials on this subject in *Monthly Review.*

60. The literature on the New Deal is now gigantic and the subject of specialized bibliographies. On the New Deal and the business community generally (excluding many case studies of particular policies), see Ellis Hawley, *The New Deal and the Problem of Monopoly* (Princeton: Princeton University Press, 1962); idem, "The Discovery and Study of a 'Corporate Liberalism,' " *Business History Review* 52 (1978): 309–20; Thomas Ferguson, "From Normalcy to New Deal: Industrial Structure, Party Competition and American Public Policy in the Great Depression," *International Organization* 38 (1984); 41–94; Kim McQuaid, *Big Business and Presidential Power* (New York: William Morrow, 1982); Barton Bernstein, "The New Deal: The Conservative Achievements of Liberal Reform," in *Toward a New Past: Dissenting Essays in American History,* ed. Barton Bernstein (New York: Pantheon, 1968); Ronald Radosh, "The Myth of the New Deal," in *A New History of Leviathan,* ed. Ronald Radosh and Murray N. Rothbard (New York: Dutton, 1972), 146–86; H. A. Winkler, ed., *Die grosse Krise in Amerika* (Göttingen: Vandenhoech & Ruprecht, 1973); Murray Rothbard, "Herbert Hoover and the Myth of Laissez Faire," in *A New History,* 111–45; Gabriel Kolko, *Main Currents of American History* (New York: Harper & Row, 1976); Peter Gourevitch, "Breaking with Orthodoxy," *International Organization* 38 (1984): 95–130; Lloyd Gardner, *Economic Aspects of New Deal Diplomacy* (Boston: Beacon Press, 1964); and Robert Collins, *Business Response to Keynes* (New York: Columbia University Press, 1981). See as well the discussions of the New Deal in Philip Burch, *Elites in American History,* Vol. III (New York: Holmes & Meier, 1980); and G. William Domhoff, *The Higher Circles: The Governing Class in America* (New York: Random House, 1970).

2/The Life of the Party: From the New Deal to Nixon

1. The literature on party realignments is enormous. The seminal statements were made by V. O. Key. See his "A Theory of Critical Elections," *Journal of Politics* 17 (February 1955): 3–18. For a bibliography of important subsequent works by Walter Dean Burnham, James Sundquist, David Brady, Gerald Pomper, and many others, see Bruce A. Campbell and Richard J. Trilling, eds., *Realignment in American Politics: Toward a Theory* (Austin: University of Texas Press, 1980), 329–32. The somewhat stylized summary of the literature here is of course no substitute for direct acquaintance with this work.

Note that one could support revisionist Democratic policy positions without making any particular claim about the nature of political change in America. But the realignment perspective quite clearly informs the current discussion about "new coalitions" within the Democratic Party and the challenge Reagan's success is said to pose to the party.

2. Walter Dean Burnham, *Critical Elections and the Mainsprings of American Politics* (New York: W. W. Norton, 1970), 10.

3. Recent criticisms of realignment theory include Alan J. Lichtman, "Critical Election Theory and the Reality of American Presidential Politics, 1916–1940," *American Historical Review* 81 (April 1976): 317–48; idem, "Critical Elections in Historical Perspective," California Institute of Technology Working Paper 420; Jerome M. Clubb, William H. Flanigan, and Nancy H. Zingale, *Partisan Realignment: Voters, Parties, and Government in American History* (Beverly Hills: Sage, 1980); J. Morgan Kousser, "History QUASHED: Quantitative Social Scientific History in Perspective," *American Behavioral Scientist* 23 (July–August 1980); 885–904; Richard L. McCormick, "The Realignment Synthesis in American History," *Journal of Interdisciplinary History* 13 (Summer 1982): 85–105; Lee Benson, Joel Silbey, and Phyllis Field, "Toward a Theory of Stability and Change in American Voting Patterns: New York State, 1872–1970," in *The History of American Electoral Behavior,* ed. Joel Silbey, Allen Bogue, William H. Flanigan (Princeton: Princeton University Press, 1978); and Ferguson, "Elites and Elections."

Following the lead of the so-called Michigan School of election analysis, most realignment theorists have understood individual voting primarily in social-psychological terms. On such a view, which is now being modified or supplanted by "rational choice" and other accounts which emphasize the cognitive aspect of voting, voters' party identifications normally change only slowly, since they result largely from nonrational or arational group-socialization processes. Most critical-realignment theorists then explained changes in the long-run partisan balance that they believed occurred during realignments in terms of the dramatic effects high-stimulus, issue-oriented campaigns have on voters' party identifications. Essentially a "landslide" theory of wholesale "conversion" (or perhaps the sudden mobilization of previously unaffiliated nonvoters), this view of political change virtually requires that all levels of elections move similarly, for if voters are able to discriminate carefully between parties at different levels of government, they can hardly be experiencing overpowering "conversion effects." In emphasizing the differences in results at different levels of government, more recent research thus raises questions about the whole underlying mechanism of realignment. Newer "rational choice" models of voting, which emphasize the instrumental character of voter motivation, do not suffer from this drawback. But it is no accident that many analysts deploying such "economic" theories of voting behavior are skeptical of the realignment literature.

4. See, for example, the analysis in Lichtman, "Critical Elections in Historical Perspective," and Ferguson, "Elites and Elections."

5. See, for example, Clubb, Flanigan, and Zingale, *Partisan Realignment*, in particular chapters 2 and 3.

6. Clubb, Flanigan, and Zingale, *Partisan Realignment*, 119.

7. See the discussion in McCormick, "Realignment Synthesis"; Martin Shefter, "Bureaucracy, and Political Change in the United States," in *Political Parties: Development and Decay*, ed. L. Maisel and J. Cooper (Beverly Hills: Sage, 1978), 211–66; Benjamin Ginsberg, *The Consequences of Consent* (Reading, MA: Addison-Wesley, 1982); and Ferguson, "Elites and Elections."

8. Thomas Ferguson, "Party Realignment and American Industrial Structure: The Investment Theory of Political Parties in Historical Perspective," in *Research in Political Economy* 6, ed. Paul Zarembka (Greenwich, CT: JAI Press, 1983), 1–82. This innocent-sounding formulation, however, conceals a host of methodological problems that have to be faced squarely if the "investment" approach to the analysis of political coalitions is not ultimately to become as porous as electoral versions of realignment theory. Who, or what, for example, qualify as "major" investors? How does one identify them, and why should they receive disproportionate attention (particularly in recent years, with the development of at least some legal limitations on contributions)? How can the existence or stability of various political coalitions be established? Such questions are particularly important for this study, because the answers guide our analysis (discussed in more detail below, in the Appendix) of data from the Federal Election Commission. For reasons of space, however, they cannot be discussed here; interested readers are referred to Section 3 of "Party Realignment and American Industrial Structure," which outlines the justification for the methods adopted in this study. See as well our Appendix, below.

9. A number of analysts have observed the formidable barriers in cost, time, and information scarcity that face ordinary voters when they attempt to control the state, and have identified these, in varying degrees, as potentially undermining democratic control of policymaking. At several points in his classic *An Economic Theory of Democracy* (New York: Harper & Row, 1957), for example, Anthony Downs clearly indicated that information costs might by themselves render voters incapable of controlling policy. Following his work, and the discussion of the "logic of collective action" by Mancur Olson in his *The Logic of Collective Action: Public Goods and the Theory of Groups* (Cambridge: Harvard University Press, 1965), skepticism has grown appreciably. See, for example, Randall Bartlett, *Economic Foundations of Political Power* (New York: The Free Press, 1973); Charles Lindblom, *Politics and Markets: The World's Political-Economic Systems* (New York: Basic Books, 1977), and Cohen and Rogers, *On Democracy*, chapter 3.

Though most representatives of "public choice" tend, when challenged, to defend some version of "electoral sovereignty," skepticism about voter control does surface occasionally in that literature's treatment of "fiscal illusions" and related topics. See, for example, Peter Aranson and Peter Ordeshook, "Alternative Theories of the Growth of Government and Their Implications for Constitutional Tax and Spending Limits," in *Tax and Expenditure Limitations*, ed. H. F. Ladd and T. N. Tideman (Washington, DC: Urban Institute Press, 1981), 143–76.

Other notable recent work that either expresses or implies at least some skepticism about the strength of the "electoral connection" includes Ginsberg, *Consequences of Consent*; Shefter, "Party, Bureaucracy, and Political Change"; Benjamin I. Page, *Choices and Echoes in Presidential Elections: Rational Man and Electoral Democracy* (Chicago: University of Chicago Press, 1978); Roger Benjamin and Raymond Duvall, "The Capitalist State in Context," in *The Democratic State*, ed. Roger Benjamin and Stephen L. Elkin (Lawrence, KA: University Press of Kansas, 1985), 19–58; and, especially for the discussion of the "System of 1896," Burnham, *Critical Elections*; and idem, "The Appearance and Disappearance of the American Voter," in *The Political Economy: Readings in the Politics and Economics of American Public Policy*, ed. Thomas Ferguson and Joel Rogers (Armonk, NY: M. E. Sharpe, 1984), 112–39. The last essay, along with Samuel Popkin, John Gorman, Charles Phillips, and Jeffrey Smith, "What Have You Done for Me Lately? Toward an Investment Theory of Voting," *American Political Science Review* 70 (September 1976): 779–805, offers a useful analysis of how the federal structure of the American state and other factors add further to voters' costs. For other aspects of "American exceptionalism," see the review by Burnham, "The United States: The Politics of Heterogeneity," in *Electoral Behavior: A Comparative Handbook*, ed. Richard Rose (New York: The Free Press, 1974), 653–725. Finally, for discussion of a cost of political action in the United States that is commonly overlooked, see Robert Justin Goldstein, *Political Repression in Modern America* (New York: Shenkman, 1978).

10. See Ferguson, "Party Realignment," 66 and following, for discussion of this formulation; and see Appendix below.

11. See Ferguson, *Critical Realignment: The Fall of the House of Morgan and the Origins of the New Deal* (New York: Oxford University Press, forthcoming); idem, "From Normalcy to New Deal." Our discussion of the New Deal here draws heavily on that article and material collected for the book.

12. Raymond Moley, *Diary*, 13 June 1936, cited in Ferguson, "Normalcy," 68.

13. This language of "broadly supported" is carefully chosen, but could be misleading. Different parts of this package aroused different levels of enthusiasm from various parts of the business community. For a detailed discussion of most of these bills, see Ferguson, "Normalcy," 86–90. See as well the discussion in Burch, *Elites*, 42–45; Domhoff, *Higher Circles*, 212–16 and 234–44; McQuaid, *Big Business*; and Collins, *Business Response*.

More immediately, the use of the term "support" in this study follows that in Ferguson, "Investment Theory," 23 and following. In this view, investors hold politicians (and, often, political commentators) quite like they hold stocks. There is therefore nothing necessarily contradictory in an investor's taking positions in both parties. The point, however, is that it almost never pays most investors to take equal positions in both parties, any more than it would pay most major investors to take equal positions in all stocks. Speaking strictly, then, our description of firms or prominent individual investors as "Democratic" means only that these firms or individuals extended substantial support to the Democrats; it does not imply that they never rendered important aid to the Republicans. See also the discussion of the methods we used to analyze campaign finance in the Appendix, below.

14. The data on union growth are from the Bureau of Labor Statistics, *Handbook of Labor Statistics*, *December 1980* (Bulletin 2070) (Washington, DC: GPO, 1980), Table 165. The investment, productivity, disposable personal income, median family income, and postwar unemployment data are from *Economic Report of the President*, *1985* (hereinafter *ER*) (Washington, DC: GPO, 1985), Tables B-2, B-40, B-24, B-27, and B-33, respectively. The 1920–39 unemployment data are from U.S. Bureau of the Census, *Historical Statistics of the United States, Colonial Times to 1970* (Washington, DC: GPO, 1975), series D-86.

15. On the trade figure, see Ernest Mandel, *Late Capitalism*, trans. Joris De Bres (London: New Left Books, 1975), 142. On the expansion of U.S. banking, see generally U.S. Senate, Foreign Relations Committee, Subcommittee on Foreign Economic Policy Staff Report, *International Debt, the Banks, and U.S. Foreign Policy* (Washington, DC: GPO, 1977).

16. The full history of this coalition remains to be written. See, however, *Prospect for America: The Rockefeller Panel Reports* (Garden City, NY: Doubleday, 1961), especially Report IV. Here is how they described what the conclusion of the book referred to (at 331) as their "New Frontiers":

As set forth in other sections of this report, we shall need, in the next decade, a greatly expanded school system to broaden and improve education. We shall need urban redevelopment on a vast scale to lift the living standards and the social and cultural content of metropolitan life. We shall need more and better highways and improved modes of transportation to spur commerce, communication, and travel. We shall need better water supply and pollution control systems to meet domestic, industrial, and agricultural requirements. We shall need more health and hospital facilities, more basic and applied research, more recreation areas. The list is extensive and, as the final section of this report sets forth, estimates indicate an increase of almost 50 percent in government purchases of goods and services by 1967. [279–81.]

See as well E. Ray Canterbery, *Economics on a New Frontier* (Belmont, CA: Wadsworth, 1968), especially chapters 1–5.

17. The multinational orientation of Kennedy's and Johnson's top federal appointees and advisers is evident from the data gathered in Burch, *Elites*, chapter 5, and the tables at 451–62. An excellent analysis of the role multinational business and finance played in formulating the Kennedy Administration's major economic policies is offered by Canterbery, *Economics*, chapters 5–6. For Ford, Rockefeller, and the tax cut, see Burch, *Elites*, 188–89, among other sources. On the "supply side" aspects of the tax cut, see Ronald King, "From Redistribution to Hegemonic Logic: The Transformation of American Tax Politics, 1894–1963," *Politics and Society* 12 (1981): 46–48. The general features of the Kennedy tax bills noted here are from Pechman, *Who Paid*, 63. For a discussion of some of the congressional politicking around the bills, see Witte, *Politics and Development*, 155–65.

18. A full-length analysis of the Goldwater candidacy is still not available, although several interesting studies are in preparation. For Goldwater's business supporters, see *Business Week*, 1 August 1964, 19–20; *Wall Street Journal*, 31 May 1966; *New York Times*, 10 October 1971; and Philip Burch, Jr., "The NAM as an Interest Group," *Politics and Society* 4 (Fall 1973): 118–21. For the import clause in the party platform, see *National Party Platforms 1840–1968*, compiled by K. H. Porter and D. B. Johnson (Urbana: University of Illinois Press, 1970), 685. Sectors promised relief included textiles, oil, glass, coal, lumber, steel, and beef.

19. For the foundations and the black movement in the early 1960s, see Mark Stern, "The Contemporary Black Suffrage Movement and the Public Policy Agenda" (Paper presented at the 1985 annual meeting of the American Political Science Association, New Orleans, 29 August–1 September 1985), especially 28–29. This paper also demonstrates that top officials in the Administration hoped to slow the movement down, but that neither the base nor the foundations were receptive (see 27–31). The estimate on the number of Southern protests and arrestees in 1963 is from the Southern Regional Council, and is reported in Manning Marable, *Black American Politics: From the Washington Marches to Jesse Jackson* (London: Verso, 1985), 90. The identification of the Democrats with the cause of civil rights was strengthened, of course, by Kennedy's campaigning in 1960, including such famous gestures as his phone call to Mrs. Martin Luther King at a time when her husband was imprisoned. Nixon's unwillingness to match this appeal certainly cost the Republicans most of whatever credit they had gained among blacks as a result of the Eisenhower Administration's interventions in the South.

20. On the tax exemption, see Stern, "The Contemporary Black Suffrage Movement." Some interesting contrasts between the role of lawyers in the civil-rights movement and the present are drawn in the letters pages of the *New York Times*, 20 October 1985, Section 4. For governmental efforts to crush similar movements in the past, see Goldstein, *Political Repression*.

21. For a partial, but very impressive, list of Johnson's multinational campaign supporters, see *New York Times*, 4 September 1964. This includes many of the greatest names in American business, including Henry Ford II, Thomas S. Lamont, Edgar Kaiser, Sidney Weinberg, Norton Simon, Paul Cabot, John Loeb, Marion Folsom, Robert B. Anderson, and Robert Lehman. See also the discussion in Burch, *Elites*, 192–210. Note also that while some of these figures had supported Eisenhower (or Nelson Rockefeller), many had longtime relations with the Democrats. Weinberg, for example, appears to have raised more money for Roosevelt in 1936 than any other single person. (Compare again the list of 1936 supporters in Ferguson, "Normalcy," 89–92.) For the multinational orientation of the major media, see the boards of directors of

the various broadcasting companies, as listed in Standard and Poor's *Directory* for the early 1960s. For the foundations and multinational businesses, see the discussion in Joseph Goulden, *The Moneygivers* (New York: Random House, 1971), chapter 8.

22. For a useful summary of the Kennedy Round, see Thomas Bradford Curtis, *The Kennedy Round and the Future of American Trade* (New York: Praeger, 1967).

23. The "welfare shift" is discussed in Huntington, "The United States," 68–70. For the increase in military spending, see Executive Office of the President, Office of Management and Budget, *Historical Tables: Budget of the United States Government, Fiscal Year 1986* (Washington, DC: GPO, 1985) (hereinafter *HT*), Table 6.1

Given the proliferation of explanations of military spending centered on its economic function, it may be worth emphasizing that the willingness to use military force as an instrument of U.S. foreign policy was unrivaled during the Kennedy–Johnson years. Over the 1963–64 period, for example, before the Dominican invasion, or the major escalation of U.S. efforts in Vietnam, U.S. military power was deployed on the average of once every nineteen days. See Barry M. Blechman and Steven S. Kaplan, *Force Without War* (Washington, DC: The Brookings Institution, 1978), Appendix B.

24. *ER*, Tables B-33 and B-39.

25. *HT*, Table 3.1.

26. A few friendly critics of our earlier essay on the 1980 election ("The Reagan Victory: Corporate Coalitions in the 1980 Campaign," in Ferguson and Rogers, *The Hidden Election*, 3–64) misconstrued our discussion to imply that the crucial factor in Reagan's victory was the support of a new power bloc of U.S. business from the South and West. Thus Fred Halliday (*The Making of the Second Cold War* [London, Verso, 1983], 108, n. 3) comments: "Whilst their focus on such elite coalitions may be unduly monist, they are right to see Reagan as having won the support of a new grouping in US business." On the contrary, our claim in both *The Hidden Election* and this study is that major firms that previously supported the Democrats heavily have switched or tapered off their support. Because the "center" has pulled out of a coalition with the "left" and allied with "right" groups that it once considered beyond the pale, new groups (and new personnel) have entered both the government and the dominant business alignment. The "center," however, remains (tensely) in power, and the far "right" does not dominate, although its influence has vastly increased. See also the various critical discussions of Kirkpatrick Sale's *Power Shift* (New York: Random House, 1975), especially that of Burch, *Elites*, 231–35.

27. David Rockefeller, "International Monetary Reform and the New York Banking Community," in *World Monetary Reform*, ed. H. G. Grubel (Stanford: Stanford University Press, 1963), 150–59.

28. For Meyer's encouragement of Kennedy, see Arthur Schlesinger, *Robert Kennedy and His Times* (Boston: Houghton Mifflin, 1978), 787. For McCarthy's campaign, see Herbert Alexander, *Financing the 1968 Election* (Lexington, MA: D. C. Heath, 1971), 50–51. For general business opposition to the conduct of the war, see David Halberstam, *The Best and the Brightest* (New York: Random House, 1969), 653; Thomas R. Dye, "Oligarchic Tendencies in National Policy-Making: The Role of the Private-Policy Planning Organizations," *Journal of Politics* (May 1978), 316–17; and idem, *Who's Running America* (4th ed.; Englewood Cliffs, NJ: Prentice-Hall, 1986), 249. Subsequent right-wing attacks on *The Washington Post* (owned by the Graham family, which at the time was probably the dominant voice in Allied Chemical), *The New York Times*, and other media concerns that became increasingly critical of the war obscure the dimensions of establishment disaffection from the war, while of course removing such disaffection from any understandable context.

29. For the oil producers' swing to Nixon, see Jack Anderson (with James Boyd), *Fiasco* (New York: Times Books, 1983), 30 and following. Anderson and Boyd ascribe the swing solely to Humphrey's old views on the oil-depreciation allowance. For some Texas firms, this may have played a role, though we suspect a close study of the Humphrey effort in 1968 will show little commitment to that issue by the candidate. It is clear, however, that many American supporters of Israel strongly backed Humphrey (see, for example, the list in Burch, *Elites*, 230); that the upcoming British withdrawal from east of Suez was scrambling the strategic situation in the Middle East; and that Nixon was signaling his strong rejection of any "isolationist"

tendencies (see, for example, Richard Nixon, "Asia After Vietnam," *Foreign Affairs* 46 [October 1967]: 111–25).

30. On the rise in real wages in the late 1960s relative to productivity increases, see Michael Bruno and Jeffrey Sachs, *The Economics of World Wide Stagflation* (Oxford: Basil Blackwell, 1984), 167 and following. Our assessment of the general business view on late 1960s wage "correction" comes from the business press of the period, and is supported by Nixon's behavior once in office. While Nixon did tighten the economy after his election, pushing the economy into recession in 1969, and producing −0.2 percent growth in GNP in 1970, he soon stimulated it again. See the discussion below.

31. For partial but quite formidable lists of multinational business figures who supported Humphrey or some other Democrat in 1968, see the striking discussion in *Finance*, July 1968, 12; *New York Times*, 28 October 1968; and Burch, *Elites*, 284, n. 7.

The need to explain changes in the business community's policy views is logically prior to discussions about its changing organization. Absent such an explanation, it is impossible to draw any conclusions about the partisan and policy significance of either increased business organization or tightening networks of corporate "inner circles." Thus, while we would not quarrel with the claims about the dense nature of corporate interlocks advanced by Michael Useem in his very suggestive *The Inner Circle* (New York: Oxford University Press, 1984), or with much of the careful and illuminating analysis of Edsall's *New Politics* (which at several points parallels our own earlier essay in *The Hidden Election*), we would not accept either as an adequate explanation for America's right turn. Both encourage the view (which is explicit in Edsall) that big business is monolithic and normally Republican, while the Democrats be analyzed mainly in demographic or electoral terms; both works also scarcely mention foreign policy, or even the pressures the international economy puts on domestic actors. Such an approach obscures the dynamics of the two main U.S. political parties, which are crucially influenced by rivalries *within* big business and by conditions in the world economy. Compare our discussion below, in chapters 3–6.

32. For representative statements of the TV hypothesis, see Sidney Blumenthal, *The Permanent Campaign* (New York: Simon & Schuster, 1982); and Edsall, *New Politics*, 34 and 94–99. For TV households, see U.S. Department of Commerce, Bureau of the Census, *Statistical Abstract of the United States 1985* (105th ed.; Washington, D.C.: GPO, 1985), 542.

33. See, for example, Thomas E. Weisskopf, "Marxian Crisis Theory and the Rate of Profit in the Post-War U.S. Economy," *Cambridge Journal of Economics* 3 (1979): 341–78.

34. Unions typically seek to consolidate their positions in organized shops by bargaining for "union security" clauses in their contracts with employers; these typically condition continuing employment in those shops on union membership (if a worker wants to continue working in the shop, he or she must join the union). Hence the expression "union shop." Section 14(b) of Taft-Hartley permits state legislatures to pass "right to work" laws prohibiting such arrangements. For an assessment of the impact of such laws on union organizing, see David Ellwood and Glenn Fine, "Impact of Right-to-Work Laws on Union Organizing," National Bureau of Economic Research Working Paper No. 1116, Cambridge, May 1983.

35. On the Labor Law Study Group's early history and membership, see Haynes Johnson and Nick Kotz, *The Unions* (New York: Pocket Books, 1972), 112–29. For a brief discussion of the maneuverings around 14(b), see Graham K. Wilson, *Unions in American National Politics* (London: Macmillan Press, 1979), 102–6. For the rise of the Construction Users Anti-Inflation Roundtable and its gradual metamorphosis into the Business Roundtable, see Thomas Ferguson and Joel Rogers, "The Knights of the Roundtable," *The Nation*, 15 December 1979, 620–25. For a general discussion of the legal constraints on union power in the United States, see Joel Rogers, *Divide and Conquer: The Legal Foundations of Postwar U.S. Labor Policy* (Unpublished PhD dissertation, Princeton University, 1984).

36. For declining expenditures on organizing per nonunion worker, see Paula Voos, *Labor Union Organizing Programs 1954–1977* (Unpublished PhD dissertation, Harvard University, 1982), cited in Richard B. Freeman and James L. Medoff, *What Do Unions Do?* (New York: Basic Books, 1984), 229. Freeman and Medoff use Voos's data to conclude that "as much of a third of the decline in union success through NLRB elections is linked to reduced organizing activity" (229). We should note that Voos herself, however, contests

this interpretation. See Paula B. Voos, "Trends in Union Organizing Expenditures, 1953–1977," *Industrie and Labor Relations Review* 38 (October 1984): 52–63; the calculations reported in our text are from her data as reported there. The percentage of private nonagricultural wage and salary workers organized through NLRB elections is calculated from *NLRB Annual Report* (Washington, DC: GPO), various issues, and *ER*, Table B-37. For the organized percentage of the work force during the 1970–80 period, see Courtney D. Gifford, ed., *Directory of U.S. Labor Organizations*, 1984–85 edition (Washington, DC: Bureau of National Affairs, 1985), 2. For the absolute private-sector loss over the 1969–79 period, see AFL–CIO Department of Research, *Union Membership and Employment 1959–1979*, February 1980, I-19.

37. The Meany quote appears in *U.S. News & World Report*, 21 February 1972, 28; cited in Edsall, *New Politics*, 151.

38. There is an enormous literature on organized labor's relation to black workers. For a good historical overview, see Philip S. Foner, *Organized Labor and the Black Worker 1619–1981* (New York: International Publishers, 1981); for treatment of some of the disputes between organized labor and radical black worker organizations, see James A. Geschwender, *Class, Race, and Worker Insurgency* (Cambridge: Cambridge University Press, 1977). Labor's relations with the women's movement have been less carefully explored. See, however, James J. Kenneally, *Women and American Trade Unions* (Montreal: Eden Press Women's Publications, 1981); Philip S. Foner, *Women and the American Labor Movement from World War I to the Present* (New York: The Free Press, 1980); and Ruth Milkman, ed., *Women, Work, and Protest: A Century of U.S. Women's Labor History* (Boston: Routledge Kegan Paul, 1985). For two views of labor's relations with the environmental movement, the first more optimistic than the second, see Richard Kazis and Richard L. Grossman, *Fear at Work: Job Blackmail, Labor and the Environment* (New York: Pilgrim Press, 1982); and Richard Grossman, "Environmentalists and the Labor Movement," *Socialist Review* 81–82 (July–October 1985): 63–87. We should note that, especially in its early days, the environmental movement received some support from at least some unions.

39. For the role of foundations in subsidizing black, women, and Hispanic organizations, see J. Craig Jenkins, *Patrons of Social Reform* (forthcoming). For a striking case study of how such funding affected the organizations' development, see the discussion of the Ford Foundation in Karen O'Connor and Lee Epstein, "A Legal Voice for the Chicano Community: The Activities of the Mexican American Legal Defense and Educational Fund, 1968–82," *Social Science Quarterly* 65 (June 1984): 245–56.

40. For the role of the AIFLD in Central and South American affairs, see Bill Felice, John Frappier, and Nancy Stein, "Boss and Bureaucrat," *Latin America and Empire Report*, May 1977; Michael J. Sussman, "AIFLD: U.S. Trojan Horse in Latin America and the Caribbean" (Washington, DC: EPICA, 1983); William Bollinger, "The AFL–CIO in Latin America: Documents and Analysis on the American Institute for Free Labor Development (AIFLD)" (Los Angeles: Interamerican Research Center, 1984); Hobart A. Spalding, Jr., *Organized Labor in Latin America: Historical Case Studies of Urban Workers in Dependent Societies* (New York: Harper & Row, 1977), 264–75. See Sussman, 7, for both the Meany quote and the list of corporate members of AIFLD.

41. The data on gross receipts is from *HT*, Table 2.2; the effective rates of payroll taxes is from Pechman, *Who Paid?*, 77 and 79. Note that we use Variant 1c, the most progressive, of Pechman's different incidence assumptions. On Variant 3c, the least progressive, the rise was less dramatic but the effective rates were higher.

42. The literature on the design of the Great Society's programs is vast, but much of it passes by the most important points. A really adequate account of how these programs came to be designed the way they were will no doubt need to take account of the enormous amount of material at the LBJ Library at the University of Texas, as well as the many advisory commissions that honeycombed the Administration, and the political and business ties of the members of the various congressional committees that produced the enabling legislation. Still, for helpful discussions, see Benjamin Page, *Who Gets What from Government?* (Berkeley: University of California Press, 1983), chapter 3; John Mollenkopf, *The Contested City* (Princeton: Princeton University Press, 1983), chapter 2; and Joe R. Feagin, Charles Tilly, and Constance Williams, *Subsidizing the Poor* (Lexington, MA: D. C. Heath, 1972), 52 and following. For the crime programs, see Richard Quinney, *Critique of Legal Order* (Boston: Little, Brown, 1974), chapters 3 and 4. For the medical programs,

see, among other discussions, Paul Starr, *The Transformation of American Medicine* (New York: Basic Books, 1982); and especially E. Richard Brown, *Rockefeller Medicine Men* (Berkeley: University of California Press, 1979), particularly chapter 5.

See also the general discussion of the Johnson Administration in Burch, *Elites*, chapter 5; and Frances Fox Piven and Richard A. Cloward, *Regulating the Poor* (New York: Pantheon, 1971), chapter 9. With sponsors like these, the emphasis on "policy mistakes" and the dashing of "good intentions" characteristic of the ever-growing literature on "implementation" is potentially misleading.

43. See, for example, Kevin Phillips, *The Emerging Republican Majority* (New Rochelle, NY: Arlington House, 1970).

44. See the careful analysis in Burch, *Elites*, chapter 6, which also includes discussion of the individuals we mention. For Nixon's textile commitment, see I. M. Destler, Haruhiro Fukui, and Hideo Sato, *The Textile Wrangle* (Ithaca: Cornell University Press, 1979), 68–69. After getting the nomination, Nixon confirmed this commitment in writing. Hubert Humphrey, meanwhile, made much weaker noises about the problem. Like many Democrats before him, and Carter later, he would probably have been unwilling to sacrifice relations with Japan to demands of national industry. For the Humphrey position, see *Wrangle*, 70.

45. On the Administration's revenue-sharing programs and their effect on traditional funding, particularly in the cities, see the discussion in Mollenkopf, *Contested City*, 122–35; and Dennis R. Judd and Francis N. Koppel, "The Search for National Urban Policy: From Kennedy to Carter," in *Nationalizing Government: Public Policies in America*, ed. Theodore J. Lowi and Alan Stone (Beverly Hills: Sage, 1978), 163–200. On Shultz's encouragement of building tensions between black and white workers, see John Ehrlichman, *Witness to Power* (New York: Simon & Schuster, 1982), 228–29. On LEAA funding, see Quinney, *Critique*, 108 and following; and Benjamin Ginsberg, "Controlling Crime: The Limits of Deterrence," in Lowi and Stone, *Nationalizing Government*, 341–57. On the many different programs of domestic espionage and spying, see Frank Donner, *The Age of Surveillance: The Aims and Methods of America's Political Intelligence System* (New York: Alfred A. Knopf, 1980).

46. On the substantial continuity between the Johnson and Nixon Administrations, see the essays in Lowi and Stone, *Nationalizing Government*. On the general rise in social spending, see *HT*, Table 6.1. On social security, see the summary of Nixon Administration changes in Paul Craig Roberts, *The Supply Side Revolution: An Insider's Account of Policymaking in Washington* (Cambridge: Harvard University Press, 1984), 260–62. On the family-assistance plan, see J. Vincent and Vee Burke, *Nixon's Good Deed* (New York: Columbia University Press, 1974).

47. On the terms of trade and wage rises, see Bruno and Sachs, *World Wide Stagflation*, chapter 6.

48. For Dunlop, Kirkland, and their Caribbean investments, see the discussion in "Lane's Friends," *The Nation*, 19 January 1980, 37–38.

49. Even the example of unsafe working conditions is not completely clear-cut. Large establishments with few employees and/or safe working conditions, for example, may well support such legislation, which will throw further costs on their smaller competition.

50. See Friedrich Engels, *The Condition of the Working Class in England in 1844*, trans. F. K. Wischnewetzky (London: George Allen and Unwin, 1952), 276–77. This study also powerfully makes a point that our discussion is not intended to dispute—that many forms of environmental pollution fall hardest on the poor.

51. For the OCAW support, see Charles Noble, *Liberalism at Work: The Rise and Fall of OSHA* (Philadelphia: Temple University Press, 1986); for the makers of catalytic converters, see Bernard Asbell, "The Outlawing of Next Year's Cars," *New York Times Magazine*, 21 November 1976, 128–31; for the "snail darter" and Southern Railway, see Kathleen Kemp, "Industrial Structure, Party Competition and the Sources of Regulation," in Ferguson and Rogers, *The Political Economy*, 105; for the Eastern coal producers, see Robert W. Crandall, "Air Pollution, Environmentalism, and the Coal Lobby," in *The Political Economy of Deregulation*, ed. Roger Noll and Bruce Owen (Washington, DC: American Enterprise Institute, 1983), 84–96; for the insurers and the air bag, see, among other sources, *New York Times*, 9 January 1985. For the regional struggles and the use of environmental legislation to slow down capital migration, see Peter B. Pashigian, *The Political Economy of the Clean Air Act: Regional Self-Interest in Environmental Legislation*,

Washington University, Center for the Study of American Business, Publication No. 51, October 1982.

52. The association of many multinational lawyers and financiers with organizations like the Natural Resources Defense Council suggests the problems with those analyses of the environmental movement, such as that offered by Pashigian, that write off the impact made by organizations that really are interested in the environment, and not simply, say, slowing down capital mobility from declining regions. See Pashigian, *Clean Air Act*, 1.

As part of the research for this section of our work we filed requests under the Freedom of Information Act for copies of IRS Form 990 (Return of Organization Exempt from Income Tax) and the original request for tax-exempt status filed by as many different environmental organizations as we could identify. We also attempted to secure copies of each organization's annual reports. But while most of the organizations cooperated readily, the Treasury Department did not, and its dilatory tactics have prevented us from offering a systematic statistical overview of the environmental movement here. Still, enough information has come through to justify the generalization in the text.

Consider first the Natural Resources Defense Council. One of the most important and aggressive of all the environmental organizations, the Council has been involved in many of the most controversial, highly publicized lawsuits and environmental campaigns. According to materials filed with its application for tax-exempt status, the organization was founded in 1970, just before the first wave of environmental legislation crested in the Nixon Administration's first term. Laurance Rockefeller helped incorporate it, and served as a trustee. The other trustees included Stephen P. Duggan, partner in the prestigious Wall Street law firm of Simpson, Thatcher & Bartlett (which includes among its other partners Cyrus Vance), and many members of wealthy, socially prominent families, including J. Willard Roosevelt and Adele Auchincloss. The powerful elite backing the Council continues to command today is evident from its board, which still includes not only Rockefeller but also international lawyers with law firms whose major clients are New York City's most powerful banks; leading foundation executives; and other top corporate personnel.

Another major center of environmental litigation and research, the Environmental Defense Fund, shows similar patterns of support. Founded in 1967 by a mixed group of scientists and lawyers considerably less prominent than the founding members of the NRDC, the EDF is now chaired by the president of the German Marshall Fund of the United States (which contributes major support to National Public Radio and the free-trade-oriented Center for International Economics). Its board includes Harry Havemeyer and many prominent lawyers, including a member of the famous New York corporate firm of Davis, Polk & Wardwell, who is also a member of the American Bar Association's Environmental Section. The EDF now spends more than $3 million a year and receives extensive support from leading foundations.

The board of the World Wildlife Fund–U.S., an organization that now spends, according to its annual report, more than $7 million a year, includes many prominent multinational business figures, including not a few whose names might well strike fear into the hearts of the world's wildlife. Among the most prominent are Robert McNamara, Citibank's John S. Reed (a self-declared Democrat), Elliot Richardson, Godfrey Rockefeller, Alexander Trowbridge (a Democrat, currently president of the National Association of Manufacturers, and formerly of Allied Chemical), Revlon chairman Michel Bergerac, and Otis Chandler, chair of Times Mirror.

The Conservation Foundation, which spends some $2 million a year, includes on its board of trustees Thornton Bradshaw, president of RCA (which owns NBC); Walter Hoadley, former chief economist for Bank of America, and now a fellow at the Hoover Institute; developer James Rouse; and Atlantic Richfield president William F. Kieschnick.

We regret that we lack the space to discuss the ties between these and other environmental groups and the mass media, which are far more extensive even than indicated by the lists of trustees here; to discuss the differences between these organizations and other groups, such as the Sierra Club, in their strategies and their responses to Reagan and the anti-nuclear movement, discussed below; or to trace the revealing implications of cases like that of David Browder, who in the 1960s led a dissident faction out of the Sierra Club to form Friends of the Earth.

But the data here are enough, in our view, to indicate why it is no particular mystery that in the 1980s environmental concerns have come to dominate even "radical" political activist movements, why a number of prominent environmental groups—including the NRDC—have now added free trade to their list of concerns, and why, as discussed below, some actively support a certain type of anti-nuclear movement.

Finally, all students of the relation between American multinational elites and the early 1970s environmental movement will wish to consult Nelson A. Rockefeller, *Our Environment Can Be Saved* (Garden City, NY: Doubleday, 1970).

53. The literature on postwar international monetary relations is vast. For useful overviews, see Fred L. Block, *The Origins of International Economic Disorder: A Study of United States International Monetary Policy from World War II to the Present* (Berkeley: University of California Press, 1977); and Leland B. Yeager, *International Monetary Relations: Theory, History, Policy* (2nd ed.; New York: Harper & Row, 1976), part 2.

54. See Robert Triffin, *Gold and the Dollar Crisis: The Future of Convertibility* (New Haven: Yale University Press, 1961).

55. For Business Council pressures on Nixon to take action, see *Dun's Review*, December 1976, 94.

56. On the import question during this period, see Ferguson and Rogers, "Corporate Coalitions," 12–15; and the useful summaries in Joan Edelman Spero, *The Politics of International Economic Relations* (3rd ed.; New York: St. Martin's Press, 1985), 104–11; and Congressional Quarterly, *Trade: U.S. Policy Since 1945* (Washington, DC: Congressional Quarterly, 1984), 62 ff. On the Japanese practices, see Scott, "Competitiveness," 55–70; idem, "National Strategies: Key to International Competition," in Scott and Lodge, *U.S. Competitiveness*, 71–143; Alan Wm. Wolfe, "International Competitiveness of American Industry: The Role of U.S. Trade Policy," in Scott and Lodge, *U.S. Competitiveness*, 301–27.

57. For a striking indication of an active search for an alternative to Nixon by some multinational businesses, see David Nichols, *Financing Elections* (New York: New Viewpoints, 1977), 108–9.

58. For the plumbers and Muskie, see Jim Hougan, *Secret Agenda* (New York: Random House, 1984).

59. For Palevsky's role in the McGovern campaign, see Laurence H. Shoup, *The Carter Presidency and Beyond: Power and Politics in the 1980s* (Palo Alto, CA: Ramparts Press, 1980), 57; for other big business supporters of McGovern, see Herbert Alexander, *Financing the 1972 Election* (Lexington, MA: Lexington Books, 1976), e.g. 557.

60. For the Nixon political business cycle, see Robert R. Keller and Ann Mari May, "The Presidential Political Business Cycle of 1972," *Journal of Economic History* 44 (June 1984): 265–76. Ordinarily the financial markets constrain such blatant manipulations by pressures exerted through the Federal Reserve. (Indeed, the Fed was originally designed to make sure such pressures are effective. On this matter of design, see, among others, Gabriel Kolko, *The Triumph of Conservatism* [New York: The Free Press, 1963], 217–54.) Much, albeit largely unwitting, evidence about business anxieties during this period is offered by the interviews reported in Leonard Silk and David Vogel, *Ethics and Profits* (New York: Simon & Schuster, 1976).

61. For wage and productivity growth in 1971, see *ER*, Tables B-39 and B-41, respectively. Bruno and Sachs, *Worldwide Stagflation*, chapter 8, trace the economic slowdown in the United States and other countries and the concurrent course of wages. While we agree with their judgment that wages were generally not a significant factor in the U.S. slowdown in the late 1970s, we hesitate to endorse their claims about the Western European case.

3/Right Turn: The Dismal 1970s

1. For the Stockman quote, and an earlier version of this basic argument, see Thomas Ferguson and Joel Rogers, "Neoliberals and Democrats," *The Nation*, 26 June 1982, 767, 781–86.

2. Net investment in plant and equipment and investment per worker from Bruce R. Scott, "U.S. Competitiveness: Concepts, Performance, and Implications," in *U.S. Competitiveness in the World Economy*, ed. Bruce R. Scott and George C. Lodge (Boston: Harvard Business School Press, 1985), 31. Productivity data are from Edward F. Denison, *Trends in American Eco:.omic Growth, 1929–1982* (Washington, DC: The Brookings Institution, 1985), 6. See as well the discussion in Lester C. Thurow, "Solving the Productivity Problem," in Lester C. Thurow, Arnold Packer, and Howard J. Samuels, *Strengthening the Economy: Stud-*

ies in Productivity (Washington, DC: Center for Democratic Policy, 1981), 9. Growth rates are from Lawrence, *Can America Compete?*, 25.

3. Data on unemployment, real gross weekly earnings, and median family income from *ER*, Tables B-33, B-39, and B-27, respectively. Recovery from the 1973–75 recession raised wages and median family income. Neither, however, reached earlier levels. At their post-1972 peak, for example, real average gross weekly earnings (in 1978) were still 5 percent below their 1972 level; real median family income (also in 1978) was 0.3 percent below its 1973 level.

4. For the U.S. shares of world trade and GNP, see Scott, "Competitiveness," 18–21. For the top 50 world firms, see Albert Bergesen and Chintamani Sahoo, "Evidence of the Decline of American Hegemony in World Production," *Review* 8 (Spring 1985): 595–611.

5. This point is emphasized in Scott, "Competitiveness," 18–19.

6. All data in this paragraph from Scott, "Competitiveness," 25–27.

7. Different analysts have slightly different estimates of import and export dependence in general and in manufacturing in particular. None of these differences, however, affect our basic argument here, since all careful analyses see a qualitative jump in U.S. integration with the rest of the world economy in the 1970s. For other data on exports and imports generally, see Scott, "Competitiveness," and other sources cited in chapter 1, n. 58. For an overview of the decline in U.S. manufacturing, including its deteriorating competitiveness, see Eckstein, Caton, Brinner, and Duprey, *The DRI Report*, especially chapter 2.

8. An overall estimate of the change from "price makers" to "price takers" is difficult to make, but must certainly be vastly larger than the percentage of firms directly threatened by imports or firms whose exports are price-sensitive. Scott ("Competitiveness," 20), for example, estimates that:

> . . . for commodity prices like oil, imports of 5–10 percent of internal demand may be enough to influence the price, as long as the market is open to additional imports. For less price-sensitive products the figure may well be higher, but with exports and imports averaging some 20 percent of domestic supply, some impact on prices from foreign competition must be accepted as a major force in most, if not all, industries.

Similarly, Lester Thurow estimates that "about 70 percent of all the goods and services produced in the United States are subject to actual and potential competition," with effects felt by the remaining 30 percent. See Thurow's comments in the roundtable discussion "Beyond Protectionism," *World Policy Journal* 3 (Winter 1985–86): 160.

Because our point here can be easily misinterpreted, we emphasize that we are not arguing that those sectors of the American economy that were exposed to international competition became "competitive industries" in the sense favored by neoclassical economists. Much of this new competition derived from foreign oligopolies, and interactions among oligopolistically organized parts of industries (either foreign or domestic) are unlikely to produce patterns of price behavior typical of "competitive industries," in the neoclassical sense, particularly in the long run.

9. An excellent criticism of most of the major explanations is offered in Bowles, Gordon, and Weisskopf, *Wasteland*, chapter 3. Of the importance of Third World industrialization for the basic structure of the world economy, see Michael Beenstock, *The World Economy in Transition* (2nd ed.; London: George Allen & Unwin, 1984).

10. On plant relocation and other business strategies, see Bluestone and Harrison, *Deindustrialization*; and Norman J. Glickman, "Cities and the International Division of Labor," Lyndon B. Johnson School of Public Affairs, University of Texas, Austin, Working Paper No. 31, 1985.

11. For detailed accounts of the growth of management consulting firms during the period, see Hearings before the House Education and Labor Committee, Subcommittee on Labor Management Relations, *Pressures in Today's Workplace*, 96th Cong., 1st and 2nd sess., 1979–80, Vols. I–IV. For the basic data on unfair-labor-practice charges against employers and NLRB "remedies," see National Labor Relations Board, *Annual Report* (Washington, DC: GPO), various issues. The calculation on the 1 in 20 chance of getting fired for supporting a union is reported in several places. See, among others, Freeman and Medoff, *What*

Do Unions Do?, 232–33; and Paul Weiler, "Promises to Keep: Securing Workers' Rights to Self-Organization under the NLRA," *Harvard Law Review* 96 (1983): 1780–81.

12. Data on the union premium from George Johnson, "Changes over Time in the Union/Nonunion Wage Differential in the United States" (Unpublished manuscript, University of Michigan, 1981); cited in Freeman and Medoff, *What Do Unions Do?*, 53. It is always important to emphasize the tremendous variation in wage patterns within the labor movement. While the average wage-and-benefit package for union members remains well above that of the average worker, in many sectors the difference is slight, and in a few, unionized workers are paid even less than nonunion ones.

13. Numbers of workers organized through NLRB elections (RC cases) and lost through decertifications (RD cases) calculated from NLRB, *Annual Report*, various issues. On the organized percentage of the civilian work force, see Courtney D. Gifford, ed., *Directory of U.S. Labor Organizations*, 1984–85 edition (Washington, DC: Bureau of National Affairs, 1985), 2. Note that this figure includes all members of any labor organization, not just unions. For a discussion of the fight over the Labor Law Reform Bill, see Thomas Ferguson and Joel Rogers, "Labor Law Reform and Its Enemies," *The Nation*, 6–13 January 1979, 1, 17–20.

14. See Ferguson, "Normalcy," 49–50, for a more complete discussion of this labor constraint. Note that what is at issue here is the willingness and ability of firms to support "liberal" labor policies at the national level. Virtually all firms resist unions at the plant level.

15. John S. Saloma III provides a detailed survey of these activities in his *Ominous Politics: The New Conservative Labyrinth* (New York: Hill and Wang, 1984). His study is one of the very few to bring out the importance of the astronomical sums of money lavished on these activities, in contrast to the customary rhetoric about the importance of "new ideas." For the PACs, see Gary J. Andres, "Business Involvement in Campaign Finance: Factors Influencing the Decision to Form a Corporate PAC," *PS* 18 (Spring 1985): 213–20. For the risk studies, "experts," and tightened bonds between business and universities, see David Dickson and David Noble, "By Force of Reason: The Politics of Science and Technology Policy," in Ferguson and Rogers, *The Hidden Election*, 260–312; and David Dickson, *The New Politics of Science* (New York: Pantheon, 1984). For the general campaign against regulation, see Saloma, especially chapters 2, 3, and 6. For the media studies in particular, which merit a book in themselves, see Saloma, chapter 9; Walter Schneir and Miriam Schneir, "The Right's Attack on the Press," *The Nation*, 30 March 1985, 361–67; and Louis Wolf, "Accuracy in Media Rewrites the News and History," *Covert Action* 21 (Spring 1984): 24–38 (note especially, at 28–29, the funds from both the "right" *and* leading multinationalists). See as well *Washington Post*, 4 January 1981, which has a useful list of multinationals involved in a growing "conservative" network.

16. Quoted in Saloma, *Ominous Politics*, 65–66.

17. On the activities of the Olin, Smith Richardson, and Scaife funds, see Saloma, *Ominous Politics*, 24–35, 75–76, 132–33; Wanniski is quoted at 34. For a detailed survey of Scaife activities over 1973–80, see Karen Rothmyer, "Citizen Scaife," *Columbia Journalism Review*, July–August 1981; for the 1977–82 grant to *The Public Interest*, see Edsall, *New Politics*, 120. For an overview of foundation support for pro-business "public interest" law firms, see Mary Anna Culleton Colwell, "The Role of Conservative Foundations in Developing Nonprofit Law Firms Which Serve the Interests of Business" (Unpublished paper).

18. See sources noted in Edward S. Herman, *Corporate Control, Corporate Power* (New York: Cambridge University Press, 1981), 384–85, n. 77; and Edsall, *New Politics*, 116.

19. We emphasize this last point. In effect, the international regulatory initiatives opened up splits *within* the multinational community.

For useful discussion of international regulatory initiatives, see Dickson and Noble, "By Force of Reason"; and Dickson, *New Politics of Science*, chapter 4.

20. For discussion of the political consequences of the grain crisis, see Charles Kindleberger, "Group Behavior and International Trade," in his *Economic Response* (Cambridge: Harvard University Press, 1978), 19–38; and Peter Alexis Gourevitch, "International Trade, Domestic Coalitions, and Liberty: Comparative Responses to the Crisis of 1873–96," *Journal of Interdisciplinary History* 8 (Autumn 1977): 281–313

21. For oil, the Democrats, and the 1936 election, see Ferguson, "Normalcy," 52, 91–92. Truman's Secretary of the Interior, Harold Ickes, resigned from the Cabinet at least in part to protest the proposed appointment of oilman Edwin Pauley to a post in the Navy Department. For Lyndon Johnson and oil, see the extensive discussion in Robert Caro, *The Path to Power* (New York: Alfred A. Knopf, 1982), passim.

22. For an overview of the energy price deregulation debate, see Joseph Kalt, *The Economics and Politics of Oil Price Regulation* (Cambridge: MIT Press, 1981). For Carter's promise to Boren and other oil Democrats, see Elizabeth Drew, *Politics and Money: The New Road to Corruption* (New York: Macmillan, 1983), 39–40. Drew reports that Boren actually wrote the text of Carter's letter himself; apparently the idea for it was dreamed up in a meeting between Boren, Robert Strauss (then chair of the DNC), and Dolph Briscoe (then governor of Texas), at the Texas–Oklahoma football game in the Cotton Bowl, in Dallas, in October of that year.

23. A striking example of the ties between regional business elites and many varieties of fundamentalism is presented by the board of governors of the Council for National Policy (CNP). Frankly intended as a counterpart to the Council on Foreign Relations (CFR), long chaired by David Rockefeller, CNP had Nelson Bunker Hunt as its vice president during 1982–83 and a staggering array of leading lights of the American right on its board. They included "Onion King" Othal Brand, beer baron Joseph Coors, Cullen Davis, columnist M. Stanton Evans, George Gilder, Heritage Foundation president Edwin J. Feulner, Lieutenant General Dan Graham (chair of High Frontier, a "Star Wars" lobby), Richard Viguerie, Howard Phillips, National Right to Work Committee president Reed Larson, Herbert Hunt, Jack Kemp, Accuracy in Media president Reed Irvine, Major General John K. Singlaub (who now heads the American affiliate of the World Anti-Communist League), Paul Weyrich, James R. Whalen (publisher of Sun Myung Moon's *Washington Times*), and more than two dozen evangelists, including Robison, Falwell, and Pat Robertson. Of the 146-member board (including members-elect), at least thirty-seven came from Texas, including twenty of the business people and thirteen evangelists. Note, however, that while huge fortunes like the Hunts' are well represented, along with figures from the defense industry, steel, and other sectors, most large Texas banks and the largest industrial concerns in the state are *not*. Neither, needless to say, are the businesses who supply the leaders of the CFR, or indeed most other major national business organizations, such as the Committee for Economic Development, or even the Business Roundtable.

24. Jerome Tuccille, *Kingdom: The Story of the Hunt Family of Texas* (Ottawa, IL: Jameson Books, 1984), discusses the various members of the Hunt family's long record of involvement with right-wing leaders and causes. For Bunker Hunt's service as a director of Falwell's "Old Time Gospel Hour," see the bond prospectus issued by Old Time Gospel, Inc., on file with the Washington, D.C., office of People for the American Way. For Davis and Robison, including their much-touted "idol smashing" of a collection of Oriental art owned by Davis, see the file on Robison on record with the same office. On Criswell, see Dick J. Reavis, "The Politics of Armageddon," *Texas Monthly* 12 (October 1984): 245–56.

25. There has been very little good work done on what might be termed the "material basis" of fundamentalist appeals or on the appeal of the "social issues" the fundamentalists promote. One notable exception for one prominent issue, however, is Kristin Luker, *Abortion and the Politics of Motherhood* (Berkeley: University of California Press, 1984).

26. Bryan, of course, ran on a platform calling for free silver, which the copper companies also mined. See the discussion in Lawrence Goodwyn, *Democratic Promise* (New York: Oxford University Press, 1976). For Anaconda in particular, see Ferguson, *Critical Realignment*.

27. For the aggregate growth rates for developing and developed countries, see Lawrence, *Can America Compete?*, 24. For the case of East Asia and the Pacific, see World Bank, *World Development Report 1984* (New York: Oxford University Press, 1984), 11.

28. For examples of the many studies and reports commissioned during the period, see Dickson and Noble, "By Force of Reason."

29. On the growth in imports among oil exporters, see Glickman, "Cities."

30. For the non-oil LDC debt and the U.S. bank share, see William R. Cline, *International Debt and the Stability of the World Economy* (Washington, DC: Institute for International Economics, 1983), 14–15.

32. For the net direct investment flows, see Richard P. Mattione, *OPEC's Investments and the Future of the International Financial System* (Washington, DC: The Brookings Institution, 1985), 32. On the debt-versus-equity issue, see Stephen Magee and William A. Brock, "Third World Debt as a Political Redistribution Game," in *The Global Debt Crisis*, ed. Michael Clauden (Cambridge: Bollinger [forthcoming]); and Jeff Frieden, "Third World Indebted Industrialization: International Finance, and State Capitalism in Mexico, Brazil, Algeria, and South Korea," *International Organization* 35 (Summer 1981): 407–31.

31. See Ferguson, *Critical Realignment*, for a longer discussion of the 1936 case.

32. Note in particular that at least some of the momentum for the efforts to expand NATO armaments in the late 1970s originated with a group of what appear to have been Democratically oriented military analysts. See Robert Komer, *Maritime Strategy or Coalition Defense* (Cambridge: Abt Books, 1984), xv. The later military buildup, however, quite transcended the aims of most Democratic Europeanists in the Carter Administration. It also emphasized different force configurations than they proposed. See the discussion below, in chapter 5.

33. For our earlier comments, see Ferguson and Rogers, "Corporate Coalitions," n. 18, at 57–58. For CIA revisions of previous estimates, see *New York Times*, 3 March 1983. For the conclusions of the Scowcroft Commission, see *Report of the President's Commission on Strategic Forces* (Washington, DC: April 1983), and the follow-up "Final Report of the President's Commission on Strategic Forces," *Atlantic Community Quarterly* 22 (Spring 1984): 14–22. For the DIA's conclusion that investment did not grow at all, see William W. Kaufmann, *The 1986 Defense Budget* (Washington, DC: The Brookings Institution, 1985), 6. For a good debunking of the "unilateral disarmament," see Robert W. Komer, "What 'Decade of Neglect'?," *International Security* 10 (Fall 1985): 70–83. For the lack of a causal connection between Soviet and U.S. spending on arms, see John R. Freeman, "Granger Causality and the Time Series Analysis of Political Relationships," *American Journal of Political Science* 27 (May 1983): 350–54.

34. This and the preceding paragraph draw from our discussion in "Corporate Coalitions," 15–17.

35. Between 1960 and 1985, there have been 138 successful coups in the Third World; 33 of these, or just under one-quarter of the total, occurred over the 1974–79 period. On the total number of coups, see Ruth Leger Sivard, *World Military and Social Expenditures 1985* (Washington, DC: World Priorities, 1985), 25; Sivard supplied us with the number that occurred over 1974–79. More telling for the character of U.S. response, the 1974–80 period comprised the third great postwar wave of successful *revolutionary* activity in the Third World (the first such wave occurring over 1944–54, the second over 1958–62). Fourteen countries fell to revolutionary forces during this period, a highpoint in the postwar era. See the discussion in Halliday, *Second Cold War*, chapter 4.

36. For the Laird quote, see Thomas Bailey, A *Diplomatic History of the American People* (9th ed.; Englewood Cliffs, NJ: Prentice-Hall, 1974), 923; cited in Richard E. Feinberg, *The Intemperate Zone: The Third World Challenge to U.S. Foreign Policy* (New York: W. W. Norton, 1983), 43.

37. See the useful discussion in Feinberg, *Intemperate Zone*, 43–56, on which we draw here.

38. On the Iranian case, the literature is voluminous. However, for a short summary, particularly attentive to the destabilizing effects of the arms buildup, and on which we draw here, see Michael T. Klare, *American Arms Supermarket* (Austin: University of Texas Press, 1984), chapter 6.

39. For discussions of the rise of the CPD, see Alan Wolfe and Jerry Sanders, "Resurgent Cold War Ideology: The Case of the Committee on the Present Danger," in *Capitalism and the State in U.S.–Latin American Relations*, ed. Richard R. Fagen (Palo Alto: Stanford University Press, 1979), 41–75; Jerry Sanders, *Peddlers of Crisis: The Committee on the Present Danger and the Politics of Containment* (Boston, MA: South End Press, 1983); and Ferguson and Rogers, "Corporate Coalitions," 17–18.

40. See the discussion of corporate divisions on the defense issue in Ferguson and Rogers, "Corporate Coalitions," 18–19.

41. Again, for the influence of the media on mass opinion during this period, see Fan, "Defense Spending 1977–84."

42. All data in this paragraph from Robert S. McIntyre and Dean C. Tipps, *Inequity and Decline: How the Reagan Tax Policies Are Affecting the American Taxpayer and Economy* (Washington, DC: Center on Budget and Policy Priorities, 1983), 13–14.

43. For the total on tax expenditures, see Witte, *Politics and Development*, 292. For the share of business loopholes traceable to the 1970s, see McIntyre and Tipps, *Inequity and Decline*, 11.

Bracket creep was more onerous for lower-income Americans for at least two reasons: (1) the standard deduction, personal exemptions, and the earned income credit are more important for lower-income Americans than higher-income ones, and were severely eroded by inflation; (2) brackets at the lower level are narrower than at the top, with the result that inflation was more likely to push a lower-income taxpayer into a new bracket. See McIntyre and Tipps, *Inequity and Decline*, 10.

44. For the Harris results, see Ladd, "The Polls: Taxing and Spending," 127.

45. The study we refer to is Robert Kuttner, *Revolt of the Haves: Tax Rebellions and Hard Times* (New York: Simon & Schuster, 1980).

46. For the American Council on Capital Formation, see a revealing account in its own 1983 *Annual Report*. Note in particular the self-congratulatory account of its "sophisticated interaction with the economic press," and its remarkable list of "institutional supporters," as well as the clear statement of the theory of corporate tax incidence offered in our main text. Tax reduction, of course, begins at home; the *Report* advertises that contributions to the ACCF are tax-deductible.

47. Simon is prominently advertised in much NTLC literature. For the ties of the organization's president, Louis K. Uhler, to the early John Birch Society, see *Group Research Report* 17 (30 May 1978): 18. The CED's later opposition to the balanced budget is evident in S. H. Park and F. W. Schiff, "The Proposed Constitutional Amendment to Balance the Federal Budget: Pros and Cons," 15 May 1982.

48. Note in particular the differences between the fundamentalists and the personnel of the Institute on Religion and Democracy. This group, funded by Olin, Smith Richardson, Sarah Scaife, and other foundations, has close ties to the corporate-dominated AEI and the Coalition for a Democratic Majority. Its main spokespersons—Ernest Lefever, Michael Novak, and Richard Nisbet, for example—are certainly not fundamentalists. See also the interesting discussion in Ana Maria Ezcurra, *The Neoconservative Offensive: U.S. Churches and the Ideological Struggle for Latin America* (New York: CIRCUS Publications, 1983); an opening essay by Rev. Michael McIntyre notes (at 9) the funding sources.

49. On funding for progressive organizations during the period, see J. Craig Jenkins, *Patrons of Social Reform*. On support for the think tanks and legal foundations, see Saloma, *Ominous Politics*.

50. For the campaign by the right to influence the press, see Schneir and Schneir, "The Right's Attack on the Press"; and Saloma, *Ominous Politics*. Since 1981, the Reagan Administration had added the power of government to these privately sponsored efforts. See the review of Administration actions in Eve Pell, *The Big Chill* (Boston: Beacon Press, 1984). For the change at the *New York Times*, see Dinesh D'Souza, "The 'Times' It Is A-Changing," *Policy Review* 30 (Fall 1984): 20–26; the quote is at 26. The Heritage Foundation's *Annual Report* for 1983 claims (at 15) that it is now a principal source of op-ed pieces in *The New York Times*.

51. See the discussion in Ferguson and Rogers, "Corporate Coalitions," 26–27; Burch, *Elites*, 313–15; Thomas R. Dye and L. Harmon Zeigler, *The Irony of Democracy* (North Scituate, MA: Duxbury Press, 1978), 253; and especially Shoup, *The Carter Presidency and Beyond*, chapters 1–3. Note that while Carter originally ran with the support of only one union (the UAW), he was supported by labor in the general election, and afforded labor considerable help while in office. In this he differs importantly from the later revisionist Democrats with whom he has sometimes been compared. While the study remains incomplete as this book goes to press, quantitative analysis of the multinational support for Carter is provided in Thomas Ferguson, "The Death of the New Deal: A Longitudinal Analysis of Major Investors in the Democratic Party" (paper presented to the Conference on "The Reagan Revolution," Centre for American Studies, University of Western Ontario, 7–9 May 1986). That discussion supports the basic contention made below; viz., that a large number of multinational firms and banks contributing to Democrats in 1976 were not willing to do so in subsequent elections. It also indicates Carter's attempt to strike some sort of accommodation with representatives of the protectionist steel industry. But because little came of these efforts, which anticipated some of the "reindustrialization" proposals Democrats pursued in 1984, we do not discuss them here.

52. For discussion of Carter Administration reform of the regulatory process, see Dickson and Noble, "By Force of Reason"; and Susan J. Tolchin and Martin Tolchin, *Dismantling America: The Rush to Deregulate*

(Boston: Houghton Mifflin, 1983), chapter 2. For a detailed study of changes in one of the most controversial areas of regulation—occupational safety and health—see Noble, *Liberalism at Work.*

53. For the 1977 water squabbles, see Charles Warren, "Subsidizing Disaster: Federal Policy on Water Development," *Challenge* 17 (July–August 1977): 46–49; and reporting in the *Congressional Quarterly Weekly Report,* 19 March 1977, 481–82 and 484; and 23 April 1977, 734–36. For the continuing tensions in 1978, see the *National Journal,* 1 July 1978, 1052. For the Environmental Policy Center, Carter, and the water fiasco in general, see Wiley and Gottlieb, *Empires,* 55–57. For Carter's urban-aid program, see Glickman, "Cities." On this, as on so many issues, considerable continuity exists between the last years of Carter and the Reagan Administration, but we emphasize the major differences—in policies toward labor, social security, the environment, and other areas. Party differences narrowed, and the whole spectrum shifted right, but the Democrats and Republicans did remain different parties.

54. Our description here follows that in Witte, *Politics and Development,* 205–6.

55. The quote from the "Washington insider" and the estimate of the distribution of the benefits of the 1978 bill are from Kuttner, *Revolt,* 243 and 249, respectively.

56. See the discussion in, among others, Bruno and Sachs, *Worldwide Stagflation,* chapter 8; and Stephen Magee and Leslie Young, "Endogenous Protection in the United States, 1980–1984" (Paper presented to the conference on U.S. Trade Policies in a Changing World Economy, University of Michigan, 28–29 March 1985). Note that this inflation certainly exacerbated divisions within the work force; it also undoubtedly irked holders of paper assets.

57. For the failure of the Administration's efforts at international macroeconomic policy coordination, see George de Menil, "From Rambouillet to Versailles," in de Menil and Anthony Solomon, *Economic Summitry* (New York: Council on Foreign Relations, 1983), 21–27; for the effects of this failure on at least some foreign elites, see Henry Nau, "Where Reaganomics Works," *Foreign Policy* 57 (Winter 1984–85): 14–37. For the dollar crisis and inflation in general, see Gerald Epstein, "Domestic Stagflation and Monetary Policy: The Federal Reserve and the Hidden Election," in Ferguson and Rogers, *The Hidden Election,* 141–95. Our discussion in the text, of course, is not intended as an exhaustive analysis of the problem of "inflation," but only as an analysis of how it affected interests in U.S. politics.

58. Ferguson and Rogers, "Corporate Coalitions," 31; Epstein, "Domestic Stagflation," 166 and following.

59. The Carlton Group's name comes from the fact that it met regularly at the Sheraton-Carlton Hotel in Washington.

60. For the trade compromise, see Nau, "Where Reaganomics Works."

61. Throughout this discussion we have drawn on our earlier essay on the 1980 election. For the last days of Carter, his residual support at the end, the meeting of investment bankers, and Reagan's accommodations with the internationalists, see Ferguson and Rogers, "Corporate Coalitions," 34–52. For a useful account of Reagan that is particularly attentive to his views in the late 1970s, see Ronnie Dugger, *On Reagan: The Man & His Presidency* (New York: McGraw-Hill, 1983). For the independent expenditures, see *New York Times,* 29 November 1981; Reagan's total was $10,601,864; Carter's was $27,773.

4/"Reaganism"

1. See as well the discussion of cross-cutting pressures on the business community in Cohen and Rogers, *On Democracy,* chapters 4 and 5.

2. The "young intellectuals" assessment is from Daniel Patrick Moynihan, "Reagan's Inflate-the-Deficit Game," *New York Times,* 21 July 1985, Section 4. As is usual where no notice is taken of the hundreds of millions of dollars invested over the previous decade in these conservative intellectuals and their ideas, the reference is as self-serving as it is silly; these are, after all, people who promised to raise the U.S. growth rate by simply cutting taxes. The most conspicuous referent, David Stockman, has had a long personal association with Senator Moynihan.

The "new class war" phrase is taken from Frances Fox Piven and Richard A. Cloward, *The New Class War: Reagan's Attack on the Welfare State* (New York: Pantheon, 1982). We should note, however, that

Piven and Cloward, unlike many other commentators, argued that the American welfare state would survive the attack and emerge stronger than ever.

3. On this appointments process and other useful insights into the Reagan Administration's calculations, see Martin Shefter and Benjamin Ginsberg, "Institutionalizing the Reagan Regime" (Paper prepared for delivery at the 1985 Annual Meeting of the American Political Science Association, New Orleans, 29 August–1 September 1985). On "defunding," see James Ridgeway, "The New Right's Campaign to Defund the Left," Village Voice, 11 January 1983, and the discussion below.

4. For complaints about the lack of foreign-policy action and definition, see the discussion throughout Alexander Haig, Caveat: Realism, Reagan, and Foreign Policy (New York: Macmillan, 1984). Indicative of its importance to the Administration, monetary policy is the first issue addressed in David Stockman's famous "Economic Dunkirk" memorandum of December 1980. See Greider, Education, Appendix.

5. See Herbert Stein, "The Coming Clamor for Price Controls," Fortune, 12 January 1981, 61.

6. Quote from Stein, "Clamor," 61. For the "credibility hypothesis," see William Fellner, "The Credibility Effect and Rational Expectations: Implications of the Gramlich Study," Brookings Papers on Economic Activity 10 (1979): 167–78. For criticism of "rational expectations" accounts of disinflation, see Robert J. Gordon, "The Theory of Domestic Inflation," American Economic Review 67 (February 1977): 128–34.

7. See Nau, "Where Reaganomics Works," 14–37.

8. The "retains sufficient power" quote is from Henry Nau, "International Reaganomics: A Domestic Approach to World Economy" (Center for Strategic and International Studies, Georgetown University, Significant Issues Series 6, no. 18), cited in C. Fred Bergsten's contribution ("The Problem") to a debate with Nau: "The State of the Debate: Reaganomics," Foreign Policy 59 (Summer 1985): 140. All other quotes from Nau, "Where Reaganomics Works," at 22, 22–23, and 26, respectively.

9. For the fear of social unrest, rising protectionism, and other doubts about monetary stringency as Reagan assumed office, see New York Times, 2 January 1981. This registers the opposition of the CED's chief economist, among others. For Kemp's view, see, for example, the discussion of 1980–81 in "The Supply-Side Strategy for Lower Interest Rates" (Remarks before the Federal Reserve Bank of Atlanta and Emory University, Atlanta, 17 March 1982).

10. Now that the recession of 1981–83 is over, virtually everyone concedes that Volcker and the Fed sought to wring inflation out of the economy by a gigantic run-up in interest rates. Some analysts have argued, however, that various misinterpretations of monetary statistics led the Fed to underestimate the disastrous effects its policies would have on the economy. See, for example, Michael Hadjimichalakis, The Federal Reserve Money and Interest Rates: The Volcker Years and Beyond (New York: Praeger, 1984). While we lack the space for a detailed discussion of the question, we cannot resist noting that by early 1982 anyone who could read a newspaper knew the U.S. economy was in desperate shape. Yet the Fed persisted in its tight-money policies. Though it eased very slightly in the early summer of 1982, it did not break definitively with its tight money policies until the Mexican debt crisis in late summer forced it to come to the rescue, not of ordinary Americans, but of international banks threatened with default on their loans. No less importantly, most scholarship on the Fed generally underestimates the extent to which the Fed targets wages and even bank profits. See, for example, the discussion in Gerald Epstein and Thomas Ferguson, "Monetary Policy, Loan Liquidation and Industrial Conflict: The Federal Reserve and the Open Market Operations of 1932," Journal of Economic History 44 (December 1984): 957–83. Compare the earlier discussion of the same case in Milton Friedman and Anna Schwartz, A Monetary History of the United States 1867–1960 (Princeton: Princeton University Press, 1963).

11. On Fed policy during the Carter term, see Epstein, "Domestic Stagflation," 169–74. Note that the Fed had eased off in the months before the 1980 election, before tightening again right afterward, and that a rise in reported inflation early in 1981 may have helped the tight money bloc muster additional support for its position.

12. Insider criticisms of the Fed's policies are reported in detail in Paul Craig Roberts, Supply Side Revolution, especially 220–25.

13. The "lovefest" and Stockman remarks to the Chamber group are noted in Roberts, Supply Side Revolution, 224 and 225, respectively. For a particularly striking instance in which the President and top

business figures, including the chair of the U.S. Chamber of Commerce, sought to rein in the Fed after it began to reflate, see *Boston Globe*, 13 February 1983. For the iatrogenic costs of this "cure" in jobs, alcoholism, suicides, homicides, and other effects, see Bluestone and Harrison, *Deindustrialization*, chapter 3, and sources cited there.

14. For Reagan's early supporters, including Simon, see Ferguson and Rogers, "Corporate Coalitions," 41–42. For the "Trojan horse" remark, see William Greider, *The Education of David Stockman and Other Americans* (New York: E. P. Dutton, 1982), 49.

15. On the politics of Reagan tax initiatives, see Richard Florida, "Entreprises et Politique Fiscales: l'Exemple Américain," *Revue Française de Finance Publiques* 1 (1983): 85–101; McIntyre and Tipps, *Inequity and Decline*; A. F. Ehrbar, "The Battle over Taxes," *Fortune*, 19 April 1982, 58–63; *New York Times*, 21 February 1981; the retrospective on 1981 provided in the *Boston Globe*, 3 May 1982; and "Business and Reagan: More Blowups Ahead?," *Dun's Business Monthly*, December 1982, 38–41. For the Carlton Group, see especially *New York Times*, 18 March 1982.

16. This and the next several paragraphs on the tax fight draw on the sources noted above (note 15), and in particular on Florida, "Entreprises"; and McIntyre and Tipps, *Inequity and Decline*.

17. For the Stockman quote, see McIntyre and Tipps, *Inequity and Decline*, 55.

18. For the Stockman quote, see Greider, *Education*, 58.

19. See Moynihan, "Inflate-the-Deficit"; Tom Wicker, "A Deliberate Deficit," *New York Times*, 19 July 1985. Moynihan voted for the original tax package. Neither he nor the general press, however, found it in their interest to make anything of the point until the summer of 1985, when they were campaigning for a tax rise.

Some close analysts of the Administration's budget policies had suspected the deliberate nature of its deficit production much earlier, and said something. See Henry Aaron's remarks in July 1983, at a conference on social welfare attended by many members of the Administration, in *The Social Contract Revisited: Aims and Outcomes of President Reagan's Social Welfare Policy*, ed. D. Lee Bawden (Washington, DC: Urban Institute Press, 1984), 243; and Thomas J. Sargent, "Confrontations over Deficits," *New York Times*, 12 August 1983. And White House insiders knew what was up from the start. Writing of August 1981, just when the Reagan tax bill was finally passed, Reagan Treasury official Paul Craig Roberts concludes: "OMB wanted deficits, but not deficits that could be laid on the doorstep of monetary policy. OMB was determined to use the deficit to focus congressional attention on the budget." See Roberts, *Supply Side Revolution*, 173.

20. One of the Chase ads appeared in the *New York Times*, 14 September 1981. Run long after the shape of things to come was perfectly clear, this notice deserves recall every time some political analyst tries to fix responsibility for the deficit debacle on the political power of "small business," or "competitive capital," or "new entrepreneurs."

21. For the combined effect of ERTA and TEFRA on effective tax rates on business, see Perry D. Quick, "Business: Reagan's Industrial Policy," in *The Reagan Record*, 298. For the declining share of federal receipts provided by corporate income taxes, see *HT*, Table 2.2. For the estimate on corporate loopholes, see Citizens for Tax Justice, "Corporate Taxpayers & Corporate Freeloaders" (Washington, DC: August 1985), 7.

22. All data from Citizens for Tax Justice, "Corporate Taxpayers," 2.

23. For the reductions by income quintile, see Marilyn Moon and Isabel V. Sawhill, "Family Incomes: Gainers and Losers," in *The Reagan Record*, Table 10.3. For the increases or reductions of the whole tax package, correcting for inflation, see McIntyre and Tipps, *Inequity and Decline*, Figure 6, and the assumptions reported at Figure 7.

24. The current dollar rise in national defense budget outlays and authority are reported in *HT*, Tables 3.3 and 5.1, respectively. We have taken the calculations of real increase from Defense Budget Project, Center on Budget and Policy Priorities, *The Fiscal 1986 Defense Budget: The Weapons Buildup Continues* (Washington, DC: Center on Budget and Policy Priorities, 1985), Table 3. Note, however, that the Defense Budget Project uses the Department of Defense price deflator in these calculations. The OMB, in its calculations of constant dollar defense spending (see *HT*, Table 6.1), uses a different deflator. Based on its figures, the rise in outlays was 36 percent. For outlays as a percentage of all federal outlays, and of GNP, see *HT*, Table 3.1.

25. For the real growth in different parts of the DOD budget, and the increasing investment share of the overall defense function, Defense Budget Project, *FY 1986 Defense Budget*, Tables 6 and 5, respectively.

26. All data in this paragraph are from Defense Budget Project, *FY 1986 Defense Budget*, 12, and Table 9. For other discussion of the Reagan military buildup, see William W. Kaufmann, *The 1985 Defense Budget* (Washington, DC: The Brookings Institution, 1984); and idem, *The 1986 Defense Budget*.

27. Reagan's claim that the United States had "unilaterally disarmed" during the 1970s was made at several points during the 1980 campaign, and he continued with the claim even after taking office. See, for example, his interview with Walter Cronkite, CBS-TV, 3 March 1981; cited in Richard Stubbing, "The Defense Program: Buildup or Binge," *Foreign Affairs* 63 (Spring 1985): 852. On the capabilities Reagan inherited from Carter, see Kaufmann, *The 1986 Defense Budget*, 7.

28. The calculation on the relative rates of growth of strategic and tactical/conventional programs is from Defense Budget Project, *FY 1986 Defense Budget*, 22. This calculation includes research and development costs but excludes related personnel costs. The relative share data on strategic versus tactical/conventional weapons are from the same source, at 7. The data on "unnecessary duplication" and quoted description of the MX and D-5 missiles are from Kaufmann, *The 1985 Defense Budget*, 47.

29. The estimate on the cost of a single carrier battle group is provided in Earl C. Ravenal, *Defining Defense: The 1985 Military Budget* (Washington, DC: Cato Institute, 1984), 12–13. The quote on different rationales for the acquisition of new groups is from Kaufmann, *The 1986 Defense Budget*, 34–35.

30. See the discussion in Malcolm Goggin, "Reagan's Revival: Turning Back the Clock in the Health Care Debate," in *The Attack on the Welfare State*, ed. Anthony Champagne and Edward J. Harpham (Prospect Heights, IL: Waveland Press, 1984), 61–85; and Karen Davis, "Access to Health Care: A Matter of Fairness," in *Health Care: How to Improve It and Pay for It* (Alternatives for the 1980s, No. 17) (Washington, DC: Center for National Policy, 1985), 45–57.

31. See *Democratic Fact Book: Issues for 1982* (Washington, DC: Democrats for the 80's, 1982), 102–6.

32. See the discussion in Edward J. Harpham, "Fiscal Crisis and the Politics of Social Security Reform," in Champagne and Harpham, *The Attack on the Welfare State*, 9–35. The estimates of benefit reductions are from Palmer and Sawhill, *The Reagan Record*, 377.

33. Timothy M. Smeeding, "Is the Safety Net Still Intact?," in Bawden, *The Social Contract Revisited*, 86.

34. A useful overview of recent (including 1970s) trends in social-welfare programs is provided by Smeeding, "Is the Safety Net Still Intact?," 69–120; the declining value of different benefit packages is at 86. On particular program cuts under Reagan, see D. Lee Bawden and John L. Palmer, "Social Policy: Challenging the Welfare State," in Palmer and Sawhill, *The Reagan Record*, Table 6.1.

35. This paragraph draws heavily on Joshua Cohen and Joel Rogers, *Inequity and Intervention: The Federal Budget and Central America* (Boston, MA: South End Press, 1986), 22–23, 35–36. See references cited there.

36. The 10 percent figure comes from Bawden and Palmer, "Social Policy," 187; the $176 billion estimate is from Congressional Budget Office (CBO), *The Economic and Budget Outlook: Fiscal Years 1986–1990* (Washington, DC: GPO, February 1985), 153. For all other data in this paragraph, see CBO, *Major Changes in Human Resources Programs Since January 1981*, (Washington, DC: GPO, August 1983); cited in Center on Budget and Policy Priorities, *End Results: The Impact of Federal Policies Since 1980 on Low Income Americans* (Washington, DC: Interfaith Action for Economic Justice, 1984), 12.

37. For all but the poverty data, see the Congressional Budget Office's 1984 report on the Reagan policies, cited in *End Results*, 11–13. For the poverty data, see Center on Budget and Policy Priorities, *Smaller Slices of the Pie* (Washington, DC: November 1985), 7.

38. The literature on Reagan's regulatory strategy is enormous. For useful overviews, see George C. Eads and Michael Fix, *Relief or Reform? Reagan's Regulatory Dilemma* (Washington, DC: The Urban Institute Press, 1984); Tolchin and Tolchin, *Dismantling America*; and Noll and Owen, *The Political Economy of Deregulation*.

39. *Democratic Fact Book 1984*, (Washington, DC: Democrats for the 80's, 1984), 298–99.

40. For the numbers of sites and cleanup progress, see *Time*, 14 October 1985, 76–77; for the Reagan

proposal to abolish the Superfund and eliminate the EPA's groundwater budget, see *Democratic Fact Book 1984*, 306 and 294, respectively.

41. For the early proposals, see *Democratic Fact Book 1984*, 299; for the grazing-land and water-projects initiatives, see Friends of the Earth, Natural Resources Defense Council, The Wilderness Society, Sierra Club, National Audubon Society, Environmental Defense Fund, Environmental Policy Center, Environmental Action, Defenders of Wildlife, and Solar Lobby, *Indictment: The Case Against the Reagan Environmental Record* (Washington, DC, March 1982), 15 and 25, respectively.

For a good overview of the Reagan Administration's environmental policies, see Jonathan Lash (with Katherine Gillman and David Sheridan), *A Season of Spoils: The Reagan Administration's Attack on the Environment* (New York: Pantheon, 1984).

42. The Reagan initiatives in antitrust, it should be noted, consolidated much earlier work; see Quick, "Businesses," 204–6. On civil rights, see Robert Plotkin, "Prologue to the Report by the Washington Council of Lawyers," and "Reagan Civil Rights: The First Twenty Months—A Report by the Washington Council of Lawyers," *Human Rights Annual* 1 (1983): 99–171; on secrecy, see Pell, *Big Chill*; Donna A. Demac, *Keeping America Uninformed: Government Secrecy in the 1980's* (New York: Pilgrim Press, 1984); and Walter Karp, "Liberty under Siege: The Reagan Administration's Taste for Autocracy," *Harper's*, November 1985, 53–67. On the Reagan estimate of "savings," and a careful criticism of this almost certainly bogus number, see Eads and Fix, *Relief or Reform?*, 237–54.

43. On Schiavone's OSHA violations, see Frank Ackerman, *Hazardous to Our Wealth: Economic Policies in the 1980s* (Boston: South End Press, 1984), 129. On Hunter's recommendations, see the "Department of Labor" chapter in *Mandate for Leadership: Policy Management in a Conservative Administration* (Washington, DC: The Heritage Foundation, 1981). On labor and Reagan generally, see Thomas Ferguson and Joel Rogers "La Défaite du Mouvement Syndical Américain," *Le Monde Diplomatique* 332 (November 1981): 11; idem, "Big Labor Is Hurting—Itself," *The Nation*, 1 September 1984, 129, 144–45; and idem, "Labor Day, 1985," *The Nation*, 7 September 1985, 164–65.

44. See Dotson's letter to the editor in *American Bar Association Journal*, August 1980.

45. Reilly came to the NLRB in March 1983. Before then, he served under Labor Secretary Ray Donovan as Acting Director of the Office of Labor-Management Standards Enforcement, the Labor Department office charged with auditing unions and otherwise superintending their compliance with the reporting provisions of the LMRDA. While there, Reilly moonlighted by representing clients in a private suit, financed by NRWLDF, against the Communications Workers of America. Reilly admitted this in congressional testimony, but claimed there was no conflict between his work for NRWLDF and the government, since he was not paid for the time he spent on the case. See *Washington Post*, 30 June 1983.

46. For the drop-off in enforcement at OSHA, see Eads and Fix, *Relief or Reform?*, 195; for general enforcement levels and the $6.50 penalty estimate, see Congress of the United States, Office of Technology Assessment (OTA), *Preventing Illness and Injury in the Workplace* (Washington, DC: GPO, 1985), 368–74 and 236, respectively.

47. On narrowing the scope of protections, see *Meyers Industries*, 268 NLRB No. 73 (January 6, 1984) and *Clear Pine Mouldings, Inc.*, 268 NLRB No. 173 (February 22, 1984); on expanding the scope of permissible employer conduct during representation campaigns, see *Rossmore House*, 269 NLRB No. 198 (April 25, 1984); on lowering the costs of unlawful employer conduct, see *Gourmet Foods*, 270 NLRB No. 113 (May 14, 1984); on relocations, see *Milwaukee Spring Div.*, 268 NLRB No. 87 (January 23, 1984) and *Otis Elevator Co.*, 269 NLRB No. 162 (April 6, 1984). On the duty to bargain, see *Creasey Co.*, 269 NLRB No. 219 (February 29, 1984); *Purolator Armored, Inc.*, 268 NLRB No. 191 (February 29, 1984); *E. I. Du Pont de Nemours & Co.*, 268 NLRB No. 161 (February 24, 1984); and *Thomas Sheet Metal Co, Inc.*, 268 NLRB No. 186 (February 27, 1984). On the policy of deferral, see *United Technologies*, 268 NLRB No. 83 (January 19, 1984) and *Olin Corporation*, 268 NLRB No. 83 (January 19, 1984).

Examples of Board bias abound during the same six-month period. In interpreting the acts' protection of employees who refuse to work under abnormally dangerous conditions, for example, the Board repeatedly found worker claims about unsafe conditions insufficient. In *Bekker Industries Corp.*, 268 NLRB No. 147 (February 16, 1984), it upheld the discharge of an employee who refused to work in a plant half a mile from the site of a chemical explosion, although local authorities had evacuated all residents living within a five-mile radius of the accident. In *L. E. Meyers Company*, 270 NLRB No. 146 (May 31, 1984), it upheld the discharge of two employees who had refused to climb a forty-foot ladder to an I-beam on a day when snow had fallen, even though a fellow worker had already slipped on the ladder. In *Asplundh Tree Expert Co.*, 269 NLRB No. 63 (March 22, 1984), the Board ruled that a worker's protest of his supervisor's failure to get medical attention for a co-worker who had been injured by a downed power line constituted quitting. The protest consisted of the worker's throwing his hard hat to the ground and refusing the employer's instruction to pick it up. This, the Board ruled, indicated that he had "opted to forsake employment." Similarly, the Board has helped further erode the law governing employer conduct during election campaigns by interpreting standing doctrine on threats and reprisals in interesting new ways. In *Bardcor Corp.*, 270 NLRB No. 157 (June 7, 1984), for example, it found that an employer who went through his plant taking pictures of employees shortly after learning that an organizing drive had begun, and whose supervisor told workers that the employer did this because he wanted to have a picture to "remember" them by, was engaged in harmless activity, while in *Benchmark Industries, Inc.*, 270 NLRB No. 8 (April 30, 1984) it held that an employer who told an employee that "a little birdie told me" the employee was handing out union authorization cards (normally 30 percent of the members of a unit have to sign such cards before a representation election will be conducted by the NLRB) was not engaged in intimidation. A favorite Board tactic in finding anti-union activity legal was to find that activity motivated by purely economic concerns or part of the reserved managerial prerogatives of business. In *Garrett Flexible Products, Inc.*, 270 NLRB No. 173 (June 13, 1984), for example, it held that an employer's firing of laid-off union supporters was legal, because it was covered by a company policy of terminating all workers laid off for more than 120 days. The Board concluded this despite the fact that this "policy" had never been previously announced to workers, and the Administrative Law Judge had found the company representative who testified on it "vague and unsure" about its origins and unable to name with certainty the other firms where he claimed it was standard practice. In *Royal Coal Sprinklers, Inc.*, 268 NLRB No. 156 (February 21, 1984), it found layoffs of employees who had voted a week before to bring in a union justified on economic grounds, even though the employer had granted wage increases the week before that. The list could go on and on. See the discussion in House Committee on Education and Labor, Subcommittee on Labor-Management Relations, *The Failure of Labor Law—A Betrayal of American Workers*, 98th Cong., 2d sess., 1984, Rept. 98, 17–22, on which we draw here.

48. See House Committee on Government Operations, *Delay, Slowness in Decisionmaking, and the Case Backlog at the National Labor Relations Board*, 98th Cong., 2d sess., 1984, H. Rept. 98-1141, 7–18.

49. For unemployment insurance coverage, see John Bickerman, *Unemployed and Unprotected: A Report on the Status of Unemployment Insurance* (Washington, DC: Center on Budget and Policy Priorities, March 1985), 3–5, *ER*, Tables B-31 and B-36.

50. See Ferguson and Rogers, "Labor Day, 1985," 164–65.

51. For union-membership trends over 1980–84, see Larry T. Adams, "Changing Employment Patterns of Organized Workers," *Monthly Labor Review* 108 (February 1985): 25–31.

5/*The Democrats' Response* (1981–82)

1. See Kaufmann, *The 1986 Defense Budget*, Table 13.

2. See the summary discussion in Bawden and Palmer, "Social Policy," especially Table 6.1.

3. On O'Neill and the open rule, see S. S. Smith, "Budget Battles of 1981: The Role of the Majority Party Leadership," in *American Politics and Public Policy: Seven Case Studies*, ed. A. P. Sindler (Washington, DC: Congressional Quarterly Press, 1982), 62. Smith implausibly claims that O'Neill thought this refusal would work against the adoption of the Administration's package. For a less strained account, see Walter Karp, "Playing Politics," *Harper's* 269 (July 1984): 51–60. Rostenkowski gets money from many sources. For his huge outside income from speeches, see *U.S. News & World Report*, 28 May 1984, 52, which notes that his income from this source exceeds that of all other members of the House (even Jack Kemp); for his remarkable PAC contributions in 1983–84, see *New York Times*, 6 November 1984.

4. "Federal Budget Cuts Adversely Affect Self-Help Groups" (Preliminary Report) (Washington, DC, Campaign for Human Development, 15 July 1982), 1–2.

5. For general discussions of the state of nonprofit organizations under Reagan, see Lester M. Salamon, "Nonprofit Organizations: The Lost Opportunity," in Palmer and Sawhill, *The Reagan Record*, 261–85; idem, "The New Budget and the Nonprofit Sector" (Washington, DC, Urban Institute, April 1985). For the survey, see "Lost Opportunity," 279; for funding cutbacks, see "New Budget," 10–14. For some of the funding restrictions, see Raul Yzaguirre, "Testimony on the Job Training Partnership Act: Implications for Hispanics" (Washington, DC, National Council of La Raza, September 13, 1983). Space does not permit discussion of the civil-rights implications of the "block grants" that are the vehicle of the New Federalism, but we believe these to be considerable, and malign.

6. See the Labor-Management Group's press release, "New Labor Management Group Formed," Washington, DC, 4 March 1981. Shapiro later retired as Du Pont chair, remaining on the board, and became involved in the Mondale campaign (see below). Labor leaders included John Lyons of the Iron Workers, Lloyd McBride of the Steelworkers, William Wynn of the United Food and Commercial Workers, and Martin Ward of the Plumbers. In the late 1970s, UAW president Fraser had loudly resigned from the LMG's predecessor, denouncing business for waging a "one-sided class war" against labor.

As in the past, Kirkland's contacts with top business figures excited his imagination. In a long interview with veteran labor reporter A. H. Raskin, Kirkland began describing an immense oil-extraction project Exxon planned for the Piceance Basin in the Rocky Mountains:

> From the rapt way in which Kirkland described the undertaking, it was plain that he is not among the skeptics. I had rarely seen him betray more signs of excitement. It was almost as if the contemplation of a new El Dorado just west of the Great Divide gave the A.F.L.–C.I.O. chief blissful surcease from the problems of his storm-rocked movement. . . . The ordinary soporific pace of his words quickened as the operation's gigantic scope seized his imagination. . . . "What we are talking about is the creation of a quarter-million construction jobs, and these would be the foundation for seven or eight hundred thousand more jobs in mining and processing and extracting oil from the shale," Kirkland said. "It dwarfs anything we have ever tackled in this country—even the Manhattan Project. For us in labor, this is our greatest challenge, even beyond the organization of women and white-collar workers, important though both of those are.

See A. H. Raskin, "A Reporter at Large: Unionist in Reaganland," *The New Yorker*, 7 September 1981, 85.

7. For labor's budgetary priorities and foreign-policy activities, see Ferguson and Rogers, "Labor Day, 1985"; and *Business Week*, 4 November 1985, 92–96.

8. The date of the formation of Democrats for the 80's was confirmed by the authors by telephone with Joan Shaffer, press spokesperson for the group, 21 August 1985. Its board membership, like that of the Center for National Policy, is publicly available. We should note that we were on the editorial board of *democracy*.

9. On the changes at Brookings, see *Industry Week*, 25 June 1984, 107.

10. For Manatt's law firm's clients, see *New York Times*, 17 August 1981 and 14 June 1982.

11. For the loan data, see records on file with the Federal Election Commission, Washington, DC.

12. Benjamin Ginsberg makes the point that much recent campaign technology is heavily capital-intensive. It therefore advantages the party best able to raise money, and disadvantages parties that rely more on volunteer workers to make up the difference. See Ginsberg, "Money and Power: The New Political Economy of American Elections," in Ferguson and Rogers, *The Political Economy*, 163–79. That Republican identifiers, if not investors, are generally wealthier than Democratic ones, is well known. As of 1983, NORC reported that among the 80 percent of the electorate making less than $35,000 a year, Democrats were favored by 65 percent, Republicans by 35 percent; among the 20 percent of the electorate making more than $35,000, Republicans outnumbered Democrats by 58 to 42 percent. See Edsall, *New Politics*, 61, for a citation to this survey.

13. Radaker said plainly that he wanted to arrest what he considered anti-business tendencies in the party.

See *Industry Week*, 25 June 1984, 80–81. The quoted description of the DBC is from a Council advertising flyer, "The Democratic Business Council," September 1984.

14. For the list of members, see "Democratic Business Council." Discussions of huge natural-gas projects were a prominent part of détente's brief career. More recently, officials of some natural-gas concerns have sharply criticized the Reagan Administration's handling of Soviet relations. See, for example, Jack H. Ray, "The Soviet Gas Pipeline Controversy: A Look Forward," in *Common Sense in U.S.–Soviet Trade*, ed. Margaret Chapman and Carl Marcy (Washington, DC: American Committee on East-West Accord, 1983), 113–18. Ray is president of Tennessee Gas Transmission and a member of the American Committee on East-West Accord, described below.

15. These data from the Forum Institute's "Search for Security: A Guide to Grantmaking in International Security and the Prevention of Nuclear War" (Washington, DC: The Forum Institute, July 1985), Tables 1 and 4.

16. For Kendall, the BAC, Felix Frankfurter, and the New Deal, see Ferguson, *Critical Realignment*.

17. The Inter-American Dialogue began with a series of meetings held between October 1982 and March 1983. The participants noted here are those active in those meetings, and the quoted conclusions are from a report of the Dialogue summarizing the proceedings, *The Americas at a Crossroads* (Washington, DC: Woodrow Wilson International Center for Scholars, April 1983), 42–43.

18. The Council report is cited in Dye, *Who's Running America?*, 252.

19. An excellent analysis of the regional and urban impacts of the Reagan economic program is provided by Norman J. Glickman, "Economic Policy in the Cities: In Search of Reagan's *Real* Urban Policy," Lyndon B. Johnson School of Public Affairs, University of Texas, Austin, Working Paper No. 26, 1984. Note in particular the discussion of the tax program, the budget, the flow of funds, the new federalism, and the explicit urban budget. Glickman does not explicitly discuss the effects of exchange rates, but see the discussion of the regional impact of "implicit industrial policy" in Norman J. Glickman and Marcia Van Wagner, "Two Cheers for Industrial Policy: A Critical Look at some Urban and Distributional Issues," Lyndon B. Johnson School of Public Affairs, University of Texas, Austin, Working Paper No. 32, 1985. While concern over high interest rates may have also agitated real estate figures their actual behavior during this period indicates a clear and compelling interest in matters of budgetary policy.

20. Ibid. For the importance of mass transit to some big city developers, see Robert Fitch, "The Family Subway," in *Research in Political Economy* 8, ed. Paul Zarembka and Thomas Ferguson (Greenwich, CT: JAI Press, 1985), 163–200.

21. On the organizational, financial, and other support for the anti-nuclear movement by business and foundations, see *New York Times*, 2 May 1982, 32; this notes the Rockefeller Family Fund's financial aid to Physicians for Social Responsibility, the New York-based New World Foundation's program to educate the public on the consequences of nuclear war, and various proposals by Rockefeller Foundation president Lyman, among others; it also includes a brief discussion of efforts by right-wing groups and foundations to counter the anti-nuclear movement. See also the discussion in *New York Times*, 6 May 1985; and "Search for Security." For the Boston real-estate and hotel magnates and the New England anti-nuclear movement, see the fleeting mention in Art Jahnke, "The Liberals' Santa Claus," *Boston Magazine*, December 1984, 189. According to a *Boston Globe* story (12 February 1984), Stanley Weiss's Business Executives for National Security was founded in 1982, and has its largest membership from Boston area concerns. Mentioned as members as of February 1984 were a number of civic and business leaders from sectors obviously affected by the Reagan budget cuts, including David Arnold, Jr., the chairman of Emerson Hospital; developer (and *Atlantic* proprietor) Mortimer Zuckerman; and William Dunfey of Dunfey Hotels. The treasurer of Polaroid, a large Boston area multinational, and Philip Villers, president of a leading high-tech concern in the area, were also members. So too was Kenneth Germeshausen, the retired founder of EG&G in Wellesley, Massachusetts, an important military contractor. (Bernard J. O'Keefe, current head of EG&G, and a self-described "card-carrying member of the military industrial complex," denounced the Reagan Administration's controversial plans to deploy Pershing II missiles in Europe during his term as head of the National Association of Manufacturers. See *New York Times*, 12 August 1983). Weiss, the group's organizer,

is chairman of American Minerals and formerly was part of a concern engaged in trading with the U.S.S.R. (see *Fortune*, 17 October 1983, 62). He also helped underwrite environmentalist Barry Commoner's campaign for the Presidency on the Citizens' Party ticket in 1980. Other important supporters of this group include Alan Sagner, chairman of the Port Authority of New York, several prominent investment bankers, and George Kennan, a member of the Committee on East-West Accord's board of directors (see *New York Times*, 3 February 1983). Since the group came together in the midst of the campaign for the freeze, it is unclear how active any particular individual member was in the movement's earliest stages, though a considerable number—notably Kennan and some of the investment bankers and real-estate magnates—undoubtedly were.

Leading business supporters of the influential campaign in favor of the Bilateral Nuclear Weapons Freeze Initiative in California included Dyson-Kittner-Moran chairman Charles Dyson, financier (and Trilateral Commission member) Victor Palmieri, Paul Warnke, Jerome Wiesner, and Harold Willens (see *New York Times*, 21 February 1982, Section 3). Retired rear admiral Gene R. LaRocque, who heads the Center for Defense Information, and endorsed the freeze, had been working with a group of wealthy donors and foundation officials (from the Stern and other funds) concerned with arms reduction and the nuclear freeze since at least the fall of 1981. Because members held at least one meeting at the New York Yacht Club, the group has become informally known as the "Yacht Club" (see *New York Times*, 2 May 1982). The Audubon Society reportedly helped push the freeze in Oregon, while officers of Friends of the Earth and other environmental groups, including Greenpeace, also spoke out for it. Two liberal East Coast foundations—the Field Foundation and the Fund for Peace—also reportedly helped support parts of the freeze campaign, while Senator Edward Kennedy's PAC, the Fund for a Democratic Majority, helped back freeze candidates.

It should also be noted that many leading critics of the Reagan arms buildup (including many, though not quite all, who had kind words for some sort of "freeze") were or soon became members of the American Committee on East-West Accord. Prominent business members of this group, which expanded rapidly in precisely this period, include Averell Harriman, Robert McNamara, McGeorge Bundy, Thornton Bradshaw (head of RCA, which owns NBC), Robert Anderson (chair of Atlantic Richfield), Robert Roosa, Stewart Mott, George Ball, and Donald Kendall (chair of Pepsi-Cola). Though the point can only be illustrative, since we have not systematically surveyed the party affiliations of the executives associated with the group, at least four of these nine qualify as prominent Democrats, while two others contributed to Mondale or other Democrats in 1980–84.

Donald Trump recently announced that he could learn "everything there is to learn about missiles" in ninety minutes, and do a much better job of negotiating weapons limitations and reductions than the Administration (see *New York Times*, 9 March 1985). See similar expressions of confidence in Ron Rosenbaum, "Trump: The Ultimate Deal," *Manhattan Inc.*, November 1985, 109–18. For Trump's early contribution to Walter Mondale, see below. Our analysis of FEC data shows contributions by Petrie and many other business figures (including a substantial number of the Forbes 400) to various anti-nuclear and arms-control groups.

Finally, although we lack the space to develop the point, we should note that many of the business groups supporting a freeze had previously assisted John B. Anderson's independent candidacy for President in 1980.

22. See *Nuclear Times*, February 1984, 11–12.

23. For Komer's criticisms of the naval buildup, see his "Maritime Strategy vs. Coalition Defense," *Foreign Affairs* 60 (Summer 1982): 1133–34, and *Maritime Strategy or Coalition Defense?*, especially chapter 7. The quotes are from *Maritime Strategy*, 74. For Huntington's suggestions, see his "Deterrence and Conventional Relations in Europe," *International Security* 8 (Winter 1983–84): 32–56.

24. A useful survey of various anti-nuclear military proposals appeared in the *Boston Globe*, 29 April 1982. For the major statement of the Gang of Four on conventional defense, see McGeorge Bundy, George F. Kennan, Robert S. McNamara, and Gerard Smith, "Nuclear Weapons and the Atlantic Alliance," *Foreign Affairs* 60 (Spring 1982): 753–68. All four of the authors are members of the Committee on East-West Accord. Smith was also a director of a major gas company, Panhandle Eastern.

The complementarity of the strategists of "coalition defense" and advocates of arms control has been emphasized by both sides. Komer, for example, states in *Maritime Strategy* (31) that "perhaps the greatest stimulus" to new conventional thinking has come from nuclear-arms advocates, and explicitly identifies the Gang of Four as influential, while Bundy, in his introduction to that work (x), states:

> I think Komer's answers are essentially right, not only on their own strategic terms but on the wider ground that they are responsive to political imperatives as well. His position is squarely in the great tradition of our postwar military political leadership, all the way back to Marshall and Eisenhower. I believe that only by what Komer calls a coalition strategy can we help to sustain the political will and self-confidence that are essential to the future safety of all the societies we need as friends.

25. As an example of the affiliation of "middle of the road" Democrats with this position, see John Glenn, "Rethinking Defense," in *Rethinking Defense and Conventional Forces* (Alternatives for the 1980s, No. 8) (Washington, DC: Center for National Policy, 1983), 13, which adopts the logic of the "nuclear stalemate" argument for increased conventional forces:

> [N]uclear parity no longer permits us to add a nuclear weapons "edge" to the scales, to offset imbalances created by vastly larger Soviet forces.
>
> Beyond that, however, conventional forces deserve more emphasis in our defense effort because to the extent that conventional forces are able to head off threats to the peace, the danger of nuclear war is diminished. Conventional forces that were adequate in an era of nuclear monopoly are not adequate now. I am well aware that conventional forces are costly . . . But if we are serious about protecting this country's interests while avoiding nuclear war, we must buy the kind of conventional forces our foreign policy demands.

Joining and complementing Glenn in this issue of the CNP's "Alternatives" was Robert W. Komer, who again made his argument for the increase in conventional forces in a period of nuclear stalemate.

26. On the support for the Democrats from investment banks and insurance companies, see the discussion below, in chapter 6, as well as the statistical analysis of campaign contributions offered in the Appendix. For an analysis that indicates the effects that deficits have on the market for long-term bonds (and specifically on the term structure of interest rates), see Robert A. Johnson, "Anticipated Fiscal Contraction: The Economic Consequences of the Gramm-Rudman-Hollings Bill for the U.S. Economy," unpublished manuscript, February 1986. Johnson's discussion centers on 1985–86, but clearly implies the effect we are claiming for the earlier period.

27. For the interest burden on RCA during the fourth quarter of 1981 (just when media coverage of the victims of the Reagan budget was becoming more sympathetic), for example, see *New York Times*, 28 January 1982. For RCA and other firms, of course, this burden continued (unevenly) throughout 1982.

28. For coverage of the late September fundraiser, see *New York Times*, 1 October 1982.

29. For the plan itself, see Center for National Policy, *Restoring American Competitiveness: Proposals for an Industry Policy* (Alternatives for the 1980s, No. 11) (Washington, DC: January 1984). For Heller's dissent, see Lenny Glynn and Elizabeth Peer, "Felix: The Making of a Celebrity," *Institutional Investor*, December 1984, 97.

30. See the announcement of the rules changes in *New York Times*, 27 March 1982.

31. On the increased turnout in 1982, see reporting in *Congressional Quarterly*, 23 July 1983, 1503–7.

32. See Joel Rogers, "The Politics of Voter Registration," *The Nation*, 21–28 July 1984, 34 and 45–51.

33. "Interoffice Memorandum" on "1984 Election Prospects" from Ann Lewis to Charles Manatt, 9 February 1984 (Unpublished).

34. For reports on early activities, see *Democracy in America: Towards Greater Participation* (New York: New World Foundation) and *Funders' Guide to Voter Registration and Education* (New York: Ad Hoc Funders' Committee for Voter Registration). Both pamphlets are undated.

6/The Campaign

1. Throughout this chapter, we draw on our examination of FEC records on candidate contributions, discussed in more detail in the Appendix. Additional notes supplement this basic data set.

2. On the making of the "new," pro-business Mondale, see *New York Times*, 7 October 1984; *Newsweek*, 22 October 1984, 77–78.

3. Press coverage of the early backers of Mondale's (and everyone else's) candidacy is, of course, very sparse by comparison with the endless rounds of stories about what the candidate was wearing, how tired he was, and how he felt in front of TV cameras. See, however, on the Mondale candidacy and Wall Street, *Institutional Investor*, April 1984, 10; on Mondale and business generally, see *Industry Week*, 25 June 1984, 72–73; *Fortune*, 14 November 1983, 46; *National Journal*, 30 June 1984, 1265–67. For an attempt to trace the role of "soft money" state PACs in the early stages of the Mondale effort, see Bill Hogan and Alan Green, "Waltergate," *Regardie's*, July 1984, 26–37. On Mondale's advisers on foreign policy, trade, and other issues, see *New York Times*, 2 March 1983, 26 September 1983, 4 January 1984, 2 February 1984, 3 March 1984; *Washington Post*, 16 September 1984; and *U.S. News & World Report*, 30 July 1984, 26–27. Additional information came from a telephone interview with Mondale campaign officials, from whom we requested lists of prominent business and foreign-policy advisers.

Note that because the dates of these articles vary and other candidates were dropping out or entering the race, some of the people listed as Mondale supporters or advisers in the later stages of the campaign were not present at the beginning. Our narrative attempts to sort these out, though it must also be read in the light of earlier remarks (chapter 2, note 13) on the use of multiple campaign contributions by investors. See as well the discussion in the Appendix, below. Note also that the list of contributors in the text includes both contributors to the formal campaign committee and the earlier PAC, the Committee for the Future of America. As Hogan and Green, "Waltergate," make clear, this was also a campaign vehicle.

4. For McGovern's views on the Middle East, see Paul Findley, *They Dare to Speak Out* (Westport, CT: Lawrence Hill, 1985), 136. Cranston, by contrast, was a strong supporter of Israeli actions.

5. For early response to the McGovern candidacy, see McGovern's own account in "George McGovern: The Target Talks Back," *Columbia Journalism Review*, July–August 1984, 27–31. For the press coverage of McGovern relative to other candidates during 1983, the Iowa vote, and McGovern's and Hart's coverage after Iowa, see William C. Adams, "Media Coverage of Campaign '84: A Preliminary Report," *Public Opinion* 7 (April–May 1984): 9–11.

6. *New York Times*, 12 April 1983, 4.

7. The probability that the association of favorable media coverage with candidate membership on the Commission is due to chance alone can be estimated quite precisely. If one accepts the ranking of the favorability of candidate media coverage for 1976 implied in Shoup (*Carter Presidency*, chapter 3), and those put forward for 1980 in Lutz Erbring ("Media Monitoring and Public Opinion Change in 1980" [Paper prepared for delivery at the Annual Meeting of the American Political Science Association, Washington, DC, August 1980; revised October 1980]); agrees that serious candidates in 1976 included Carter, Wallace, Ford, Udall, Reagan, and Jackson, and in 1980 were Carter, Kennedy, Reagan, Bush, and Anderson; and assumes that initially each candidate has the same chance of ending up number one (obviously not true for unknowns Carter and Anderson)—then calculations using the binomial theorem for sampling without replacement yield a truly microscopic value—less than 2 chances in 100.

8. On Israel, Glenn, and Mondale, see *New York Times*, 26 September 1983; on Mondale and the Coalition for a Democratic Majority, see *New York Times*, 15 November 1983. For the turmoil in the Glenn campaign over this issue, see Findley, *They Dare*, 135–36.

9. For early Hart supporters, see *New York Times*, 2 March 1983. For Sorensen and the diamond cartel, see Jonathan Kwitney, *Endless Enemies: The Making of an Unfriendly World* (New York: Congdon & Weed, 1984), 46.

10. Hart's proposals on industrial policy may be usefully compared to those offered by Thomas Watson in *Computer World*, 3 June 1983, 14–15. For McKenna, see *InfoWorld*, 23 July 1984; for Johnston, see e.g., *New York Times*, 3 April 1984. Additional information on Hart's business supporters and foreign-policy advisers came from author telephone interviews with Hart campaign staffers Beth Smith (25 June 1984) and Ginny Terzano (26 June 1984). For Hart's real-estate partnership with the *Times* staffer, see *Washington Post*, 10 March 1984.

11. In addition to the FEC, this paragraph draws on the interview with Terzano.

12. See Gary Hart, "What's Wrong with the Military," *New York Times Magazine,* 14 February 1982. Hart, in addition, had previously criticized the Navy's concentration on large, expensive aircraft carriers.

13. Independent PACs spent $100,000 extra for Mondale in New Hampshire.

14. The loans are plainly listed on the appropriate forms for Americans with Hart, Inc., the Hart campaign organization, on file with the FEC. The amounts outstanding, of course, vary by date.

15. See, for example, reporting in *The Washington Post,* 4 August 1983, which describes the bank simply as "Arabian-owned." The *Post* also quotes Hart's campaign manager as saying he had reviewed the loan for possible conflicts. Hart's "special counsel" later attempted to claim the campaign did not realize the bank was Arab-owned (see Findley, *They Dare,* 135).

16. The Jackson candidacy has already, of course, excited enormous comment and controversy. For a useful juxtaposition of views, see Marable, *Black American Politics,* especially chapter 5; and Robert Brenner, "The Paradox of Social Democracy: The American Case," in *The Year Left: An American Socialist Yearbook,* ed. Mike Davis, Fred Pfeil, and Michael Sprinker (London: Verso, 1985), 32–86.

17. On the efforts to win franchises, see *Black Enterprise,* January 1984, 36; and August 1983, 52; the latter indicates that Jackson's Operation PUSH has been the most aggressive champion of the franchise campaign. For critics' comments on the franchises of Jackson's half brother, see William P. Hoar, "Profile of a Radical," *Conservative Digest,* July 1984, 14. For Pinckney and others, see James Ridgeway, "The Company He Keeps," *Village Voice,* 10 July 1984, 1, 13–15.

18. Compare Jackson's coverage in, for example, *Time* with the account of that publication's coverage of various Middle East issues in Emerson, *American House of Saud,* 204–7.

19. See discussion in Marable, *Black American Politics,* 287–88.

20. On Arab-American funding for Jackson, see *New York Times,* 4 November 1984. On Mondale's refusal, see Findley, *They Dare,* 135. For the Arab League and Libyan donations to PUSH, see Marable, *Black American Politics,* 283.

21. The primary-vote shares for Hart and Mondale are taken from Walter Dean Burnham, "The 1984 Election and the Future of American Politics," 211. The share of delegates in late June is from *Congressional Quarterly Weekly Report,* 23 June 1984, 1504–5.

22. For Caldicott's reluctance, see *Peace Through Strength Report* 3 (March 1984): 6. We should note that this journal is published by a group closely affiliated with the ultra-hawkish American Security Council. One freeze leader identified there as prepared to endorse Mondale does not, in fact, appear to have endorsed him, at least at that time.

23. For details of Mondale's settlement on the campaign funds, see Herbert E. Alexander, "American Presidential Elections Since Public Funding 1976–84" (Paper presented to the International Political Science Association XIIth World Congress, 15–20 July 1985, Paris, France), 18.

24. For all comments on "the Glenn people," see *National Journal,* 30 June 1984, 1267, quoting San Francisco attorney Duane Garrett, a top Mondale fund-raiser. For the description and results of Mondale's hotel-suite phone calls, and the Roderick comments, see *New York Times,* 24 May 1984. Note that Roderick's comments refer only to the race between Hart and Mondale and *not* one between Mondale and Reagan.

25. For Bradley's relations with the Los Angeles corporate community and Feinstein's relations with San Francisco business groups, see Wiley and Gottlieb, *Empires,* 113–15 and 103, respectively. Additional information on Feinstein came from an author interview with an executive in one of the city's largest banks. Information on Cisneros comes from an interview with Geoffrey Rips, editor of the *Texas Observer.*

26. A special Gallup Poll commissioned by *Newsweek* right after the convention showed the candidates essentially even. See Jack W. Germond and Jules Witcover, *Wake Us When It's Over: Presidential Politics of 1984* (New York: Macmillan, 1985), 413.

The comment on "unfortunate words" came from Mondale's friend investment banker Herbert Allen, speaking of the acceptance speech and other Mondale statements, as quoted in the *New York Times,* 7 October 1984, Section 3.

27. On the business mobilization in Washington against deficits, see *Industry Week,* 25 June 1984, 88–

91; for the Jacobs quote, see 81. For the July Rubin–Altman trip to Minnesota, see *Newsweek*, 22 October 1984, 78.

In addition to their concerns about the deficit issue, it is possible that an expectation that Mondale might slow the pace of financial deregulation attracted a few investment bankers to the party. The differences between the parties on this issue, however, are minute, but the issue was briefly mentioned (in the context of a much longer discussion about the deficit) by Securities Industry Association president Richard H. Jenrette in an article urging support for Mondale among business. See his "There's Nothing to Fear from Mondale," *New York Times*, 21 October 1984, Section 3.

28. On the Reagan advisers' relief, see *New York Times*, 19 October 1984; this also notes the special pre-convention trip Senator Bill Bradley and Representative Richard Gephardt made to Minnesota to encourage Mondale to endorse tax reform.

29. For the calculation on labor's share, see *Nation's Business*, October 1984, 26, quoting Irving Shapiro. Mondale's tolerance for Volcker's behavior at the Fed is evident from his reactions to Reagan's reappointment of Volcker; see *New York Times*, 20 June 1983.

30. On the Ferraro–Zaccaro finances, and Zaccaro's business dealings, see *New York Times*, 16 August 1984; 20 August 1984; 13 September 1984; 8 January 1985; and 13 January 1985, Section 4. The charge to which Zaccaro eventually pleaded guilty involved attempted fraud against fewer than ten persons; as such, it ranked as a misdemeanor, and not a felony. For contrasting media treatment of Republican leaders Ray Donovan, Paul Laxalt, and Charles Wick, see, e.g., Mark Dowie, "How ABC Spikes the News: Three Reagan Administration Scandals That Never Appeared on 'World News Tonight,'" *Mother Jones*, November/December 1985, 37–39, 53.

31. For the O'Connor quote, see Germond and Witcover, *Wake Us*, 486. For the percentage of newspaper endorsements of Mondale, see *Editor and Publisher*, 3 November 1984, 9–11. The endorsement process occasioned some dispute, with publishers often leaning hard on editors who wished to go the other way; on this, see *Editor & Publisher*, 10 November 1984, 20.

32. As the Appendix to this study demonstrates, investment bankers were disproportionately supportive of the Democrats, for what appear to be quite understandable reasons, in the 1984 campaign. This does not, of course, imply that all were, and one is led naturally to wonder about those who were not. While we cannot develop the point here, the "star wars" industrial policy alternative, with its implicit stance in favor of continued free trade, may be a good place to begin developing an explanation.

33. Quoted in Germond and Witcover, *Wake Us*, 485.

34. Mondale is quoted in Robert Kuttner, "Ass Backward," *The New Republic*, 22 April 1985, 18.

35. For the Ford suggestion, see *Newsweek* (Election Extra), November–December 1984, 81.

36. See the "Dear Mayor" letter of Charles Manatt, Democratic National Committee, 24 September 1984 (Unpublished).

37. Throughout this discussion of the voter-registration effort in 1983–84, we have drawn on interviews with Richard A. Cloward and Frances Fox Piven, and on their "Voter Registration Treadmill: A Call for Institutional Reform" (Unpublished paper), which contains a careful review of the voter-registration efforts in 1983–84. Parts of this paper were subsequently published as "Trying to Break Down the Barriers," *The Nation*, 2 November 1985, 433–37; and "How to Get Out the Vote in 1988," *The Nation* 23 November 1985, 547–49.

Note on the language on "7 million new people registered through group activity": this excludes those who Cloward and Piven estimate would have registered anyway, without any group efforts. Of course, different analysts give different estimates of the effectiveness of the voter-registration drives, and assign credit in different places. A *New York Times* editorial of 10 October 1985, for example, cites with approval a study of registration efforts conducted by Interface, "a New York think tank," which credits the nonpartisan voter-registration drives with 2.5 million, while the *Times* itself credits each of the major political parties with having registered 4 million. Asked by Cloward how they knew the parties had actually registered this many (something that continues to be a subject of intense dispute), a *Times* staffer said simply that that was what the parties claimed. As to the 2.5 million figure of Interface, we note only that the methodology of the study was widely and sharply disputed, particularly by those groups that conducted "wholesale" registration in social-service centers and elsewhere. Some of the harshest critics of the registration efforts, who echo such revisionist Democrats as Huntington, should by this time know better. See Thomas B. Edsall, "Politics and the Power of Money," *Dissent* 32 (Spring 1985): 149–52.

38. On Grace, see *Corporate Taxpayers & Corporate Freeloaders*, 6.

7/Aftermath: The Legacy of 1984

1. For Stein's comment on "full employment," see Herbert Stein, "Why Americans Should Thank Japanese Exporters," *International Herald Tribune*, 10–11 August 1985, 4.

2. Here an extra dash of wariness is stimulated by all the premature predictions of Republican collapse generated by the 1982 recession. Out of goodwill toward our professional colleagues, we will not append here any note to these. But we should note that the close of our "Corporate Coalitions" essay, finished well before the recession hit, contained the claim that, in the absence of a major war, Ronald Reagan was "likely" to fail to complete two terms. While the remaining years of his second term may save this prediction, it appears now to be wrong. In mitigation, we note that the prediction failed only because it underestimated the Reagan Administration's tolerance for a gargantuan deficit—needed both to satisfy its business constituency and to produce the massive political business cycle that returned the President to office. We are happy to stand by nearly all our other forecasts—of the shape of the cities in 1984, of the Administration's inability to increase weapons spending without massive cuts in social expenditures, of conflict over policy toward the U.S.S.R., the Middle East, and Japan, and of the likelihood of many "noisy resignations of top officials" in the government (see "Corporate Coalitions," 54–55).

3. On this last point, see Dickson and Noble, "By Force of Reason."

4. For a useful discussion of the problem of funding progressive movements, see David M. Gordon, "Where Will the Money Come From?," *The Nation*, 23 February 1985, 205–8. The figure on combined 1983 spending by Olin, Pew, and Scaife is at 206. The cumulative Scaife figure is reported in Schneir and Schneir, "The Right's Attack on the Press," 365.

5. For union net income, see Leo Troy and Neil Sheflin, *Union Sourcebook: Membership, Finances, Structure, Directory* (West Orange, NJ: IRDIS, 1985), Table 4.2; note the comment on "Sources and Methods" at 4-1. Corporate profits are from *ER*, Table B-83.

6. The estimate on the natural attrition rate of the union share is from Freeman and Medoff, *What Do Unions Do?*, 241. In our calculations, we used the estimate of the 1984 private nonagricultural work force in *ER*, Table B-37; and the reports of election activity before the NLRB in *NLRB Election Report*, various issues. Note the language on "net" new workers; in 1984; unions actually gained 92,000 members through representation elections, but they lost 24,000 current members through decertifications.

7. The reference is to the Council's discussion of the need for "power sharing and a military truce" with rebels in El Salvador. See Council on Foreign Relations, *Annual Report 1982–83*, 24; cited in Dye, *Who's Running America?*, 252. For opposition within the labor movement to present policy in Central America, see Ferguson and Rogers, "Labor Day, 1985," and *Business Week*, 4 November 1985, 92–96.

8. Data in this paragraph were supplied by Robert Armstrong, of NACLA, in an author interview conducted 31 October 1985. The estimate of annual costs of current U.S. policies toward Central America and the Caribbean is from Cohen and Rogers, *Inequity and Intervention*, Section 3.

9. We should note that Cox-Chambers at least formally grants each of its papers' editorial boards freedom of choice in making Presidential endorsements.

10. For a discussion of the soft-money contributions from Watson, Moldow, and others, see *PACs and Lobbies* 6 (16 January 1985): 1–6. The Republicans, of course, used essentially the same techniques on a far broader scale. On Kirk's background, see *Boston Globe*, 20 December 1984.

11. On the Kirk–Jackson conflict, see *Boston Globe*, 3 February 1985. On Kirk's neutrality pledge, see *New York Times*, 30 January 1985. On criticisms of Sanford, see Emerson, *American House of Saud*, 300–1.

12. On the Crotty–Kirk struggle, see Jack Anderson's column in the *Austin American Statesman*, 25

February 1985. For early reporting on the Democratic Leadership Council, see *New York Times*, 1 March 1985.

13. On productivity growth after Reagan, see Peter K. Clark, "Productivity and Profits in the 1980s: Are They Really Improving?," *Brookings Papers on Economic Activity* 1984 (1): 133–67; and Robert J. Gordon, "Unemployment and Potential Output in the 1980s," *Brookings Papers on Economic Activity* 1984 (2): 555–56.

14. On MIGA, see *New York Times*, 14 September 1985.

15. As this book goes to press, the dramatic drop in the world price of oil has temporarily soothed anxieties about a revival of inflation, permitting the Fed to lower interest rates more rapidly than most observers expected. To protect their export surpluses, Japan, Germany, and other allied countries have finally lowered their interest rates in early March 1986. Because these moves promise to quicken the pace of economic expansion in the world economy, they are likely to afford policymakers a bit more breathing space. Top Fed officials and other U.S. policymakers, however, are continuing to pressure the Germans and the Japanese for fiscal policy expansion, and the analysis here retains its force.

16. Some of the dilemmas of macroeconomic coordination are explored in Gerald Epstein's useful "The Triple Debt Crisis," *World Policy Journal* 2 (Fall 1985): 625–57.

17. For Weinberger, see *International Herald Tribune*, 9 January 1986.

18. For the Business Council meeting, see *New York Times*, 12 October 1985; for the changing business alignment on taxes, see *New York Times*, 27 November 1985.

19. For the Saudi oil-pricing strategies, see *New York Times*, 28 January 1986.

20. Even many of the multinational companies, however, might find a U.S. oil tariff attractive as part of a package that involves sequential moves by other countries to put a floor under the price of oil. See, for example, the plan co-authored by a leading international oil industry consultant: Walter Levy and Milton Lipton, "The Dark Side of Oil-Price Reductions," *New York Times*, 31 January 1986.

If the oil tax were not rebated to lower-income groups, of course, it would also be severely regressive. It could be argued that these groups would benefit from the government programs which the tax would fund, but this would probably be true only for a few programs, and not in general. Such a move would essentially duplicate the tax history of the 1960s and early 1970s, when rising social security taxes left ordinary Americans a large part of the bill for their own programs. See Page, *Who Gets What?*, and the discussion above, in chapters 2 and 3.

21. The trade issue, of course, is prominent, and prominently divisive, in both parties. Within Republican ranks, see the continuing defense of free trade in Jack Kemp, "The Recipe for a New Depression," *International Herald Tribune*, 13 August 1985, 4; for Gingrich's view, see *International Herald Tribune*, 22–28 July 1985; for continued pressures from GOP manufacturers, see *International Herald Tribune*, 10–11 August 1985, 9. For Democrats and the trade issue, see *Financial Times*, 9 August 1985, 4.

22. For the Japanese attitude, see *Financial Times*, 9 August 1985.

23. For business critics of bank-rescue plans, see *New York Times*, 10 February 1983; for domestic industry, see Sylvia Ann Hewlett, "Overview and Policy Options," in *The Global Repercussions of U.S. Monetary and Fiscal Policy*, ed. Sylvia Ann Hewlett, Henry Kaufman, Peter B. Kenen (Cambridge: Ballinger, 1984), 212–13. For the criticisms of a prominent Rand economist, see *New York Times*, 11 September 1985. See as well the amusing exchange between *Atlantic* publisher Mortimer Zuckerman and Citibank vice-chair Thomas C. Thoebald in *New York Times* 11 January 1985 and 20 January 1985. For criticisms of the funding of the World Bank's insurance plan for multinationals, see *Wall Street Journal*, 24 September 1985.

24. On European attitudes toward the current U.S. fiscal and monetary policy, see Samuel Brittan's comment in *Financial Times* (29 July 1985): "The least bad outcome for the rest of the world, in the absence of timely action on the budget, may be U.S. toleration of some extra inflation in the later 1980s."

Concern about the repercussions of such a move is pervasive. The papers are full of analyses by economists and business figures concluding that a "soft landing" of the dollar either does or does not impend, and correlative debates over whether the Fed should, or should not, lower interest rates some more. Though we cannot pursue the point here, most of the current dispute over the meaning of Federal Reserve monetary aggregates is really over this and related issues (see, for example, *New York Times*, 4 March 1985). Note, incidentally, that reductions in the deficit will by themselves simply remove a cloud that now hangs over the long-term bond market. They will thus make it that much more attractive to *hold* dollars. See the very careful discussion of this point in Henry Kaufman, "Complexities of U.S. Stabilization Policies in an International Context," in Hewlett, Kaufman, and Kenen, *Global Repercussions*, 6–7.

25. On criticisms of Reagan from the right even before his first inauguration, and the talk of blocking his renomination, see *Boston Globe*, 4 January 1981; and *Washington Post*, 20 January 1983.

26. The extraordinary arrangement with Robertson receives a paragraph of coverage in *The New York Times*, 27 October 1985. If Robertson runs, he would probably hurt the candidacy of Congressman Jack Kemp, Bush's archrival. Bush, it may be added, has wide support in Texas, where he claims residence. Note that since the *Times* article appeared, the Bush supporter appears to have distanced himself somewhat from Robertson's campaign.

27. On the growing dispute within the party over protection, compare the strong free-trade position outlined by Center for National Policy president Ted Van Dyk (see *New York Times*, 19 September 1985) with Congressman Gephardt's defense of legislation he introduced mandating 25 percent surcharges on imports from countries whose sales to the United States exceed purchases by 65 percent and which decline to reduce their trade deficits by 5 percent within a year (see *New York Times*, 8 October 1985). Gephardt asserts correctly that he is far from espousing unqualified protectionism. But this position is also represented in the party and indicates how contentious the issue now is.

Appendix

1. This simple statement of the theory, of course, masks a host of knotty methodological issues. Again, a more systematic presentation of the view is provided in Ferguson, "Party Realignment," Section 3.

2. For the operationalization of the original coalition, see Ferguson, "Normalcy," 64–66.

3. For the *Forbes* listing of the 400 wealthiest Americans, see *Forbes* Special Issue, 1 October 1984. All the real-estate figures we tracked came from this list.

4. The Fortune 500 largest industrials for 1984 are reported in *Fortune*, 30 April 1984; our list of major service firms comes from *Fortune*, 11 June 1984.

Whether assets, or sales, or profits, or net revenue, or some other magnitude is the theoretically best criterion to use to rank the concerns need not detain us here. We know the problems with each, including the criteria we used, but as indicated above, we wanted to achieve comparability with the earlier Ferguson study, and we must in any case work with readily available data. The real question is whether different criteria would change our results. We very much doubt it would.

The *Fortune* "service" directory includes two other categories, for "retailing" and "diversified service" firms. Because most of these firms are much smaller than leading firms in other categories, however, it is probably a mistake from the standpoint of the investment-theory perspective to lump them with the rest. We have, however, what are by far the two largest diversified service companies (RCA and Phibro-Salomon) in our file, RCA being grouped with the *Fortune* industrials and Phibro-Salomon with the investment banks; we also added in data for Sears, which dwarfs all other retailers, into the "industrial" list.

5. The emphasis on the very largest of investors is noted in Ferguson, "Party Realignment," 70, n. 44.

Our use of "controlling," and our list of those owners who are, follow Philip Burch, *The Managerial Revolution Reassessed* (Lexington, MA: D. C. Heath, 1972). We have updated where possible, looking for "active" owners who were on the board or otherwise closely associated with the firm.

6. For the top investment banks (for January–June 1984), see *Institutional Investor*, September 1984, 173. These rankings almost certainly do not reflect the strength (both financial and political) of major foreign-owned firms like Schroeders, as well as firms like Brown Brothers Harriman. Leading figures from these houses, however, played important political roles, particularly within the Democratic Party. Because of a momentary downturn in its fortunes, another leading firm with prominent Democratic activists, Hambrecht & Quist, also does not appear in our sample. As a consequence of our relying on the *Institutional Investor* list, then, we probably slightly *underestimate* the attraction of the Democrats to investment bankers.

One other aspect of our working procedures probably also biases our estimates of Democratic strength slightly *downward*. For statistical purposes (though not in our text), we assigned PAC contributions by firms to the head of the firm only, instead of to all four top officers. Unless the other three contributed personally, therefore, they are not reckoned as contributing. This qualification applies to all sectors aside from investment banking, where we counted only individual contributions in our totals—to err, once again, on the side of conservatism, and avoid all chances that we were counting more Democrats than there really were.

Two individuals in our sample, we should note, were assigned to specific party candidates on the basis of highly detailed press reports of their campaign activities, even though they did not turn up in the fundraising lists for any Presidential candidate. One was a Republican, the other a Democrat.

Two other points probably merit notice. In our significance testing, in the "all investors" category against which we tested individual industries, we included even investors who did not make any contribution in the Presidential race, as well as, obviously, those who only contributed to Republicans. This again makes our results for the more Democratic industries more impressive, since we are truly making it difficult to qualify. Also, it should be obvious that in addition to the problems of small numbers mentioned in the text, questions of definition make it quite impossible to mechanically test "every" possible industry for Democratic leanings. Some firms or individuals are so specialized that the categories easily break down, and one has to aggregate at some arbitrary level.

7. Once again, we are treating "support" as a variable that can be divided in various proportions between Democrats and Republicans, and trying to identify who gives at least some aid to the Democrats. Note again that non-contributors count as part of the "base" of total investors; readers should *not* jump to the conclusion that the percentage of Republican contributors equals 100% minus the Democratic percentages reported in the table.

8. This is not, of course, to claim that this statistical analysis proves that the multinationals exited from the party at the time our text suggests they did, in the late 1970s, or that they once constituted a New Deal bloc for the Democratic Party. For clear evidence of the latter, however, see Appendix note 2, above. For the quantitative assessment of the multinational exit from the Democrats over 1976–84, see Ferguson, "The Death of the New Deal," which shows a striking and very large number of multinational firms and banks contributing to Democrats in 1976 but not in 1984.

Index